VOICE, CHOICE, AND ACTION

VOICE, CHOICE, AND ACTION

The Potential of Young Citizens
to Heal Democracy

Felton Earls & Mary Carlson

THE BELKNAP PRESS *of* HARVARD UNIVERSITY PRESS
Cambridge, Massachusetts, and London, England · 2020

Library of Congress Cataloging-in-Publication Data

Names: Earls, Felton, author. | Carlson, Mary, author.
Title: Voice, choice, and action : the potential of young citizens
to heal democracy / Felton Earls and Mary Carlson.
Description: Cambridge, Massachusetts : The Belknap Press of
Harvard University Press, 2020. | Includes bibliographical
references and index.
Identifiers: LCCN 2020008255 | ISBN 9780674987425 (cloth)
Subjects: LCSH: Children and politics. | Children's rights. | Youth—
Civil rights. | Youth—Political activity. | Political participation.
Classification: LCC HQ784.P5 E17 2020 | DDC 320.083—dc23
LC record available at https://lccn.loc.gov/2020008255

WE DEDICATE THIS BOOK TO DEMOCRACY—
THE TRUEST KIND OF DEMOCRACY
THAT INCLUDES ALL ITS CHILDREN.

Contents

Prologue

How can we adults claim to see our world clearly and completely without incorporating the perspectives of its youngest inhabitants, its children? Believe it or not, children can contribute insights and solutions to profoundly difficult circumstances confronting their communities. The question is not whether they have something to say but whether today's children will be encouraged and expected to voice their opinions, make informed decisions, and coordinate their chosen actions. What will we adults—parents, neighbors, educators, scholars, and leaders—do to engage them?

This book draws on childhood development science, intensive fieldwork, and real-world social action to show how to improve society by ensuring that children become respected participants in the public discourse. Our definition of children follows that of UNICEF, as the international standard: "every human being below the age of eighteen years." In these pages, we explore how even very young people can be introduced to the idea of human rights and citizenship and provided with the tools to deliberate among themselves. *Voice, Choice, and Action* collects decades of research into one definitive text to demonstrate that children have the awareness and competence to claim citizenship roles in democratic society.

We show children doing just this—whether growing up in a Chicago neighborhood riddled by violence, surviving homeless on the streets of Brazil, or facing the loss of parents to HIV in Tanzania. In Chicago, children initiated a probing dialogue to question the violence threatening their neighborhoods. In Brazil, children formed their own political movement to help forge a child rights statute in the country's new constitution that changed the identity of children from that of lesser "minors" to that of empowered "rightsholders." These successes helped to inform a fully developed Young Citizens program that was rigorously evaluated in Tanzania. There, young citizens started a public health movement in their local communities that led to a dramatic increase in voluntary testing for HIV, a critical intervention in a devastating national crisis.

To be sure, equipping a child to participate in public discourse begins in infancy. In Romania, we encountered abandoned infants living in state institutions by the thousands, denied the most basic social contact required to become fully human, let alone citizens. Yet nurture alone is not sufficient to give children voice, prepare them to make choices, and embolden them to take action. This is not charity. Rather, we need processes for discovering children's social, communicative, and rational capabilities and supporting them in being recognized and respected as increasingly competent deliberative citizens.

The Young Citizens program described in these pages offers possibilities—and does so at a vital moment in history. Across the globe, birth rates are dropping, in many places quite rapidly. As the world's population ages, societies will depend ever more upon the open minds and boundless energy of children.

Today, in America, children are leading a national effort to tackle the crisis of gun violence. Around the world, children are coming together to awaken their communities and nations to the global health and ecological threat of climate change.

Freshly inspired by their actions, we synthesize here the results of our long careers' work. Framed in social theory, guided by scientific inquiry, and grounded in proven participatory practices, may innovations like the Young Citizens program help to bring more children into democratic deliberations, and to keep our democracies vibrant.

VOICE, CHOICE, AND ACTION

Introduction

The science of human development must account for two forces: the unfolding of the *innate* expectations of the human infant, and the formative influence of *environmental* supports in guiding those expectations to maturity. The fact is that humans are born in an extremely immature state relative to other existing primates, and this exposes them much more profoundly to the physical and social environment. Our work has been devoted to a probing, scientific exploration of the textured contexts in which development occurs, with a particular focus on urban contexts and on what circumstances are adequate or deficient to serve a child's basic requirements for security, attention, and encouragement. A challenge we accept in advancing this story is that the perspective, capability, and agency of the child must be brought, accurately and respectfully, into the core of our inquiry. Our goal has been the introduction of a method for integrating children into the realm of the community life and its endless pursuit of democratic ideals.

DEANDRE IS as handsome and inquisitive a thirteen-year-old as you will ever meet. He is the youngest of a half-dozen teenage interns on a research project examining exposure to violence in their Chicago neighborhoods. They meet in the project's offices, on the top floor of a bright new office building with large windows overlooking the Kennedy Expressway, just outside the Loop.

On this summer day in 1997, the group is learning about the Convention on the Rights of the Child—adopted eight years earlier by the United Nations General Assembly to recognize children as social, economic, political, civil, and cultural actors—and discussing the relevance of this international human rights treaty to their lives as children growing up in Chicago. The United States has recently signed the treaty, although it has not gone so far as to ratify it. (Indeed, fast-forwarding to 2020, the United States remains the sole UN member not to ratify the Convention.)

Up to this moment, Deandre hasn't had much to say, although his posture and gaze indicate that he is a good listener. Now he appears surprised. "You mean these rights apply to me?" he interrupts. The whole notion of being endowed with rights seems novel to him. He recalls having to pass a test on the Bill of Rights to move into eighth grade last year, but adds, "Nobody said they applied to me."

His reaction is understandable. America's Founders did not have Deandre, an African American male, in mind when they began drafting the Constitution in 1787. Deandre's seventh-grade history teacher apparently had not made the connection for him between our nation's founding documents, our legal history, and our modern lives. Passing a multiple-choice test allowed Deandre to progress to the next grade level but left him clueless about his own political rights or worthiness to influence civic life in his own backyard.

Deandre is now wondering: What does one do with rights, especially as a child?

Beyond Electoral Citizenship

Democratic societies cannot be sustained unless children are recognized, beginning at birth, as valuable members— as citizens—of their communities. This radical idea makes various demands on society, including that it must provide for the adequate socialization of all children. Deliberations about enhancing community welfare must include considerations of children's emerging capacities for language and reasoned and informed action, and how these are best nurtured.

This book synthesizes the findings of a series of ground-breaking research projects that have led to a new under-standing of human development. What is new is the argument that children should be regarded as contributing members of their society starting as early as possible. Above all, we show that children have the capacity to be effective citizens and that, when they are encouraged and enabled to contribute as citizens, their communities benefit. Ignoring their voices—and excluding them from participation in decisions that affect their care and socialization—weakens societies.

This is not about lowering the voting age. It is about raising expectations. We wish to showcase the downsides of *electoral citizenship*, which, by assuming that political power comes with voting rights, necessarily excludes certain residents from being taken seriously as political actors. In its place, we propose a model of *deliberative citizenship*, which is not narrowly defined by legislation to exclude some inhabitants.[1] Deliberative citizenship requires no proof of residency or of age. It depends only on possessing basic abilities to think, communicate, decide, question, and assemble; to obtain, share, and evaluate information; and to be heard and respected. These are not requirements that can be met only by adults. Setting aside the constraints of electoral citizenship allows for a critical discourse that enables young citizens, especially acting collectively in local groups, to plan and execute social actions in public spaces in their local communities. Indeed, they may even be able to go beyond the impact that the adults around them, of more stunted consciousness, can achieve.

Deliberative citizenship expects a group to reach consensus on what issues to address in preparation for informed, shared social actions. For example, high school students participating in a summer program in Cambridge, Massachusetts, showed us deliberative citizenship in action when they decided to take on a problem they were surprised to experience in their generally progressive school: a high level of self-segregation by race and ethnicity. Meeting in our offices overlooking Harvard Square, they investigated this phenomenon through heated dialogue, surveys, and videotaped interviews probing their own and their schoolmates' motivations. They took time to develop trust, to acquire useful new information, and to achieve a common understanding that provided the basis for planning an action relating to deep structural changes in the school's organization.

Today, the world's population is approaching eight billion. More than half of us live in cities. In 1960, there were an estimated one billion children, representing 35 percent of the global population.[2] This percentage will drop to 20 percent by 2050 as birth rates decline and older adults live longer. In this sense, those born today face an entirely new habitat and social ecology, in which young people will be outnumbered as never before. The demographic transition underway makes it all the more urgent to win a greater measure of social and political respect for children.

From Voice to Choice to Action

What began as a study of children growing up across the city of Chicago, informed by observations made in Romania and Brazil, reached its full maturity in a field experiment on neighborhoods in a small city near the base of Mount Kilimanjaro in northern Tanzania. New knowledge gained along this path informed our longitudinal and experimental studies of children, our thinking about what constitutes child well-being, and ultimately our ethical stance on how best to advance the rights and actions of children.

In Tanzania we rolled out a unique, four-part program that took these discoveries and put them into practice through a curriculum organized into four modules. Its four steps are relevant to generating politically competent young citizens anywhere in the world:

- *Group Formation* introduces activities to encourage getting to know each other, building trust, taking others' perspectives, and sharing information, while making reasoned choices to establish an egalitarian group structure.

- *Understanding our Community* entails learning about the neighborhood: meeting elected local representatives, walking the boundaries of the district, noting how public spaces are used, conducting interviews, and considering demographic make-up.

- *Health and our Community* employs active learning methods to understand local threats and obstacles to well-being. In this step, an egalitarian group plans and decides how best to improve health and promote competence in its neighborhood.

- *Taking Action in our Community* guides the group out into the world with its newly acquired knowledge, to engage and reason with their fellow citizens and to enable their youthful insights to have impact.

In Moshi, Tanzania, children worked through these four modules to tackle an extreme danger to their community: the spread of HIV. In particular, they targeted the stigma around testing and widespread fears and uncertainties about how and why such an illness spreads. In the course of their efforts to address this public crisis in a network of neighborhoods, a large cohort of young people transformed themselves into young citizens. Our account of the struggles and successes of the Tanzania program will show how children in their own communities can acquire similar benefits.

This book is divided into four parts, each focused on its own theme while also speaking to the broader concerns of the whole book and of the Young Citizens program.

Part I, Nurture, reveals how profoundly influential the earliest periods of life are. How children are nurtured from the time they are infants through their teenage years constitutes the bedrock of human society. These are the deep roots of the Young Citizens program, a unified program of education and action that grew out of seemingly unconnected fields: neuroscience, sociology, political science, ethics, and more.

In Part II, Voice, we learn how the UN Convention on the Rights of the Child inspired young people throughout the world to assemble, to find common cause, and to speak up about their concerns. Voice is the necessary first step for all manner of social change, especially for young people who are so often ignored, even in decisions explicitly targeted at their lives. This part's chapters focus on pioneering studies and groups in Chicago, Illinois, and Cambridge, Massachusetts. It also describes the "voice" modules of the Young Citizens program that would be formally organized and evaluated in Tanzania, allowing the Tanzanian children to quickly surprise, impress, and ally with adults in their communities looking for change. All children, we demonstrate, have the capacity to articulate what happens in their lives, how it affects them, and what they need to thrive.

In Part III, Choice, we draw on theoretical work by Jürgen Habermas to understand how mothers and childcare professionals in Chicago reached consensus regarding best practices in out-of-home care for infants at risk.[3] Applying Amartya Sen's theory of capability, we examine how the limited choices of institutionalized infants in Romania and homeless adolescents in Brazil led to social deprivation and capability failure, in contrast to children in families with options to achieve well-being.[4]

Finally, in Part IV, Action, the focus returns to the Tanzanian community health program and its tremendous success. The children conduct a massive public education campaign, showing their parents and neighbors the reality of HIV and how to combat it. By engaging the community through participatory drama that balances education with activism, the young citizens speak to the heart of their community's needs, fears, and hopes. Going above and beyond the project's initial scope, the young citizens even organize a series of health fairs that educate adults and, most importantly, offer testing for the dreaded and deeply stigmatized disease. A tour de force of political action and democratic decision-making, the Tanzanian young citizens' final project shows that children's engagement in citizenship can enhance well-being. We'll suggest that this radical program can be adopted by children all around the world. Our overarching goal is to demonstrate how young people—and those who support them—can use voice, choice, and action to generate new insights and improve their communities.

An Introduction to the Authors

The Introduction to a book describing a prolonged quest should perhaps also include an introduction to its authors and how they gained the "prepared minds" to engage with its questions. We, Tony and Maya, have been partners—in science, in scholarship, and in marriage and child-rearing—for many decades. The strands of our research interests and expertise have woven together again and again, in some cases by chance as our similar insights and complementary experience overlapped, but more often deliberately as we pursued projects that blended our distinctive ways of thinking and contesting issues. Throughout this book, our intent is to present our research and its implications. But given the level of personal engagement we have had with the people we will talk about here—not only in our respective disciplines, but in experiments, expeditions, and conversations—it is inevitable that our own lived experiences will be part of the narrative.

Born in New Orleans and raised in a large, extended, Creole family, Tony arrived on the campus of the University of Wisconsin in Madison after completing Howard University Medical School. His expectations of what it would be like to live considerably north of the Mason-Dixon Line, in a European American community, were shaped by the belief that the civil rights movement had improved race relations.

Maya was born in Madison—indeed, in the same complex as the Laboratory of Neurophysiology where she and Tony

would eventually meet. Her father, the son of Swedish immigrants, served in the state legislature in the heyday of the
Wisconsin Progressive Party, of which he was a founding
member. She spent most of her childhood in Madison, where
the Wisconsin State Capitol stands on one hilltop, and Bascom
Hall, the University's center, stands on another hilltop half
a mile away. They constitute a visual symbol of the "Wisconsin
Idea" in which Maya's resolve to connect the political and the
academic is deeply rooted.[5]

Our early careers intersected in 1967 when we were postdoctoral fellows in the laboratory. Maya's interest was in the
evolution of sensory areas in the primate neocortex. Tony
studied both sensory and motor areas, while considering a
career in neurosurgery. It was astonishing to discover that we
had both lived in the same New Orleans neighborhood,
Uptown, and both on Chestnut Street. We had been separated
by merely nine blocks and nine years.

During those years known as the tumultuous sixties, an era
marked by assassinations, endless war, burning cities, and civil
unrest, a question arose spontaneously: Could a better understanding of the human brain—the evolutionary triumph of
our species—provide insight into these disturbing and disruptive events? The quest launched by that speculation has been a
mutual adventure. Rather than tell the story in tandem, however,
let us each move temporarily to the first-person singular to
tell our individual stories, before reverting to a shared voice
for the journey ahead.

Tony's Journey

My response to the assassination of Martin Luther King, Jr.,
on April 4, 1968, in Memphis, Tennessee, was to seek a new
career. I had been on a thirty-six-hour stretch in a soundproof

laboratory, mapping the reception of acoustical tones across the surface of a cat's brain. When I emerged, the campus was in an uproar. *And where have I been?* It happened that I knew the street where King was shot like the back of my hand. Once upon a time, my father's promotion required our family to move from New Orleans to Memphis, where I attended Booker T. Washington High School, a mile up the road. I passed the Lorraine Motel and glimpsed that balcony every day on my walk to school. When I heard about the assassination, visual images of the murder scene flooded my consciousness.

From that day, I never again felt comfortable too far removed from the world. With the laboratory and surgical suite no longer seeming relevant, my calling became to continue the human rights struggle that King had led. I knew, too, that in the creation of a just society, children must be involved. Leaving my research career behind, I left Madison to begin an internship in pediatrics at New York City's Metropolitan Hospital.

The hospital's neighborhood, East Harlem, was a hot spot for all forms of urban ills, from drug use and domestic violence to underemployment and deteriorating housing. My first patient was an infant born addicted to heroin, who died in agonizing withdrawal two days after her birth. I did not sleep at all during the forty-eight hours of her life.

My second patient was a fifteen-year-old boy who arrived in the emergency room having been stabbed. I stabilized him and he was quickly transferred to surgery. Normally, that would have been the end of our contact. But he remembered my name and a few days later, before being discharged, he asked to see me. "Will you be working in the emergency room tonight?" he asked. "Because I'm going to send the mother-fucker who did this to me in here—and I want you to treat him like you treated me." It took me a moment to understand, but I translated this as a call for equal impact: He stabbed me, and it is my duty to get him back. But he didn't kill me, so I don't want him to die either. He added: "If you are as good a doctor as I think you are, you will know what to do."

But what exactly *was* I to do? My chief resident advised calling the police, but I chose a different tack. I went home with the boy, met his parents, and tried to defuse his need for revenge. I don't know what happened; I never saw him again. I felt, however, that I had done what was right. I had entered his social orbit, the neighborhood whose dynamics he knew all too well. Our brief conversation had made it clear that his parents' perspective did not square very well with his. But as danger was erupting in his life, they had an opportunity to listen to his account.

This event and others like it awakened a new realization. Hospitals were endpoints for a spectrum of health issues. By breaking ranks and leaving the hospital with an angry adolescent, I had entered another zone. It was a dangerous neighborhood, but I liked the idea of moving upstream from the ultimate impacts of drugs and violence. My interest turned from the endpoint to the origins, and the hope that community programs could protect children from succumbing to inequities and urban blight. The calculus was simple: either I could labor, probably in vain, to save one newborn junkie, or, with the same amount of effort, I might be able to prevent hundreds of children from being exposed to community violence and its consequences. And so I embarked on a career in child psychiatry and public health.

My first achievements as an independent scientist were with epidemiological methods to determine the prevalence, persistence, and causes of early-developing emotional and behavior problems in preschool children. The research was

conducted in neighborhoods in northeast London and replicated in the permanent population of the island of Martha's
Vineyard in Massachusetts.[6] The main objective was to see
how accurately one could detect true psychiatric disorders in
children as young as three years old. This project generated
useful new knowledge but also, perhaps even more importantly for me, solidified my self-confidence as a conductor of
complex and innovative social science research. At Washington University's medical school, I spent the 1980s building
on this early experience. I assume these are all reasons I was
recruited to lead what became the Project on Human Development in Chicago Neighborhoods.[7]

That's when the work described in these pages was launched.
In what was to be "my turn," this study would survey the lives
of thousands of children living in all types of neighborhoods
in a city of extremes. The aim was to uncover the causes of
urban violence and therefore find ways to stop the cycle. We
would prove what my experience with that fifteen-year-old
patient in East Harlem had foreshadowed: that what goes
on in neighborhoods is a primary driver not only of levels of
violence but of poor health and risky behavior generally.

Maya's Journey

Conversation about politics often dominated dinner table time
with my father. We, his children, were a captive and attentive
audience. Today, I would call this political socialization. I
thought it was what most families did at supper. The topics
were typically about local matters, bread-and-butter politics.
All that changed when our US Senator, Joseph McCarthy,
mounted his "red scare" campaign. Through his unsubstanti-
ated, often preposterous, claims of communist infiltration

throughout the country, this red-baiting, blacklisting dema-
gogue ruined many lives and careers. McCarthy tarnished
the image of Wisconsin politics as much as Robert "Fighting
Bob" La Follette had once burnished it.[8]

This bogeyman changed the tone at our dinner table and
soon took over our living room, too. In April of 1954, when
I was fifteen, my father bought our first television set, even
though the cost was beyond our family's means. Joe McCarthy
was going to be on live television as the US Senate mounted
an investigation of his shoddy dealings with the US Army. Our
television turned out to be the only one in the neighborhood.
A standing-room-only situation resulted when all the folding
chairs were occupied. Neighbors flocked to watch the political
pugilism unfold for the next two months, until the bout ended
with a knockout by Boston lawyer Joseph Welch. His now
iconic line was "Have you no sense of decency?" Despite the
ugliness, I did not give up interest in politics. I did think there
might be a better way to do it.

In my senior year of high school, I found political salvation
in an elective course called Problems of Democracy. It offered
a new view of politics, different from that of my father the
practitioner. The course was organized from the perspective
of science! And not just political science: psychology, sociology,
and economics were integrated into the curriculum. Learning
to think about how the principles and methodology of the
behavioral and social sciences could be applied to contemporary
political issues and debates was energizing. Our final grade
depended on our selection of a topic of current interest, and
development of a position we could defend in an oral presentation. While the assignment had real impact on me at the
time, today I recall the theme, not the content. I began with
the familiar opening lines of "The Ballad of East and West"

by Rudyard Kipling: "Oh, East is East, and West is West, and
never the twain shall meet . . ." I paused, thinking there might
be laughter, but hearing none I launched into my own words:
"But they never said anything about the North and the South."
As my topic, I had chosen to argue that the racial situation in
America's South could be improved by northern states' efforts
to change attitudes in southern states.

These two experiences—neighbors huddled around a fuzzy
television set eager to see if justice prevails, and my readiness
to examine structural racism as a problem to be tackled
through science—were the first building blocks of a career
aimed at resolving the tensions between science and politics,
and between biology and justice. My scientific achievements
are rooted in exposure as an undergraduate at the University
of Wisconsin to Harry Harlow's provocative experiments in
maternal deprivation. Here's the simple way I like to sum up
the main theme of his research: A monkey isn't really a monkey
without a monkey mother. As a research assistant in Harlow's
laboratory, I observed both maternal- and surrogate-reared
infant monkeys and became convinced that the bizarre behavior of the surrogate-reared monkeys was a consequence of
their being deprived of the sensation of being touched. The
human implications of this phenomenon seemed too fundamental to be ignored.

In October of 1960, having the opportunity to greet John F.
Kennedy as he disembarked from his plane and headed to a
campaign rally on the university campus drew me once again
into a political mode. In conjunction with a social psychology
course I was taking, I designed and implemented three surveys
of attitudes toward the two candidates, Kennedy and Richard
Nixon, before and twice after the upcoming election. This work
became my ticket to graduate school in social psychology at

Northwestern University and my first publication as an independent scientist.[9] The progressive era of 1961 to 1969 kicked off with Kennedy's New Frontier vision and policies, saw his assassination, and ushered in Lyndon Johnson's Great Society reforms—yet all this political upheaval was not enough to keep me from returning to my primate research roots. I delved into social deprivation and chimpanzee vocalization for my master's thesis, after which I followed my thesis supervisor and former Harlow lab colleague, Bill Mason, to Tulane University and a new primate research center opening up in that region.

As I was engaged in my dissertation research, I became increasingly interested in the evolution and development of the primate brain. The best place to go for that training at the time proved to be a homecoming. As a postdoctoral fellow in the Laboratory of Neurophysiology at the University of Wisconsin, I expanded my competence in the theory and methods of neurobiology as I shifted back to concern with the role of touch in early development.

I had the opportunity to explore two more areas of research, experimental neurology and clinical neurology, before settling down to focus on potential links between brain-behavior and early experience in neural and behavioral development. Until a few decades ago, answers to questions in this realm were beyond reach. When I found my niche in the diverse, multidisciplinary setting of Harvard Medical School, supplemented by our tenure at Washington University School of Medicine, there was a sense that personal and professional permutations were unlimited.

After twenty-five years of laboratory research in neurobiology, with a special focus on the organization and behavioral capacities of sensory areas of the primate cerebral cortex, I moved in a direction that surprised some friends and colleagues:

I began attending the Harvard Kennedy School, drawn by contentious debates on the role of social welfare policies for children, given vast global and national inequalities. This was a time when studies of brain development were generating increasing optimism about such phenomena as plasticity and exuberant connections of neurons and neuron groups. Yet welfare policies had become dominated by calls for more measurable return on investment and understanding of market processes for allocating scarce resources. Energized at becoming a student again, I seized the opportunity to work on an independent study with Amartya Sen, noted welfare economist at Harvard College, to understand how his enlightened perspectives on human development and well-being challenged the gloomy predictions of the science of scarcity.

Progressing Together

In the 1970s, we lived in Boston's South End, a neighborhood made famous by J. Anthony Lukas's book on its busing conflict, *Common Ground*.[10] Tony was in his residency training at Massachusetts General Hospital and Maya had an appointment at Harvard Medical School and a laboratory at the New England Primate Center. We lived among the citizens portrayed in *Common Ground*: adjacent to Rachel Twymon and her family in Methunion Manor, and a few blocks from the Diver family in Rutland Square. Along with many others, we were not just residents but urban pioneers, gentrifiers, and social activists. The Twymon daughters were bused to Charlestown schools, and our seven-year-old daughter, Leigh, was bused in 1974 and 1975 to schools in Roxbury. The violence associated with the busing crisis in those years earned Boston the reputation of the "Selma of the North."[11] This experience of living on the front lines of a racially-based urban conflict, and watching as children were required to carry the torch, made us see political challenges across the world in a different way: from the children's perspective. It is fair to say that living in that neighborhood at that time was as influential as anything before or since in determining the professional paths we have taken.

During the 1980s, two new connections proved to be turning points in our careers: in 1981, we made an impromptu visit to the United Nations Mission of the African National Congress, and in 1993, Maya established our first contact with the United Nations International Children's Emergency Fund (UNICEF, now formally the United Nations Children's Fund).

When the African National Congress had only observer status, and country membership was still in the hands of the apartheid regime, we wanted to support the liberation movement by volunteering to work on refugee children's health. Johnny Makhathini, head of the ANC mission to the UN, quickly set us straight. "You don't approach a liberation movement by telling us what you want to do. . . . Any damn doctor can do that. . . . If you want to help us, then go back to St. Louis and organize an anti-apartheid coalition and a divestment campaign." Accepting his challenge, we began a search for individuals and groups interested in forming a coalition around South African divestment.

After a series of community meetings, we succeeded in organizing a broad-based coalition of trade unions, religious organizations, and civic groups. Maya and Ora Malone (a well-known local activist and national figure in the Coalition of Black Trade Unionists) were elected as co-chairs. In the summer of 1987, after five years of coalition-building, lobbying, and bringing investors, anti-apartheid leaders, and other experts to provide testimony at the state capitol, we saw Missouri become the twenty-third state to legislate divestment from South Africa. The bill required state employee pension funds to divest over six billion dollars in shares of institutions doing business with South Africa.

In 1986, as the campaign was moving toward victory, we visited an extraordinary school complex run by the African National Congress in Tanzania. It served as a safe haven for the waves of young political refugees who escaped South Africa after the Soweto uprising in 1976.[12] Its purpose was to train high-school-aged citizens for a post-apartheid, liberated society of the future—part of the broader social and economic campaign for a peaceful transition to democracy. In the spring of 1990, we were on our way to Mozambique for an international African National Congress health conference on AIDS and primary health care. Passing through Johannesburg, we were able to meet Nelson Mandela, two months after his twenty-seven years of imprisonment had ended, and had the experience of being acknowledged for our role in the divestment campaign.[13] Mandela seemed delighted by the photographs we presented to him of our raising his image at the highest point in Africa, Mount Kilimanjaro, which we had climbed in 1986. Our takeaway from this remarkable first adventure in real politics was a sense of political confidence: we had contributed something to a truly challenging liberation movement. And we could do it again.

We found our next preoccupation in the World Health Organization's prediction that by 1993, in sub-Saharan Africa alone, as many as eight million children would be orphaned by HIV / AIDS. We were moved by an idea we found in a booklet from Tanzania while at UNICEF headquarters in New York City: "Children have the potential—and the right—not only to survive to adulthood, but to develop *capabilities* to play a useful and fulfilling role in society." This small book, along with others about African AIDS orphans, were especially persuasive because they avoided calling the children "vulnerable." After several hours of conversation with the knowledgeable UNICEF librarian, Maya left with two tote bags filled with the latest publications addressing the plight of "Children in Especially Difficult Circumstances" (which UNICEF shortened to CEDC) and detailing how the recently endorsed United Nations Convention on the Rights of the Child was establishing a radical redefinition of childhood.

Staff at the New York headquarters encouraged us to visit the UNICEF Innocenti Research Center in Florence, Italy. The Center is housed in what was the world's first orphanage, commissioned in 1419 specifically to care for orphans and abandoned children. We met with staff there across several days. They encouraged us to work in a rights-based, participatory style with children infected with or affected by the HIV virus. One resource they shared was a video documentary, *Raised Voices*, which effectively made the case for what the UN Convention called participatory rights. Another was a book on the special challenges of children raised in urban areas around the world.[14] These documents became the source material for a course we taught at the School of Public Health at Harvard called The Urban Child in Global Perspective. That course in turn prompted more contact with UNICEF. We visited its offices in Romania to explore the situation of infants exposed to profound early deprivation. We asked its offices in Brazil to help us organize and manage an expedition that would expose us to the deprivations experienced and the forms of services appropriate for that country's vast numbers of street and working children.

Eager to study such conditions in an American context, Maya joined the Project on Human Development in Chicago Neighborhoods. In collaboration with Tony and Jeanne Brooks-Gunn, she implemented a means of evaluating the quality of early childcare programs. Informed by our recently acquired international perspective, we theorized that an important source of deprivation for young children might be inadequate out-of-home care. This research would test the added value of bringing parents and childcare professionals into a deliberative process of finding ways to assess that deprivation.[15] Despite our different origins, we became allies in extending the mantle of citizenship to all people, of all ages.

IN 1992, in the waning years of the apartheid regime, over two hundred children between the ages of twelve and sixteen from all regions of South Africa convened in Cape Town to discuss the problems facing them—the lasting effects of apartheid that were expected to endure long after its official end. The children's courage and intelligence were all their own, but they drew additional authority from the UN's recently adopted Convention on the Rights of the Child. They employed its Article 13, entitled Freedom of Expression, which guarantees the right "to seek, receive and impart information and ideas of all kinds." These were children determined to voice their opinions and to be consulted when big decisions about their lives were being made.

Their objective was to draw up a Children's Charter that would be incorporated into South Africa's new constitution. These young delegates approached the rare opportunity they had been given with real gravity: "Representing other children back home makes me feel very, very proud," said one young girl from the Transkei homeland. "I mean, I've got the chance to come—that's why I think I am going to do my best." She elaborated: "I am speaking for *them*, so I have to do my best, 'cause I want the best for *them*." Like many others in the group, she also intended to keep using her voice: "We are going to carry on with this even back in the Transkei. I don't think that we will speak once, and they will hear you, and everything will stop. We are going to continue."[16]

Here is a child's capacity and determination to express her ideas, fulfill her potential, and serve her community. She had no way of knowing it, but she was providing an answer to the question Deandre would pose five years later and half a world away. As Caroline Webb, a UNICEF filmmaker who documented the historic event, explains: "When the raised voices of children are truly heard, the world may have grown up a little more."[17]

PART I

Nurture

1

Known City

Chicago is the known city; perhaps more is known about it,
how it is run, how it kills, how it loves, steals, helps, gives,
cheats, and crushes than any other city in the world.

—RICHARD WRIGHT

Why do some neighborhoods experience high rates of
crime, violence, and substance abuse, while other,
seemingly similar neighborhoods are relatively peaceful and
law-abiding? What is it like growing up in a violent neighborhood? Why do some young people become "career criminals,"
while others of their peers who have had trouble with the law
ultimately become productive citizens? What can families,
communities, and governments do to promote positive social development, and where and when should they do it?
Most importantly, can we learn how to change neighborhoods
for the better?

Young citizens flourish best when they are cared for in
healthy, interconnected neighborhoods where their emotional
and physical needs are met and where their aspirations—their
dreams of what they want to do and be in their lives—can be
realized. In this chapter, we'll explore the true reasons that

neighborhoods rise and fall, and why the children whose voices should be heard are too often excluded. Later we'll see how this new understanding of community well-being was applied proactively in the Young Citizens program in Tanzania (a program this book will look to again and again for its lessons). It shows not only this newly discovered truth about communities, but that children can lead their own transformations.

Before children can become young citizens, they first must be young neighbors. They need healthy neighborhoods and communities in which to grow up.

How It Kills

In the summer of 1994, Robert "Yummy" Sandifer died. A child of one of Chicago's most violent neighborhoods, Sandifer was born to an addicted teenage mother and a father then in jail. He was raised primarily by his grandmother, in a three-bedroom bungalow shared with ten aunts and uncles and at least twenty other children. "He just wanted to be loved," one neighbor recalled of Sandifer, adding that he could be disarmingly kind. "He'd say thank you, excuse me, pardon me. He loved animals and basketball and had a way with bicycles."

Still it was true that most neighbors disliked him. By the time he was eight years old, Sandifer had been in and out of protective custody, had dropped out of school, and was known as a bully and a thief. He attached himself to a street gang called the Black Disciples and, as a child too young to be prosecuted, proved useful enough at doing some dirty work.

At the end of August 1994, Sandifer went out into a neighborhood street with a gun, started shooting at rival gang members, and managed to kill a fourteen-year-old girl walking her friend home from a barbecue. Three days later, on September 1, he was whisked away by two members of his own gang, just as he was preparing to surrender to police, and shot execution-style. He was eleven years old. The story made national news, including the cover of *Time*.[1]

Six weeks following Sandifer's death, it was five-year-old Eric Morse, another Chicago child, who captured media attention. Two older boys had been pressuring Morse to steal candy for them from a local store. When he refused, the older boys decided to punish him. They forced Morse and his eight-year-old brother Derrick up to an abandoned fourteenth-story apartment in a public housing complex and dangled Morse out the window. His brother held on to his arm as long as he could but was eventually forced to let go. Morse dropped to his death.

These two tragically early deaths highlighted a long-running, multilayered social failure: American cities' inability to control escalating rates of youth violence. The crisis had been growing since the 1960s, when white residents who could afford to flee cities for the suburbs had done so. Much industry and many livelihoods went with them. The big industrial cities, primarily in the East and Midwest, were left to rust. But they did not descend into decrepitude silently; they exploded. The first big riots took place in Los Angeles in 1965 and in Detroit and Newark in 1967.

In July 1967, a federal commission was established by President Lyndon Johnson to investigate the causes of the eruptions. Johnson asked for answers to three basic questions: What happened? Why did it happen? And what can be done to prevent it from happening again? In February 1968, the Kerner Commission's report was released. It detailed notable racial "disorders" in over 150 urban centers over a

three-year period. Its first page reassured that "this deep-
ening racial division is not inevitable" and that "choice is still
possible" but also warned sternly that action must be taken:
"To pursue our present course will involve the continuing po-
larization of the American community and, ultimately, the
destruction of basic democratic values."

It went on to emphasize that this was a problem that white
America could not turn its back on:

> The alternative is not blind repression or capitulation to
> lawlessness. It is the realization of common opportunities
> for all within a single society. . . .
>
> Segregation and poverty have created in the racial
> ghetto a destructive environment totally unknown to most
> white Americans.
>
> What white Americans have never fully understood—
> but what the Negro can never forget—is that white society
> is deeply implicated in the ghetto. White institutions cre-
> ated it, white institutions maintain it, and white society
> condones it.[2]

Twenty years later, whatever optimism was generated by
the Kerner Commission's many pages of recommendations
had faded. There was a prevalent doubt that people living in
disadvantaged urban neighborhoods could still be reached.
The heavy costs of anti-poverty programs were criticized as
worse than wasted money, with skeptics blaming welfare for
growing, not shrinking, the number of Americans living in
poverty. During the 1980s, the nature of urban violence had
changed. The perpetrators were younger, and so were many
of their victims. Drug abuse had introduced a new type of
newborn to the delivery suites of public hospitals. "Crack babies," exposed to the drug *in utero*, were born in a state of

withdrawal. Once home, they were at risk of lead poisoning, blighted housing, and dangerous neighborhoods.

The heavy use of crack also generated informal economies and gangs. Older youth took to the streets, communicating in menacing hand signs and rap rhythms. In urban centers all over the United States, residents were afraid to use local parks, travel on public transportation, or allow their children to walk two blocks to school. Over the two-year period of 1990 to 1991, the number of homicides in the United States hit an all-time high: nearly twenty-five thousand per year. Over two-thirds of these homicides happened in urban centers.

Our friend Alex Kotlowitz, whose celebrated book *There Are No Children Here* captures the lives of two brothers caught up in this urban nightmare, said at the time, "We journalists have done our jobs. . . . We have stuck this true story in the public's face. Now it is your turn." And so, our "Chicago project" was born. The lead questions were these: Could the science of human development suggest better ways to reduce crime and violence? What would it take to find out, and then to design and carry out endeavors with substantial impact?

What Makes a Neighborhood?

In the six weeks between Sandifer's and Morse's deaths in 1994, the Project on Human Development in Chicago Neighborhoods collected the first pieces of what would become a mountain of evidence about the causes of youth violence in urban centers. It would turn out to be one of the most extensive social science research projects ever undertaken on this subject.

This Chicago project was a unique, decade-long study of the city's neighborhoods, which were also seen as proxies for different kinds of cities and communities across the country and around the world.[3] The general view going in was that urban neighborhoods had suffered a thirty-year period of decline; one of the project's aims was to evaluate urban neighborhoods as child-rearing or nurturing environments, and assess how their shortcomings in that regard contributed to soaring rates of youth crime and violence.

What commanded the attention of the social science world was that some of these urban neighborhoods were succeeding, not failing, at protecting their youth from crime and violence. The Chicago project discovered a phenomenon that made some neighborhoods secure even if they were economically underprivileged, and in the midst of other, dysfunctional neighborhoods. The surprising phenomenon is called *collective efficacy*. Later we'll learn how the Young Citizens program—the culmination of our decades of research in the Chicago project and beyond—enables children in diverse communities to create collective efficacy in their own lives. But first, we need to learn what collective efficacy is and why it is so very important today.

The traditional view at the time was that neighborhoods could be described and understood using structural or compositional factors (such as race and ethnicity, wealth versus poverty, residential stability and home ownership, and so on). Such a view required studying the characteristics of the residents themselves to determine how a neighborhood functions. In other words, to understand Chicago neighborhoods, the project had to interview Chicagoans. The concept of collective efficacy grew out of a set of only ten questions embedded in an interview package of many questions used in a survey of residents across all neighborhoods of Chicago. These questions concerned issues of employment, safety and security, awareness of human services, civic and political engagement, supervision of neighborhood children, attitudes about policing, and opinions about moral and legal matters.

Within the orbit of the Chicago project, the understanding of collective efficacy was shaped by the work of Harvard sociology professor Robert Sampson, one of the project's scientific directors. The project defined it as *the willingness of residents of a neighborhood to intervene constructively in matters reflecting common interest.* The "common interest" in the case of the project was youth development.

The most elaborate definition was introduced by Stanford psychologist Albert Bandura, known for his work on self-efficacy, who saw it as core to a group's level of resolve: "People's shared beliefs in their collective efficacy influence the types of futures they seek to achieve through collective action, how well they use their resources, how much effort they put into their group endeavor, their staying power when collective efforts fail to produce quick results or meet forcible opposition, and their vulnerability to the discouragement that can beset people taking on tough social problems."[4] Bandura's eloquent explanation of the importance of perceived collective efficacy also hints at why it is so difficult to observe, let alone encourage. How *do* people develop such shared beliefs?

Collective efficacy is not always pretty. For example, it can take the form of a neighborhood "defending against outsiders" who are racially or culturally different from the typical resident. Watch groups, elaborate security systems, and social clubs can all operate for the purpose of exclusion.[5] So collective efficacy is an open-ended social construct, for good and for ill. It encourages collective actions to exert a sense of informal control, sometimes for negative reasons, as with racially charged surveillance, and sometimes for positive reasons, as with monitoring and nurturing the behavior of neighborhood children. That positive collective nurturing was happening in the less violent and least crime-ridden neighborhoods was the most surprising discovery of the Chicago project, and it became the foundation for the Young Citizens program.

There are many types of institutions in a neighborhood that make up its formal organization—schools, police and fire departments, businesses, churches, and more. By contrast, neighbor-to-neighbor relationships are informal. People get to know each other and their children through casual contacts. The mere fact that someone lives on your block is sufficient reason to recognize and exchange greetings with them, and perhaps, in an emergency, to ask a favor of them. Neighborly informality permits old and young residents to acknowledge each other and perhaps even to trust each other.

Neighborhoods high in collective efficacy protect spaces for children to play under formal and informal supervision. In such neighborhoods, adults other than children's parents can be relied on to watch out for them, to discourage fighting and the destruction of property, and to understand this quasi-parental oversight as an ordinary responsibility of group living. Neighbors can also provide positive experiences that extend parenting relationships beyond the family, such as coaching teams, organizing block parties, practicing collective hobbies, and sharing skills.

We chose to focus on collective efficacy after serious deliberation.[6] The term was not nearly as well known as self-efficacy, Bandura's coinage, and some social scientists and policymakers thought it sounded arcane. But the more popular term *social capital* was problematic, because it cast neighborhood social ties as a commodity—like money, which is transferable. Both concepts do point to the value of trust, but collective efficacy carries a greater sense of neighbors united in pursuit of the common good, and willing to intervene even when doing so causes them trouble or inconvenience. Overall, social capital just didn't encapsulate all that we theorized was happening in safer neighborhoods.

And the *broken windows* theory, frankly, couldn't be bothered to try. In his commanding 2012 book, *Great American City: Chicago and the Enduring Neighborhood Effect*, Robert Sampson carefully considers the claim that cosmetic signs of disorder in neighborhoods invite more serious crime.[7] This argument deserves real scrutiny because it has notoriously been used to justify police crackdowns on minor infractions such as throwing stones through windows and covering walls with graffiti. The promise of reducing serious crime provides cover for disproportionate punishments that damage citizens and communities in enduring ways. Sampson's analysis includes data from the Chicago project's interviews and extensive videotaped records of interviewees' neighborhoods. The results convincingly show that "broken windows policing" mistakes correlation for cause: more likely, it is a neighborhood's level of collective efficacy that explains both its serious crime rates and its physical signs of property damage and neglect. Police crackdowns probably do more harm than good to residents' sense—especially young residents' sense—of security, safety, and collective efficacy.

The Chicago Project

A long incubation period preceded the launch of the Chicago project. Many scientists from a wide variety of disciplines were consulted about the design of this large-scale and multifaceted research project and the type of organization required to carry it out. Without the strong support it received from the National Institute of Justice and from the John D. and Catherine T. MacArthur Foundation, the project would not have survived, let alone attracted this valuable early-stage input.[8] This was a partnership and investment that these two organizations considered of great value to American society.

The research design outlined two separate studies within a single project: a neighborhood study and also a longitudinal study of children developing from birth to age eighteen within those varied neighborhoods. Because we are most concerned for this book's purposes with the implications of the neighborhood study, our focus here will be on it more than the longitudinal study.[9] Descriptions of both components can be found in the fourth chapter of Sampson's *Great American City*.

In 1994, when the project officially launched, there were 2.78 million official residents within Chicago's city limits. These inhabitants were distributed across 866 census tracts of some two thousand to four thousand residents each. These census tracts often serve as the units of analysis for demographic, geographic, and political analyses of many kinds. They are small enough to reflect patterns of segregation by race or ethnicity, immigration, or socioeconomic status—yet large enough to allow for within-tract analyses. Census tracts don't necessarily map neatly to neighborhood boundaries, which are defined by historical, physical, cultural, and political ties—but they do roughly approximate Chicago's neighborhoods as most residents understand them. In some instances, the project considered two adjacent census tracts to constitute one neighborhood.

A random sample was constructed of households from the tracts and one adult was selected from each household to be interviewed.[10] Researchers then posed questions to discover what was most essential to neighbors' ability to work together on neighborhood improvements. Four basic components of collective efficacy were identified as a result. The first was *social cohesion*. Can people in this neighborhood be trusted? Is this a close-knit neighborhood? Are neighbors willing to help each other? Does it matter when neighbors do not share the same values? Do neighbors get along? The answers are all indicators of social cohesion.

The second component was *intergenerational closure:* Can you count on adults in this neighborhood to keep an eye on children to keep them safe and to make sure they don't get into trouble? Are there adults in this neighborhood children can look up to?

The third component was *informal social control:* If a child showed disrespect to an adult, defaced property, or skipped school to hang out in the streets, would people in your neighborhood be likely to scold that child? If a fight erupted near your house, would neighbors likely intervene to keep someone from being beaten up?

These first three components were all directly child-centered, but the fourth one was more infrastructural: If the fire station closest to your house was being closed, how likely would your neighbors be to protest? This question, like broader survey questions about participation in organized group activities (for example: Have you, or anyone else in your household, attended a meeting of a neighborhood group about a neighborhood problem or neighborhood improvement?) was designed to discover whether the neighborhood was perceived as an entity. Neighborhoods with a strong sense of membership were likelier to exhibit collective efficacy.

An essential aspect of the project's design was the independence of the neighborhood and the longitudinal components.

For us to be able to tell if neighborhood differences contributed significantly to differences in children's development, we had to sample children across many different types of neighborhoods. A sample of all neighborhood residents was required, not just families with children. In many neighborhoods, the majority of households were elderly people or those without children, and we had to account for them, too. And finally, while hearing residents' impressions of their surroundings was essential, it was also important for us to observe firsthand how the neighborhoods looked and functioned, so as to compare the perceived neighborhood with the observed neighborhood.

For this more intensive data gathering on neighborhoods, a random sample of eighty neighborhoods was selected to be videotaped from the citywide sample of 343.[11] The observational component of the community study was situated in this smaller (yet still representative) sample of all neighborhoods, and so was the longitudinal-developmental component of the overall design.

Collective Efficacy in Chicago

While the project began as a response to escalating rates of crime and violence in American cities, it did not take long for it to evolve into a study embracing several fields of inquiry. Jeff Morenoff, a graduate student at the University of Chicago at the time, used geographic information systems (GIS) technology to produce maps comparing the addresses at which homicides occurred with those where mothers giving birth to underweight infants lived. Seven years' worth of data, beginning in 1990, revealed a striking spatial concordance. Seeing the data superimposed onto Chicago's 866 census tracts, any observer is forced to ask: What could be a common denominator for these seemingly unconnected events?[12]

The data collected by the longitudinal study was expanded to include not only delinquent, criminal, and violent behavior, but also birthweight, any history of asthma, obesity, anxiety, or depression, and age of first sexual intercourse.[13] This marked a decisive turn toward public health and health promotion.[14] A valuable archive was created at the University of Michigan to make available to the public the data collection methods employed, the raw data, and selected publications by the project.[15]

It is all too easy to assume that a neighborhood's level of collective efficacy depends exclusively on its own residents' beliefs and actions. In truth, neighborhoods radiate their character and influence outside their formal spatial bounds. One neighborhood's activity can spill over into an adjacent one, affecting it positively—as might be the case with Little League baseball—or negatively, as would be expected in the case of illegal drug markets. Studying the spatial dimensions of neighborhoods can reveal their interdependence.

Perhaps most importantly, the Chicago project revealed the distinctive spatial disadvantage of African American neighborhoods and the spatial advantage of predominantly European American ones. African American neighborhoods with high levels of collective efficacy were almost always surrounded by neighborhoods with low collective efficacy, while European American neighborhoods with low collective efficacy were almost always embedded in regions of high collective efficacy.[16] There were no European American neighborhoods of cumulative disadvantage, as defined by demographic and family factors such as employment status, educational background, and marital status of the head of household. About two-thirds of African American neighborhoods do exhibit cumulative disadvantage. It is well established that it is in these types of neighborhoods that residents are exposed to the highest rates of violence. When these structural factors become ingrained in such neighborhoods, sweeping approaches are needed to build collective efficacy.

An African American child raised in a racially segregated neighborhood with high collective efficacy must someday encounter children from the low-collective-efficacy neighborhoods that surround his own. Gang members from the low-collective-efficacy neighborhoods, for example, may confront well-socialized, nonviolent children from the higher-collective-efficacy neighborhoods and coerce them into joining their gangs. But there could be a hopeful aspect, too—if only we knew how to enhance collective efficacy.

Immigrant Effects

Thinking along different lines, although immigrants arriving from Mexico tend to be economically poor, one might expect them to have the capacity to form neighborhoods with high collective efficacy. A number of factors might contribute to this. Their families might be more stable, with married parents and a working father, than equally poor African American families. Their neighborhoods might feature more of the aspirational quality that supports collective efficacy. Immigrants often believe in the American dream, and aspire to become US citizens, purchase homes, and raise their children's educational attainments and standards of living. This hopefulness stands in stark contrast to the atmosphere in neighborhoods of equally poor African Americans, who, in the post–Martin Luther King era, have become more jaded

about their likelihood of becoming fully accepted and as-
similated Americans.[17] While aspirational qualities are true
for first-generation immigrants, second- and third-generation
descendants often lose the first generation's optimism. Their
social behaviors and physical health deteriorate. Birth weights
decrease successively. Rates of asthma, school problems, and
delinquency increase. Even depression and suicide have been
shown to increase from the first to the second generation
among immigrants.[18]

Research into this so-called immigrant paradox is ongoing.
Even if people who choose to immigrate tend to be healthy,
strong, and optimistic, these favorable attributes can be worn
down over time. Finding themselves disenfranchised by appearance, poverty, and insecurity, those who do not achieve
their dreams might succumb to an all-too-familiar pattern
of cynicism and hopelessness. Perhaps this accounts for the
overall modest level of collective efficacy found in Latino
neighborhoods.

Chicago's past and present tell us much about the effects of
the rise of industrialization and the post-industrial economy;
about patterns of immigration from Europe, Latin America,
and the Deep South of the United States; and about spatial
segregation by wealth and ethnicity. Like London in the
nineteenth century, today's Chicago is arguably the best
understood city in the world. The novelist Richard Wright was
right to deem Chicago the "known city." The completed spatial
analyses added to that knowledge by revealing a picture of
three separate Chicagos—an African American Chicago, a
Latino American Chicago, and a European American Chicago.[19] The residents of these, all citizens of one world-class
city, ride the same trains yet coexist in social isolation. This is
the modern city. It is a great experiment that partially works

but leaves full democracy and true social justice just out of reach, urging us ever onward. This has not changed much over the last two decades.

The knowledge gains of the Chicago project could also be generalized, however, to cities across the world. Researchers today find that collective efficacy helps to protect a community from crime and illness in places as far-flung as Stockholm and Brisbane and, as we shall see, Moshi, Tanzania.[20]

Chicago, the known city of radical community organizers, academic urban sociologists, architects, and poets, was the ideal place to plant this first study of collective efficacy. The study changed the discourse on the importance of community to the health, security, and well-being of city dwellers. As it grew from a study narrowly focused on criminal behavior to an endeavor concerned with public safety and public health, the Chicago project took on global significance for the quality of life in cities.

Chicago's Voice

This extraordinary new knowledge would not have been discovered if the project had not listened to the people of the city. The team of research assistants responsible for conducting thousands of interviews were struck by how generous people were in raising their voices, even about the harshest aspects of their lives.[21] Here are comments made by just three research assistants, which were echoed frequently by other team members:

> It amazed me all the time how people understood our mission and would give you everything from their brother having murdered someone to other personal things. I found there is a great dignity and trust in science.

I would never have thought people in Chicago would let you into their homes. In training, I used to sit there and think, "This is not going to work. These people are not going to let us into their homes." But so many people invite you in and they'll just talk! If you don't cut people off, you can leave a house knowing everything about their lives!

I went to interview a boy and his dad. As we were leaving the tiny apartment, I noticed the father in another room, putting a big gun in his pants. He knew I noticed. He was hiding it from his son. He escorted us with this big gun. . . . We found out this dad accompanies his boy to the bus every day like clockwork. He waits for the boy to get on the bus and waits for him to get off. On the entire ride home, my partner and I had this great conversation about how it's difficult to put ourselves in that environment and how we're blessed to not be in that environment. We talked about how on a daily basis people's environments are life-threatening—a life of fear—and we attempted to understand that a family's economic situation is not necessarily correlated with a family's (social) environment. It opened my eyes a lot. Six weeks later, three girls were killed on the corner where we had been—where this dad escorts his boy every day to the bus stop with a gun.

The stories the research assistants were telling us, like our later close encounters in Romania and Brazil, were not just sources of data. These stories invited us into the lives and world of the children. What was the son thinking as his father took him to the bus stop? But the concept of collective efficacy also taught us not to see only negative or harmful interactions. We had to document the many positive encounters that occur in neighborhoods. We wanted to go deeper into the lives of children and the neighborhoods in which they were socialized.

Missing from the project's comprehensive study were the perspectives of youth as the subjects of the research, and careful considerations of their rights to participate in matters that naturally apply to them.

There were two reasons to accept this invitation into children's lives. One was to get closer to them and gain a more valid understanding of how children experience external control over their lives, especially in urban neighborhoods. The other was to bridge the gap between science and action, and go beyond studying the lives of children to improve them. All the findings pointed to the conclusion that "downstream" solutions—like arresting delinquent youth—were more effective when "upstream" efforts were also made to engage with, listen to, and encourage children.

We had a new goal: to learn how to cultivate collective efficacy in communities that desired strong local democracy and better health for their citizens of all ages. Eventually we would realize this goal in the Young Citizens project in Tanzania, but along the way we found that there are two sides to the process of cultivating collective efficacy. The adult-centric side is to deepen an understanding of the kind of supervision and guidance that grows out of respect for the child. The child-centric side recognizes the child as a rights holder and legitimate community member with an active role to play. It recognizes the child as someone who can contribute to the generation and durability of collective efficacy. These two perspectives need not be conflictual. The surest way to achieve and maintain collective efficacy is to value and facilitate multigenerational citizenship. The formula is straightforward: respectful and involved adults together with respected, valued, and heard children produce and promote collective efficacy.

Listening to the voices emanating from neighborhoods was the first step toward understanding the rudiments of nurturing young citizenship. In all of its detail and comprehensiveness, the Chicago project allowed us to look backward, to the nurturing and well-being of children from the earliest ages, and also to look forward, to the natural consequences that follow when children's and communities' wishes or concerns are respected—or ignored. In the next two chapters we continue tracing our quest to learn all that happens when human rights are denied. Much optimism resulted from the Chicago project's discovery that the well-being of children, and indeed of entire communities, originates in the social environment. But that optimism needs to be critically examined against its bleak counterpoint: that children's rights and lives are far too often violated, even on a national scale.

2

Lonely Cradles

Having never watched any parent raise himself, he could not even comprehend what such a relationship should be.

—TONI MORRISON

F amilies raise children to be able to raise children; communities nurture citizens to secure citizenship for future generations. So, what does it mean when communities and societies not only fail to nurture their citizens, but spectacularly fail to care for their children at all? What happens when a government requires families to give birth to infants— whom they must then surrender to state institutions to raise—as a means of expanding the nation's workforce? Just such a barbarous demand was made by the Romanian state beginning in 1966, and the results are an admonishment to all subsequent human societies: the way we raise our children is fundamental to the enduring humanity of our species, as well as the functioning of our societies.[1] Children must have the protection, provision, and participation rights outlined in the UN Convention on the Rights of the Child—especially if they are to survive and to thrive in the fabricated environments and massive bureaucratic structures that have come to govern community and family life.

The key to human development lies in the science of nurturing: the ways in which the young are valued and guided to become and remain effective members of their communities. Understanding this process requires that scientists have ways to determine whether children are receiving what they need to maintain sturdy developmental trajectories to full maturity. Accurate tracking of this might even tell us where as a species we are headed.

In this chapter, we will explore how this science applies to the endangerment of society's youngest members, which children and communities are prospering, and which are endangered. Before children can become engaged and effective young citizens, they must first be nurtured into wholesome, functioning human beings—and the responsibility for doing this rests not only with parents but with local communities and society as a whole.

How do children acquire the knowledge and skills they will eventually need to raise their own children? This vital learning process begins much earlier than many people might suppose, and the consensus is that it is not as simple as watching a parent. Instead, the key to good parenting might be in the parent's own early experience with touch: being held, cuddled, embraced. In the past half-century, studies of adult brain activity and behavior—as well as of human infants, other primates, and other mammals—have been revealing. They show that the most crucial time for social development is the earliest part of life. We now know that the key to infants' development lies in the nourishing of their sensory systems as they are exposed to the feel of others' touch, the sight of others' smiles, and the sounds of familiar voices. We know, too, that some of these first developmental experiences must occur within a critical window of time. Although many years of contact are required to realize our full potential as humans, the foundation for this long development must be laid when, as infants, we are most helpless and in the hands of others.

Regrettably, much of what we have learned about this crucial time in human development has come from observing neglected infants—children denied the most fundamental elements of care during crucial stages of development. Let's look at how such inhuman conditions came to exist in certain places, and how they have contributed to our current understanding of the costs of neglect.

Alone Together

Bucharest, Romania, 1995. The scene is of voiceless infants staring into space, captive in the nursery of a state-run institution for forsaken newborns. We were invited to this *leagăn* (also the word for "cradle," the plural of which is *leagăne*) through a contact in the local UNICEF office and are hosted by a professional staff member. All the small residents, between two and six months of age, lie in cradles on their backs, tightly swaddled in cotton blankets. Their metal beds form regimental rows and columns, roughly five across and five deep. The initial impression is of an orderly array of dormant cocoons.

The only sounds of life are our own muffled gasps and cautious footsteps. We are overcome by a feeling, in this crowded room, of being very much alone. Could it be the infants have just emptied their bottles and fallen asleep? No sign of bottles or holders in their cribs. Is this their nap time? Nap time is all day, every day. Open, empty eyes stare blankly into space. Walking from crib to crib, bending to make eye contact and utter soft sounds, we elicit no response. The infants show no awareness of human presence or of any feature of this sterile environment. We sense they are alive—often their eyes are open—but they are not reactive. We make dozens of attempts to be recognized, to make them aware of our presence, but they do not even blink. No expression, no movement, no utterance. The word *infant* comes directly from the Latin for "unable to speak," but here is voicelessness taken to a terrifying extreme.

The cribs in which these isolated children spend their days, months, and years define their entire, lonely world. They are rarely touched by human hands, except for bathing and redressing. They are not socially engaged in human exchanges such as eye contact and smiling. They do not respond to their names. They do not acknowledge the others adjacent to them, unable to speak, and neither are they encouraged to. But everyone knows that babies cry. Why do we not hear even a single wail? It turns out that if the early cries of newborns produce no consequences for days or weeks, they fall silent.

In this room, it is as if someone has pushed a "mute" button. We have entered their restricted and homogeneous world and presented ourselves as attentive and animated strangers, expecting the babies either to warm to our presence as an unaccustomed stimulation or to reject it as a distressing novelty. But instead they simply do not react—not even with a focused gaze. After repeated efforts to evoke species recognition from this supine young population, our need to leave becomes urgent.

Decree 770

In 1966, believing that an increase in population would lead to a larger workforce and therefore improve his nation's economy, Romania's despotic president, Nicolae Ceaușescu, pushed through Decree 770. The new law banned abortion and birth control and was expected to increase the nation's population from twenty-three million people to thirty million within a few decades. Under the surveillance of Ceaușescu's brutal secret police, women underwent mandatory pelvic exams at their place of work. Any detected pregnancy was monitored up to delivery. There were also tax penalties and other economic incentives to encourage more childbearing.[2]

Ceaușescu's chilling rationale for Decree 770 was that "the fetus is the property of the entire society." To manage this "property," a new kind of government system sprang up. This system provided institutional care for any infants turned over by mothers who knew they would not have the resources to support the child they had been required to carry.

These state-operated children's residential institutions in Romania would, regrettably, prove to be ideal settings in which to examine, and mourn, the developmental consequences of severe touch deprivation and social deprivation. For institutionalized children raised in this form of custodial care, survival needs were met but psychological needs were not. Hundreds of thousands of infants and children from birth to age three lived in the leagăne over a period of three decades. Around age three, these young people were moved to other state accommodations, intended to provide education as well as subsistence, under the auspices of the Ministry of Education (the Ministry of Health was responsible for the leagăne). It was in such government housing that the leagăn populations would spend the remainder of their formative years. At eighteen years of age, they would be released to survive on their own.

These invasive and coercive pronatalist policies proved to be both a human rights and an economic disaster, especially as Ceaușescu's other policies crippled Romania with the inefficiencies of central planning, declining technological competitiveness, and a loss of foreign markets for its goods. Severe domestic austerity measures to reduce the national debt brought more adverse impacts on living standards, resulting in massive shortages in food, energy, and medical and household supplies. Increasing hardships across the country contributed significantly to the brief but bloody revolution in 1989 that culminated in the Christmas Day executions of Ceaușescu and his wife. So ended the last of the Soviet empire in Eastern Europe.

Yet the long-term effects of Romania's harsh intrusion into reproductive behavior and family life could not be reversed by the revolution and repeal of Decree 770. During the more than twenty years that the decree was in effect, an estimated two percent of Romanian children were cared for, housed, and educated by the state. Five years after the 1989 revolution, the situation for the leagăn children was still bleak. The political transition had stabilized, and some family planning policies had been relaxed, but parents had long accepted the leagăne as part of society. Economic conditions remained harsh for most families. These notorious "orphanages," which had brought such shame on the country at the end of Ceaușescu's reign, were still admitting tens of thousands of infants and young children a year. Impoverished mothers still left maternity homes without their newborns; such infants would be transferred to the leagăne until the family had the means to care for them. Whatever initial hopes their parents had, in reality most leagăn infants were seldom visited, let alone retrieved, by their birth families. Leaving them in the care of an indifferent and neglectful state institution became all too easy.

This practice of institutionalizing healthy newborn infants (as well as disabled, or, as they were called, "irrecoverable" children) continued for years. It was only in 2007 that the European Union deemed the reforms to the leagăn system sufficient to permit Romania to claim membership in the union.[3]

These lonely cradles had even more extensive consequences as a generation's deficiencies in nurturing got passed on to the next, through diminished social awareness and deficient parenting skills. Infants raised in the leagăne had little chance of becoming fully socialized adults with the capacity to nurture their own offspring. The leagăne's effects trickled down through subsequent families, as we saw for ourselves that same day.

Motherless Mother

Down the hall from the leagăn's nursery we encountered an agitated young woman in her twenties who had come to convince the administration that she was ready to take her daughter home for another trial visit. This young mother was well known to the staff, as they had been responsible for the care of her child since its birth.

In fact, this mother herself had been raised in a leagăn until she turned eighteen. At that age, after a life in custodial care, these dependent, unsocialized "adults" were either placed in factory jobs or simply released to the streets to fend for themselves. This woman, upon release from her leagăn, had found a job as a domestic servant with a family in Bucharest. She vaguely described to the leagăn staff a nonconsensual sexual encounter, which she might or might not have understood to be the cause of her pregnancy, when she first visited the infant daughter sent there from the maternity home. Now she was pleading her case through stunted gestures and strained utterances typical of those raised from their early months in institutions, seeking her daughter's release from the leagăn to her care. She yearned to keep her child at home, even though she was barely able to care for herself.

The limited professional staff available to work with "motherless mothers" recognized her regrettably common dilemma, seeing in it evidence of the devastating transgenerational legacy of the lonely cradles. In their minds, the only viable recourse, however problematic, was to commit the offspring of these post-institutionalized mothers to the same gloomy institutionalized childhood, repeating the cycle of early social impoverishment.

The leagăn professional staff, as well as caretakers, had little to no awareness of the history and consequences of institutional care beyond what they observed in their own institutions. This was in part because, beginning in 1977, Ceaușescu had banned research and instruction in psychology, believing the field could undermine public order. University departments were abolished and funding was discontinued. These moves were not reversed until the early 1990s, giving staff members of these leagăne little opportunity to learn how their common, substandard practices were impoverishing the social and mental lives of their young charges.

The alternative, unacceptable to the leagăn staff, would have been to place the child in this motherless mother's custody, threatening it with unintended neglect and abuse. The staff had witnessed her maternal deficiencies. She did not know how to hold her baby or bathe her. She could not be counted on to remember to feed her, and she might on occasion leave the baby unattended. The caretakers could handle at least these basic physical necessities, and so the leagăn was a marginally better alternative for this infant.

The mother begged repeatedly through her improvised language to be trusted, and when defeat was obvious, she wept.

Untouched

The consequences of Romania's criminal state neglect were plain to see: children progressed from mute and motionless infants to self-directed, motorically repetitive, noncommunicative toddlers, who were unprepared for the demands of society beyond the institution. But what can science reveal about how such deficient practices yield their inhumane outcomes? What biological potential goes untapped when a child is untouched, unnamed, and never claimed? What fundamental social interests are never awakened? What happens when our social species is raised within the confines of a lonely cradle? What is the science of nurture, and what can we learn from the science of neglect?

The lasting effects of early deprivation have been documented for two centuries. As a young medical student in 1801, Jean Marc Gaspard Itard attempted to socialize a "feral" child who had been spotted living in the woods of southern France. Having worked with deaf children, he believed that with patient tutoring, this child, who appeared to be about twelve years old, could learn to conform to social customs and to speak normally. Five years of persistent, personalized effort revealed to Itard the deep extent of the boy's social and linguistic impairments. François Truffaut's 1970 film *L'Enfant Sauvage* is an adaptation of the story; his portrayal of the frustrated Itard conveys how impossible remedial socialization becomes when efforts are undertaken too late in a child's development.

In the 1940s, early social deprivation attracted the interest of psychoanalysts. Working in South American orphanages, René Spitz coined the term *hospitalism* to describe the persistent emotional consequences for children reared in impersonal, regimented settings.[4] In the same era, British psychiatrist John Bowlby came to a similar conclusion based on his study of delinquent boys. Delving into their backgrounds, he found that a substantial number of these boys had experienced prolonged separations from their mothers; the longer the period of separation, the more "affectionless" they were—the more emotionally barren. The World Health Organization commissioned Bowlby to review the literature on maternal deprivation, and published his summary in 1951; the monograph *Maternal Care and Mental Health* condemned institutional care for young children and urged frequent parental visitation for hospitalized children, despite the prevalent concern that hospital visitors were a dangerous source of infection.[5] This had an immediate impact on early child-rearing. The worldwide dissemination of the publication across multiple editions prompted improved training for institutional workers in the psychological development of children in long-term care.

Surrogate Mothers

Around this same time, psychology professor Harry Harlow was studying infant learning in monkeys. In 1952, Harlow had established a primate laboratory in a former factory near the University of Wisconsin-Madison and begun researching cognitive development. At that time the laboratory's immediate challenge was to raise rhesus monkeys—the most common nonhuman primate used in research—under hygienic and standardized conditions. To reduce the variability that monkeys raised by their own mothers exhibit, due to differences in nutrition, infection, and injury, Harlow designed the now famous surrogate mother to be integral to his monkey subjects' standardized care routine. To make surrogate mother bodies, he started with cones of wire mesh and covered them with padding and washable terry cloth covers. This soft, fuzzy thorax featured a narrow slot to hold a doll-sized nursing bottle to provide nutrition. Topping it was a wooden head with beady eyes to suggest facial features.

In one experiment, infants were equipped with two "mothers," only one of which had a covering. The other was bare wire. Half the infants got their meals from their soft mother and half were fed by their wire mother. But all spent most of their time with the soft mother. And although surrogate-raised infants' physical growth often exceeded that of mother-reared infants, when they were exposed to their mother-reared peers, their social behavior was distinctly abnormal. The surrogate-raised infants failed to exhibit normal monkey social interactions such as the approach-avoidance or rough-and-tumble play so common in the maternal-raised and feral infants. Even worse, they spent their waking moments engaged in unnatural, repetitive mannerisms such as rocking, swaying, self-clinging, and non-nutritive sucking. They showed no interest in play objects and social interactions with available playmates. Clearly, early maternal nurturing—especially touch or "contact comfort"—is necessary but not sufficient for infants to acquire interest in their social and physical surroundings.

The surrogate-raised monkeys' deficiencies and oddities would continue to hamper their lives even as they reached reproductive age. Early deprivation prevented both males and females from breeding successfully. If artificially bred, socially deprived females were deficient in rearing their infants. It was a dreadful foreshadowing of Romania's "motherless mothers."[6]

Why did depriving monkeys of maternal touch lead to such enduring deficits in social development? Why did it eventually disrupt both reproductive behavior and maternal behavior?

These behavioral studies demonstrate a critical period: deprivation needs to begin before a certain age to be an enduring deficit. But what might be the underlying brain locus and mechanism that is fundamentally altered? What accounts for the irreversibility after that certain age? Most importantly, what does this mean for the development of the human brain? Are there specific parts of the brain that require wiring or programming at an early age to ensure "normal" socialization—without which human infants struggle to become human, let alone young citizens?

Unlicked and Dysregulated

In the early 1990s, an intriguing line of new research redirected Maya's attention from the role of touch in early socialization of primates to the early development of rat pups. Her long-standing interest in early social deprivation in monkeys had broadened during her graduate studies to include the development of vocalization in laboratory- and mother-reared chimpanzees.[7] After devoting three decades to neurophysiological research on the organization and development of the somatic sensory system in primates, she felt she was not getting any closer to a neural mechanism that might explain the lifelong consequences of early tactile deprivation.[8] She was ready to make a change. Her growing interest in the plight of institutionalized infants in Romania prompted her to look up a study she had once flagged in Tony's stack of *Science* magazine articles. Freshly reminded of research on the adrenal cortex of newborn rats, she decided to look into how tactile deprivation in pre-weaned rat pups leads to permanent changes in some parts of the nervous system she had not considered in primates.

Rat mothers always lick their newborn pups vigorously in the first three weeks of life. Pups who are denied this intense level of contact suffer lifelong changes in memory processing and ability to control the secretion stress hormone corticosterone (a rodent equivalent to cortisol). This dysregulation of stress hormone takes place in an area of the brain area called the hippocampal cortex, so named for its resemblance to a seahorse. From an evolutionary biology perspective, it is an area of the brain more primitive than the neocortex. In addition to its memory functions, the hippocampus contributes to the regulation of the hypothalamic-pituitary-adrenal (HPA) system in its role of stress hormone regulation and therefore contributes to an individual's level of "stress reactivity."[9] Dysregulation of this vital function can be detected by measuring hormone levels before, immediately after, and within an hour of an acute stress event; a well-functioning HPA system activates quickly in an emergency situation and then ramps down afterwards, allowing vital body functions to return to their basal levels. Rat pups experiencing insufficient maternal licking (that is, touch or tactile stimulation) prior to weaning fail to develop an efficient "thermostatic regulation" function of the HPA system. This compromises not only their bodies' response to threatening life events, but also the regulation of their demands for energy.

Prior research documenting hippocampal damage in "unlicked" newborn rodents was important, but what captured our greatest attention was the question of what this implied for primates, and particularly humans, similarly deprived of tactile input in infancy. Thinking of the institutionalized infants in Romania, we imagined that the HPA axis might play many crucial roles, and resolved to explore, as quickly and diligently as possible, what noninvasive methods could be used to measure the stress hormone cortisol in these infants. We designed a protocol for salivary cortisol collection, and recruited and trained US and Romanian colleagues in the saliva collection procedures. We glimpsed the possibility that such research in humans could help to establish that the hippocampal and adrenal cortices play a role in the mediation of early tactile deprivation and behavioral consequences already well-defined in non-human primates.

Stressful events activate many of an organism's higher cortical processing regions, whose function is to assess immediate levels of distress and danger. This information is then fed back to the all-important hypothalamus at the base of the brain, which controls the nearby pituitary by both neural connections and hormonal secretions. The pituitary, in turn, activates the adrenal glands located atop the far-away kidneys. These are the three key components in the HPA axis. The inner core, or medulla, of the adrenal gland immediately secretes the "fight or flight" hormones adrenaline and noradrenaline as part of a set of responses to a disturbing event. Around the same time, the outer layers of the adrenal gland start secreting cortisol at a slower pace, and the process of restoring the balance of critical metabolic and immune functions begins. Cortisol's function in responding shortly after the release of the fight or flight hormones is to regulate activity in those metabolic systems that are taxed by the initial emergency response until homeostasis (or allostasis) can be restored. This regulatory mechanism of dampening the consequences of the fight-or-flight response is characterized as a negative feedback loop. Most emergencies do not last a long time, so the stress component of the HPA axis is dampened soon after the disturbing event is resolved.

This beneficial function can, however, turn from adaptive and protective to maladaptive if cortisol is chronically activated by frequently occurring, prolonged, or unpredictable stressors. If the regulatory capacity of the HPA axis is impaired such that chronic secretion of cortisol occurs, the action of cortisol can instead become harmful, resulting in damage to many organ systems, including the nervous system itself.[10]

With this totally novel understanding came a barrage of questions. How similar were the neural mechanisms of touch deprivation in rat pups to those of surrogate-raised monkeys in a laboratory, or of swaddled infants in a leagăn? What are the consequences of touch deprivation for the regulation of the HPA stress system? Does the system show persistent abnormalities throughout early development that relate to deficits in mental and motor development? Could the leagăn children ever be made whole again?

Given the knowledge accumulated over the last century on the detrimental consequences of institutional rearing on both physical growth and psychological development, the gross neglect of the leagăn children was and is unfathomable. As these neglected infants matured, their passivity, muteness, blank facial expressions, social withdrawal—and later, their development of bizarre, stereotypic movements—all bore a strong resemblance to the behavior of the socially deprived macaques and chimpanzees of Harlow's laboratory.

Voice of the Voiceless

It was time to forge a link between the hippocampal effects discovered in rodents and those of early social deprivation of legions of infants in Romania—victims of poor economic planning and top-down and untested public policy. But what would be an acceptable strategy to examine the children's acute response to stress—that is, their reactivity? We decided to undertake a new neurobehavioral research project to find a noninvasive method of collecting cortisol samples, based on a recent discovery that cortisol could be measured as accurately in saliva as in blood. This offered the chance to avoid the distress typically associated with venipuncture.[11] Knowing this, we could envision identifying an available population of human infants who were subject to prolonged neglect, and measuring three separate features of their pathological adaptation to it.

First, we would measure the fluctuation in their cortisol levels over the course of a twenty-four-hour period (a diurnal cycle). This would yield a picture of the children's preparedness to engage in routine social and physical activities. In a normal child, cortisol levels are highest upon waking; studies had already shown that, by twelve weeks of age, this early-morning peak in diurnal secretion is an established pattern.[12] Presumably the body intends to activate energy stores following a night of fasting. Perhaps it would be otherwise with the leagăn children. They might lack not only the motivation to seek human touch but also the energy to engage in reciprocal social interactions, however rare opportunities for those might be.

Second, we would test how they responded to a single stressful event; this would help us evaluate their capacities to regulate the hippocampal HPA system following challenges and to return vital bodily functions to a normal state. Recent evidence suggested that stress-reactivity regulation was mature by six months of age (and more recent evidence suggests it might be mature as early as one month of age).[13]

Third, using these two profiles of the stress system, we would assess the children's motor and mental development to discover whether dysregulated cortisol secretion could help explain their awkward, withdrawn behavior, lack of agency, and even serious growth retardation despite the availability of adequate nutrition.[14]

The next step was to identify an institution in Romania where we could study the diurnal and reactivity regulation in infants or young children. We learned that Joseph Sparling, a developmental psychologist at the University of North Carolina, had been doing research in a leagăn since 1991. He had received funding for "an experimental and humanitarian effort to try to improve the quality of life, mental health, and developmental progress of young children in a Romanian Orphanage."[15] When we reached out to him for ideas, we heard about his new enrichment study of a large group of children in Iaşi, Romania's second largest city, some of whom had been randomly chosen for an enriched childcare intervention and the rest of whom would be subject to standard care settings in the leagăn. He welcomed our interest in stress regulation.

Sparling's program was based on his extensive prior experience with high-risk children in the United States, designing interventions to improve the quality of care and early education received in center- and home-based programs.[16] His fundamental research question, which we would adopt, was this: Could enriched institutional care practices improve the social, emotional, and cognitive development outcomes for children in the leagăne?

When we began our communication in 1993, Sparling had already trained a Romanian team of recent high school graduates as active and sensitive caregivers. They were now completing a year-long social and educational intervention, based on his randomized experimental design, involving thirty-five "enriched" infants and thirty "deprived" (meaning non-enriched) infants, beginning on average at six months of age. In the enriched group, each trained caregiver was assigned to a small sibling group of four children. Each small sibling group had its own room for play and sleeping and was cared for by the same person seven hours a day, five days a week, over the twelve months of intervention. The caregiver engaged the children by name, encouraged social communication, and provided educational games and psychosocial stimulation similar to those commonly offered in high-quality early education settings. The deprived group received the custodial care generally available in such institutions.

After obtaining funding, recruiting a small group of collaborators, and defining our method to sample cortisol in saliva, we received permission from Sparling, Harvard Medical School's Committee on Human Studies, and the director of the leagăn representing Romania's health ministry. The plan was to collect daily saliva samples from these two groups of children, the enriched and the deprived, to examine basal levels of cortisol throughout the day, and how cortisol levels varied in response to a challenging situation. We would measure their stress reactivity in response to a routine physical exam. At the same time, we planned to assess motor and mental development.

The deprived group remained in individual metal cribs in the large "standard" rooms with around twenty other children. Care in this setting took the form of diaper changes, bathing, dressing, and feeding. Each caregiver was responsible for twenty children on average. Under these standard conditions (which are in truth substandard), the untrained and overwhelmed staff spent most of their time on custodial activities: mopping floors, doing laundry, changing sheets, preparing and serving meals, and cleaning dishes and cooking utensils. There were no planned activities or outdoor exercises, and social interaction was not encouraged. While not surprised, we were saddened to see these children so self-contained. They occupied themselves throughout the day by repetitively rocking and jumping in their barren cribs.

The enriched and the deprived children had been separated into different rearing conditions from ages six months to eighteen months, but when we arrived to collect our cortisol and behavioral data they were, on average, twenty-four months of age and were back living together and receiving the same custodial care in the large standard rooms.

For purposes of comparison, rather than using existing data on cortisol levels obtained from American children, we managed to obtain both cortisol and behavioral measures from family-reared Romanian children of the same age recruited from a local day care setting. This group is referred to as the *creşă* children. We collected data from them at the same three times of day in their day care center, and we obtained their stress reactivity samples by the same methods. The same pair of physicians performed a brief physical exam as the social stressor.

Behavioral development was assessed using a battery of age-calibrated indices known as the Bayley Scales of Infant Development.[17] Bayley scores measure how closely mental and motor scores match the expected level of performance in various domains of brain and behavioral development. We took saliva samples multiple times over two consecutive days to examine both daily cortisol levels and reactivity to a mildly stressful event, the physical examination.

We collected saliva first in the child's homeroom to obtain basal levels, and then in the leagăn examination room following the physical exam to obtain stress levels. While a caretaker held the child, the child was shown a cotton roll and asked to suck, not chew, on it. One end of the roll was gently placed in the child's mouth and left there for about one minute. Afterward the saliva was squeezed into a labeled, color-coded collection tube and refrigerated. Our team did this at 8 AM, noon, and 7 PM on two consecutive days.

On the second day, in addition to the morning and noon collections, the team took samples immediately before the physical examination, fifteen minutes after the examination, and forty-five minutes after the examination. These reactivity samples were collected in the afternoon, starting between 5 PM and 6 PM, with the final post-stress sample taken around 7 PM (which for day one served as the evening diurnal sample but for day two served as the post-stress measure).

The prediction was that the enriched group would have values midway between the creşă and deprived groups, both in cortisol regulation and in mental and motor development. The basis for this expectation was that the enriched group had significantly higher growth and behavioral scores relative to the deprived group after the twelve months of special sibling group care and social and educational activities they experienced between the ages of six months and eighteen months. These scores included both physical growth measurements and behavioral development assessments using the Denver Developmental Screening Test.[18] At the time of our arrival, when the children averaged twenty-four months, the burning question was whether the enriched group's advantages had widened, diminished, or been maintained in the aftermath of the intervention. The summary of the findings using the full array of all the hormonal and behavioral data on these three groups collected at ages at twenty-four and thirty-six months follows.

The findings (which have been supported by more recent studies) indicate that both basal and reactivity regulation profiles are established as early as the first weeks of life.[19] This is when many of these infants are in nurseries at the maternity home where they were delivered, and where they stay until space is available in a leagăn. Because we had the opportunity to return for a second set of cortisol and behavioral assessments when the children were on average age three, we gained additional evidence of the stability of the initial treatment effects on behavior and HPA regulation.[20]

Turning now to the results, let us spend a moment on what these groups of children looked like. The home-reared children attending weekly day care were characterized by normal mental and motor development.[21] Those leagăn children who had not received enriched care had obvious difficulty walking, holding crayons, and even voicing single words—well below the standard metrics for their age. The leagăn children as a group were even smaller than home-reared creşă children. We noticed that most enriched leagăn children appeared to have retained basic social skills, such as making eye contact and smiling, but because it was important not to bias the assessments with knowledge of specific children's groups, we did not dwell on this observation.

We have previously reported, in a variety of scientific publications, our findings from hormonal and behavioral data collected from these three groups at ages twenty-four and thirty-six months.[22] This is the first in-print description of the age-three data for the three Romanian groups. Rather than going to the same depth and detail here, we will focus on the main question we set out to explore: Are salivary cortisol methods at a stage where diurnal and reactivity profiles can serve as markers for early social deprivation? Finding the answer required a disciplined approach to profiling diurnal cycles and stress reactivity.

To construct the diurnal profiles we adhered to a scheduled collection protocol, and then searched for correlations between different diurnal profiles and the groups' varying developmental scores. This study was one of the first to compare diurnal profiles in family-reared and neglected children, using a randomized controlled design. It enabled the reporting of any abnormal morning diurnal values in socially deprived children compared to age-matched family-reared children. Preparing the children for the diurnal collections was coordinated by our Romanian colleagues with assistance of the staff responsible for each of the large leagăn rooms; care was taken to minimize disruption of daily routines during the process. Samples were taken adjacent to their homerooms, while each child was held by a familiar person, on Day 1 at 8 AM, noon, and 7 PM and on Day 2 at 8 AM and noon. All these diurnal samples were taken before meals.

In the first collection period of cortisol at age two, the family-reared creşă group showed the typical diurnal profile of high morning values followed by a rapid drop at noon. (They did not show a decline to an expected level by 7 PM). Strikingly, these expected early-morning cortisol peak levels are absent in both the enriched and deprived leagăn groups. Given that high levels of stress hormone are often (mistakenly) seen as bad, what does it mean that the deprived leagăn children have only half the morning level as the creşă children? How could this be worrisome? In fact, it is a problem because a stress hormone does more than respond to threatening circumstances—and the level is typically high in the morning, after which it drops quickly by noon and falls to a nearly undetectable level by evening. A high morning peak in stress hormone is a normal, healthy sign; it has been shown to promote morning wakeup after fasting, and even promotes motor learning. Elevated evening levels, by contrast, are not healthy; having dropped by noon, and then dropped more by evening, the typical cortisol profile remains low until the next morning's peak.

At age three, the general shapes of the creşă and leagăn groups' diurnal profiles were similar to those at age two, but the creşă children showed a modest morning decline from their age-two average. Meanwhile, both leagăn groups showed a slight rise in morning levels, suggesting that their flat profiles found at age two might be moving toward a more typical diurnal profile.

Table 2.1 shows the significant correlations between diurnal cortisol values at the three diurnal periods and Bayley scores at ages two and three years. These correlations suggest the significance of atypical diurnal profiles for child development.

Look first at the data for the creşă group. These children's normal group values in the morning and at noon did not show significant correlations with Bayley scores. Their evening level (which had not dropped as normally expected) showed a negative correlation, but only with the Bayley tests' motor development scores. Although both leagăn groups had relatively low hormone levels in the morning, the enriched group surprisingly showed a positive cortisol-behavior correlation in the morning. What does that mean? In this case, it indicates that those enriched children in the group who had the highest morning cortisol values also had the highest mental and motor

Table 2.1 Diurnal Cortisol Averages and Bayley Scores by Year and by Time of Day

Group	Age Two			Age Three		
	Morning (8 am)	Noon (12 pm)	Evening (7 pm)	Morning (8 am)	Noon (12 pm)	Evening (7 pm)
Creşă			Negative Motor			
Enriched Leagăn	Positive Mental and Motor		Negative Mental and Motor	Positive Motor		
Deprived Leagăn		Negative Mental and Motor	Negative Mental		Negative Mental	Negative Mental

scores. This is possible even if the enriched group's average is not in the same normal range as the creşă group's.

This intriguing finding of a positive cortisol-behavior correlation for the enriched group persisted to age three, though only for high cortisol and high motor scores at that age. At noon, the deprived group's cortisol values were significantly higher than the enriched group's—bad news for the deprived group, given that noon levels typically drop. In contrast to the enriched group's positive correlations in the morning, the deprived group's higher noon cortisol levels were negatively correlated with its mental and motor scores (that is, children in the deprived group with the highest noon levels had the lowest mental and motor development scores). This same pattern of positive correlation with high cortisol and high behavior scores for the enriched group was found at both age two and age three. The age-two finding for the deprived group of an atypical noon peak, negatively correlated with mental and motor scores, held at age three, as well (although the correlation was significant only for the motor scores). Evening was the only time of day when the creşă group showed a significant cortisol-behavior correlation—and even then, only at age two, not age three. Given that the enriched and deprived groups had relatively elevated evening levels, higher than the creşă group at ages two and three, it is not surprising that they had negative correlations with developmental scores at age two. Only the deprived group continued to show significant correlations in the evening—again, negative ones.

The second kind of profiles this research demanded were "stress reactivity" profiles. Again, compiling these required adherence to a scheduled collection protocol, so that we could look for significant correlations with developmental scores. Our findings are summarized in Table 2.2 below, but before

Table 2.2 Reactivity Cortisol Averages and Bayley Scores in Relation to Stressful Event

| | Age Two | | | Age Three | | |
Group	Pre-Stress (~45 minutes before)	Stress Event (within 15 minutes of onset)	Post-Stress (~15 minutes after)	Pre-Stress (~45 minutes before)	Stress Event (within 15 minutes of onset)	Post-Stress (~15 minutes after)
Creşă	Negative Mental	Negative Mental and Motor	Negative Mental and Motor			
Enriched Leagăn	Negative Mental and Motor	Negative Mental and Motor	Negative Mental and Motor			
Deprived Leagăn		Negative Mental and Motor	Negative Mental and Motor		Negative Mental	Negative Mental

turning to them, we should first describe the procedure used to detect changes in hormone levels over a short time period. Central to the method is staging an acute "stress event"—in this case, the children were exposed to a fifteen-minute physical exam. Cortisol was sampled at three times: pre-stress, during stress (within fifteen minutes of the onset of the stress event), and post-stress (forty-five minutes after the stressor). Stress reactivity is typically measured late in the day, prior to bedtime, when the diurnal cycle is approaching a low point and reactivity changes are most easily detected.

The typical reactivity profile features a low level of cortisol at pre-stress baseline, a rising level that reaches a peak value soon after the stressor, and a decline in the post-stress period to a level similar to pre-stress value. Both the enriched and the deprived leagăn groups displayed this typical pyramid profile. One unexpected result for us was that the creşă group showed what appeared to be an anticipatory response—as if they detected that a stressful event was about to happen. At age three, the profiles of two of the groups—creşă and enriched—were very similar to what they had been at age two. The profile for the deprived group, however, changed in a disturbing way. Although these children had shown a typically regulated stress response at age two, their reactivity profile flattened at age three. They had become less responsive.

Recall that we found one positive correlation between diurnal hormone levels and behavior scores (for the enriched group at ages two and three). The reactivity assessment produced no significant positive correlations between cortisol and behavioral scores. Revealed was a pervasive pattern by which the children with the highest cortisol values, at any or all phases of the reactivity response, were those most delayed in mental and motor development (with the exception, already noted, that the deprived group had atypically low cortisol levels in the morning to go with its lower developmental scores). Here is where, if we set aside its positive role in the morning, cortisol earns its bad reputation as an unhealthy hormone.[23]

In the pattern seen at age three there are fewer correlations, all negative. These are significant only for the enriched group and only with mental scores. In that group, lower stress reactivity as measured by cortisol levels in the stress and post-stress periods is correlated with higher mental development. The persistence of this negative correlation in the enriched group at age three can be interpreted as a positive sign that the enrichment program had an enduring effect. This group remained more tuned into their surroundings relative to the deprived group, which by that point had experienced thirty-six months of uninterrupted "privation."[24]

Two irregular patterns observable across the three groups and two measurement episodes (at ages two and three) deserve closer analysis. The first is the reactivity profile for the creşă group mentioned above, which does not resemble the expected pattern—a particularly surprising result given the apparent normality of the profiles for the two leagăn groups. We noted that this seemed to be an anticipatory response to the physical exam stressor, and that it was seen at both age two and age three. One theory is that this reflects a difference in how the institutionalized versus daycare children would experience this exam. Children in the leagăn received relatively frequent exams and might have gained more familiarity with the spaces in which they were conducted. For the creşă children, both the exam and the space where it was administered were more novel. As for the enriched group at age three, they showed the typical low-high-low peak configuration, but overall, the values were more in keeping with the creşă group than with their own values at age two.

A second pattern inviting more explanation is the deprived group's lack of reaction to the stressor, as reflected by its flat reactivity profile. In the diurnal profiles discussed above, the flat profiles for both leagăn groups at age two improved by age three as the morning values rose closer to that of the family-reared creşă children. Of all the outcomes observed, the flat profile for stress reactivity in the deprived group is the most forbidding. It is most suggestive of a critical period for early social contact which, if missed, leaves a child with enduring social deficits.

The results of this study show that there is a signal—call it a voice—to be detected in the two regulatory profiles of cortisol secretion. The severity of the deprivation experienced, and the lack of statistical power to detect what may be small effect sizes, limits our capacity to hear it. Is it responsible, then, to recommend cortisol as a reliable and valid bioassay? Could it be used as a screening or diagnostic tool as we seek to understand the various ways in which socialization fails or flourishes during human development?

Our immersion in the leagăn study was driven as much by the ethical issues surrounding such systematic and massive violations of the rights of children as it was by the scientific question of developing cortisol as a useful bioassay. In the end, the study made progress on both fronts. It documented enduring cortisol irregularities in these neglected children. It also showed that cortisol dysregulation had a close, though not well understood, relationship to behavioral deficits. The purpose in working with this vulnerable population was not simply to show that the studies of deprived rat pups could be generalized to our species. Rather, our intent was to employ measurement of a biological marker in neglected children as a proxy voice. The cortisol levels could signal to scientists, parents, policy makers, and global citizens that these silent children were "stressed."

The enriched group appeared to be responding to their social context when the Romanian team walked into their rooms and called their names. Many of the enriched children would orient themselves toward the stimulus, make eye contact, and smile most of the time. Children in the deprived group remained completely self-directed in their stereotypical movements, giving them a sadly distinctive appearance. Their failure to show any HPA activity in response to the stress event at age two testing, but slightly improved morning diurnal regulation from age two to age three, implies that it is not a matter of HPA deficiencies but more a matter of increased withdrawal from their social context.

Given that diurnal cycle and stress reactivity regulation are established during the neonatal period, the ideal research design would have involved beginning the cortisol samples at one month of age and monitoring diurnal profiles and behavioral development in deprived and never-deprived infants over a two-year period. Such an approach might reveal that the normal profile is never developed in the deprived infant, or perhaps that the capacity to develop a normal cycle is lost at some later age within the first twenty-four months. In the absence of that ideal, the work of Sparling and his colleagues, conducting their intervention trials under challenging conditions, paved the way to a remarkable opportunity for us to conduct at least this exploratory investigation.

The use of cortisol as a method of detecting child mal-treatment is as much an ethical matter as it is a scientific one. Generalizing from the disastrous situation in Romania to other contexts—in which children cannot disclose their status as victims of neglect or abuse—must be pursued with an abundance of caution. We will return to this theme in Chapter 6, where we introduce two different deliberation groups in Chicago, and see them landing on radically different positions regarding the utility of measuring cortisol as an indicator of protracted stressful life circumstances. For now, we move to Chapter 3, prepared to learn next from the street and working children of Brazil.

A Critical Period Revisited

John Bowlby and Harry Harlow met in 1958 and became fast friends. Although they agreed on the critical requirement for touch in infancy, they differed on how to define the nature of the bond established by a mother and her infant.[25] Harlow believed that the requirements of socialization were nonspecific—that is, that sufficient interaction with any human being, serving as a caretaker, could adequately socialize an infant. Bowlby claimed that a single attachment figure, the mother, was the exclusive requirement for normal psychological development during infancy. It is true that their work was carried out when the field of neurobiology was still emerging, yet neither even speculated that missing this critical period might involve brain mechanisms. The kind of evidence that captured their interests was of a behavioral and social nature. Harlow died in 1981 at the age of seventy-six, and Bowlby in 1990 at the age of eighty-three. Probably they were both unaware of Romania's pronatalist policy and its flagrant dismissal of their scientific contributions to human development.

What if Meaney's findings in rat pups, or the research on the visual system that Maya pursued with Hubel and Wiesel had been as well established as Harlow's studies on deprivation in monkeys and Bowlby's work on human infants were in the 1960s. Would science have had the power to pull the rug from under Ceauşescu's feet?

If Harlow and Bowlby were alive today, they would surely be gratified by the extent to which neurobiological evidence had bolstered their behavioral studies. They would also be interested in the adoption studies that have followed the life course of infants who were removed from the horrible institutions and placed in secure family settings just after the fall of Ceauşescu. As the plight of the Romanian babies became known, hundreds of thousands of families around the world sought to adopt them. Initially, the Romanian government welcomed international adoption with enthusiasm, but in time it applied the brakes to what had been essentially unregulated activity.

The large number of infants adopted provided an opportunity to carry out what researchers call a natural experiment. The use of the term *natural* implies that the action resulting in an outcome of scientific interest is not determined by the investigator, but rather is caused by circumstances that operate beyond the investigator's control, as in an environmental disaster or the introduction of a new government policy. In such cases, investigators can advance knowledge without making an experimental intervention that defies ethical considerations or indeed is not feasible. They can plunge right in and study conditions and results as they find them. The "natural" event in the case of institutionalized infants was their discharge to much more favorable rearing environments provided by adoptive parents.

In the first few years following the discovery of the vast network of orphanages, the English and Romanian Adoptees Study recruited 165 Romanian infants and their British parents into a long-term follow-up study. The health, behavior, and socialization of Romanian children were periodically assessed during childhood, adolescence, and early adulthood and compared to age-matched English-born adoptees.[26]

The results of this quasi-experiment confirm that a critical period does exist. Social and emotional behavior were distinctly more impaired in the Romanian adoptees, and the gap actually grew as they reached adulthood. Some of the impairments resembled autistic behaviors (obsessive mannerisms and oddities in social interaction). But these outcomes were pronounced only in adoptees who as infants had remained in the orphanage longer than six months. This implies that the critical period for early socialization spans more than six months, but less than twenty-four months (or the average age of adoption). For the authors, the conclusion was clear: "We provide compelling evidence that time-limited exposure to severe adversity . . . can have a profound and lasting impact despite subsequent environmental enrichment in well-resourced and supportive families."[27]

Does all this really matter to the welfare of the adult Romanian orphans? To the point of this book's argument, discovering the importance of a critical period in socialization of humans mattered not only for the institutionalized children in Romania, but also for American children about to be targeted by welfare reform policies that could land them in day care centers of low quality (as early a one week of age). When such care is coupled with the increasing number of children under age five whose parents are poor, the enduring negative effects on child well-being constitute a violation of the rights of infants and young children. The standards by which childcare providers are judged are too often limited to structural criteria—such as child / staff ratios, caretaker training, and the types of materials available. But this science reveals that the quality of childcare should also be judged on the basis of social reciprocity and the extent to which the infant or child experiences control and predictability. This is how human rights ought to be practiced with our youngest citizens.

3

Mean Streets

Democracy is not just a question of having a vote. It consists
of strengthening each citizen's possibility and capacity to
participate in the deliberations involved in life, in society.

—FERNANDO HENRIQUE CARDOSO

Societies raise children to become members of society.
What happens when large numbers of children live at the
margins of a society that fails to protect them from hunger,
violence, and exploitation? This was the reality in the 1980s
as the power of a twenty-year military dictatorship dwindled
in Brazil. With its new Constitution of 1988 taking shape, the
nation's children generated a movement for their rights to be
included. Quoted above is the man who became president in
the 1990s. When Cardoso spoke of strengthening capacity to
deliberate, did he have them in mind?

These abandoned Brazilian children stepped up and did
incredible things. By banding together in groups, they formed
their own small societies that eventually developed ties to civil
society and sought to enact political change to benefit all of
Brazil's children. Paradoxically, Brazil became the first nation
to enact child rights legislation. What would a country that

valued children's political ideas—and responded to their political will—look like? How does a youth movement create a permanent space for future youth political action?

This chapter reveals the extreme degradations of Brazil's street children and describes the extraordinary collective action they pursued beginning in the late 1970s and early 1980s. While many obstacles remain, Brazil's melding of human rights, citizenship, and children's rights offers important lessons to the rest of the world. But before Brazil became an example of positive change, it was a tragedy. There had been a complete breakdown in the norms that say a society protects and nurtures its youngest members rather than abandoning, exploiting, and attacking them. This had been a low period in Brazil's history marked by decades of military rule, a sagging economy, and growing economic disparity.

Close Encounters

São Paulo, November 1993. On a Sunday morning, we are sitting in the Praça da Sé, the site of the São Paulo Cathedral with the majestic twin spires. We have come back to observe Brazil's infamous population of street children, this time without our interpreter and guide, Martinha Arruda, who is spending the day visiting friends. Many homeless children congregate here, especially around the fountains. Among the hundreds of children who make the square their home turf, we have communicated, through Martinha, with thirty or forty. But today we are alone and can only try to communicate with the children through gestures, facial expressions, and pantomime.

The idea of visiting this country had surfaced during visits to UNICEF Headquarters in New York and its research center in Florence, Italy, earlier that year. We had become captivated by UNICEF's rich documentation of poor and marginalized children standing at the vanguard of a popular human rights movement. Might that movement hold promise for American children like Deandre? Could the experience of these Brazilian children inform the Chicago Project in a unique and positive way?

We are sitting having our breakfast on benches far from the fountains where most of the children congregate. When they spot us, a small group of young boys approaches to ask for money. It's clear they see us as easy targets. We simply smile, shrugging our shoulders to indicate that we do not understand Portuguese. So, they start to gesture instead, indicating that they want something from us. After a few minutes of give and take, we offer a particularly persistent boy half of an egg sandwich. He accepts with a smile.

This exchange is more than an anonymous transaction, more than a simple offering from a stranger to a beggar. It is a victory in communication. The interchange is entertaining to them and to us, making for a strong sense of sport in the air as they put their skilled gestures to work negotiating. We are as pleased with the result as they are. Grinning, they turn away to seek a new challenge in their negotiation for survival.

Soon, another child approaches from behind. She looks to be about eight years old. Her face, with its pale brown skin, is beautiful—but blank—and brown curls gather loosely at her shoulders. Her sleeveless cotton dress is nearly transparent from wear. She is barefoot. She passes Tony, heading toward the empty end of Maya's bench. Maya looks into her face and smiles. This silent greeting startles her away, much as an edgy stray cat approaching a bowl of milk will flee if the person who set it out appears.

So, we are surprised when the girl approaches again, but this time Maya looks up slowly and only glances in her direction, with a neutral expression. Again, the child scampers. Even fleeting eye contact exceeds her threshold for interaction with an adult. Maya decides to avoid showing any sign of interest if she returns again. And she does reappear, this time with Maya sitting motionless, tracking her only with peripheral vision.

Very cautiously, the girl climbs onto the bench and settles against the armrest, about five feet away. Over the next few minutes, she slides along the bench, inching to within a foot of Maya. Her thin legs dangle. Cautiously, she lifts her feet to the bench and tucks her knees up. Then, leaning on her right elbow, she lowers her head into Maya's lap. It's a shockingly intimate gesture. Maya remains motionless, arms at her sides, hands resting on the edge of the bench. After a moment, the girl reaches across with her left arm to grasp Maya's right wrist. With great care, she pulls Maya's hand to her soft brown curls and starts to move it in a circular motion across the back and around the crown of her head.

We know that, to this abandoned child who has selected Maya, she is merely a random woman in a public space. But it does not feel random. As a mother, Maya has stroked the heads of our own young daughters in just this way. Careful distance becomes impossible to maintain.

After some moments, Maya judges that it is safe to participate in this fragile exchange, and gently moves her hand across the child's head, first with trepidation, then with reassurance that she will not startle. The two share a poignant moment of genuine trust, partaking in this innocent exchange in the midst of the hundreds of street children in the Praça da Sé.

Then, as surreptitiously as she appeared, and without acknowledgment, the girl darts away to rejoin her companions.

Next morning, we meet Martinha early and tell her we would like to hurry to the square to find some of the children we encountered the day before. As we approach the fountains, we see dozens of children climbing among the waterspouts. Among them is a girl sitting on a back wall with a few older boys around her, her size, curly hair, sweet face, and threadbare dress all recognizable.

But today she holds a crumpled plastic bag to her face. As she lets it fall, we see the unmistakable whitish ring around her mouth and nose from the glue she has just been sniffing. She seems disoriented and fatigued: symptoms of a child whose brain is altered by toxic fumes. Glue sniffing is extremely common among street children. It helps them fight off the pain of hunger, fear, and exploitation that they—especially the girls—suffer in this environment. This instance of it, however, is especially hard to witness.

And so is the other common experience on display: one of the older boys is fondling her through her wet cotton dress. Police and street educators throughout this area do not intervene when children abuse themselves and others with glue and sexual predation. The adults seem to sense the futility of such efforts, given the scope and duration of the phenomenon. But it is too much for us; we are now in a hurry to leave.

Maya speaks the next day with staff at the *Cruzada do Menor*, a nongovernmental organization (NGO) that works with street children in the square, with whom we have been visiting over the last few days. Perhaps they know the name of the girl and even know her story? A staff member immediately recognizes her description as a girl who first appeared in the square about a year earlier. She has at times participated in their outreach program, but the staff do not know much about her story. They do know her name: Liliana.

Recollections of that encounter still shake Maya. If she is still alive, Liliana is in her mid-thirties by now. Perhaps she has returned to her mother's home, or maybe she still lives on the streets. It is unlikely we would recognize her today, but Maya's fantasy is that we would encounter her, still looking as lovely as she was as a child, and now holding a girl of her own—looking into her eyes, smiling, and rubbing that child's small head.

Street and Working Children

For decades, Brazil has been known for having one of the world's largest populations of street children. In the 1990s, there were crude estimates that several million children worked and lived without formal shelter in Brazil's large metropolises. Not only were they despised and excluded from society; often they were physically attacked and casually killed. For a long time, there was only a whisper about this crisis in the outside world, but now Brazil's particular brutality toward these children is legend.

Our encounter with Liliana in November 1993 came shortly after an infamous incident now known as the Candelária Massacre. On July 23, 1993, a band of off-duty military and civilian policemen fired into a group of more than fifty young people who were sleeping alongside the Candelária Church in the center of Rio De Janeiro. Eight boys were killed, one of them only eleven years old. This elegant church, famed for its heritage and architecture, had been one of several places where children living on the streets felt safe enough to gather and sleep. Now it became a symbol for the brutality the country inflicted on its dispossessed children.

The shootings, occurring openly at a major tourist destination, trained worldwide attention on Brazil and sparked widespread condemnation of police violence. But the boys' deaths may not have been much mourned by many proprietors of local shops. The children's constant begging, thieving, and hustling of tourists in this area were bad for business. Store owners felt that local authorities, police, and social services were not doing enough to control the problems, and some were willing to take matters violently into their own hands. The Candelária event was a shocking escalation of a broader, ongoing war on these children. Stories abounded of street children being rounded up, loaded into vehicles, and taken to the countryside to be threatened or killed. Public perception of these children as vermin gave vigilantes the cover they needed to use extreme violence.

The Candelária Massacre occurred after international human rights advocates had begun to scrutinize violence against children. In June 1990, Amnesty International documented a shocking record of torture and extrajudicial execution in Brazil. It warned that death squads were killing minors, mainly black boys aged fifteen to eighteen, at the rate of one per day.[1] Its investigators found poor children "treated with contempt by the authorities, risking their lives simply by being in the streets."[2] Within Brazil, a think tank reported in 1989 on "the marked presence of organized actions for the elimination of people, in this case children and adolescents, with a view to 'cleaning up the streets,' 'removing witnesses,' or 'guaranteeing the security' of a given area."[3] In March 1991, responding to Amnesty International's claims, the State Assembly of Rio de Janeiro established the Parliamentary Commission of Inquiry to Investigate the Extermination of Children and Adolescents in Rio de Janeiro State.[4] After many years of judicial proceedings, three police officers were convicted of the Candelária Massacre and each was sentenced to between two hundred and three hundred years behind bars. All three have since been released.[5]

The fact that grown men, many of them fathers, could kill unarmed children huddled together for comfort and security is incomprehensible. Why was the situation in Brazil so severe? History provides some answers.

The constant political and economic changes in Brazil from the 1960s to the 1990s were dizzying. In 1964, the country's democratic government was overthrown in a military coup. Rapid and intense industrialization and growth followed. Often referred to as "the Brazilian Miracle," the economic transformation was largely fueled by industrialization in the south. But the country's global reputation as a marvel of growth was soon shadowed by its massive inequality. The rapidly increasing geographic difference in income and wealth distribution resulted in massive migration, from the northeast to the south, of landless peasants seeking jobs. This led to chaotic and inhumane living conditions within the notorious, sprawling *favelas* that now encircle Rio and São Paulo—the shantytowns where so many displaced migrants make their home. To make matters worse, the 1973 oil crisis precipitated deep economic and political woes. The following years, dubbed "the lost decade," were characterized by rising foreign debt, steep inflation, the waning of military power, and a gradual return to democracy. Direct presidential elections were reestablished in 1990.

Through the last quarter of the twentieth century, as Brazil's population increased, its economy stagnated and income disparity worsened. The poor become poorer. The near collapse of the economy in the 1980s had the most severe impact on children.[6] Many were forced out by parents too poor to support them. Many took to the streets to support themselves or to help their families.

One pioneering study carried out in 1992 by Irene Rizzini and colleagues at UNICEF was based on in-person interviews with poor children and their family members in the western Brazilian city of Goiânia. It confirmed what many already believed: that children who live on the street should be distinguished from children who work on the streets but still live with their families. The first group are properly referred to as *street children,* while the latter group should be called *working children.*[7] Others have distinguished between children who are "pushed" versus "pulled" to the street, with the former perhaps fleeing abuse at home or being rejected by parents, and the latter being drawn to the street's opportunities to generate income for themselves and their families.[8] Not surprisingly, street children contribute less to total family income than working children. Indeed, finding other children in the same predicament, the street child is likely to adopt peers as family, for emotional support and for survival.

After her encounter with Liliana, Maya asked many questions about Brazil's street children and their relationship with society. Are these children irreparably damaged, as is often the case following early social deprivation—like the docile, lonely children of Romania? Or does the deprivation experienced by these millions of street children have its own distinctive developmental consequences? The moment of trust and intimacy that Maya shared with Liliana hinted at the latter.

The answer lies in the fact that these street children *have* experienced adequate early socialization. Street educators, who are trained and employed by Children's Councils to provide outreach services and support, work with street children on a daily basis and their sense is that these children typically were raised in homes where they experienced affection. Unlike the leagăn children, such family-raised children learn to seek the comfort and support of adults in their first years of life. These social skills, once nurtured in infancy, prove

surprisingly durable. This would account for the laughing, negotiating boys and the careful, comfort-seeking girl in the
Praça da Sé.

In contrast to the Romanian infants suffering from *early*
deprivation, these Brazilian children are subject to *late* deprivation: they are marginalized from their families and communities of origin only after early nurturing has been experienced. In spite of being pushed into the streets by poverty,
deprivation, or abuse, they retain the social capacities of their
early years. Observers vouch for just how caring these children
can be toward one another. Within their self-organized groups,
these "families" of children commonly share resources and
offer mutual protection.

The novel *Captains of the Sands,* written by Jorge Amado
more than eighty years ago, portrays such mutually protecting
families of street children. Set in the city of Salvador, the story
traces in a romanticized but insightful way a variety of paths
children take toward life on the street, and the strong social
bonds they can develop once there. On one carefree day,
Amado writes, "the city was like a great carousel where they
turned on invisible horses, the Captains of the Sands. At this
moment of music, they felt they owned the city. And they loved
each other, felt brothers because they were all without affection
and comfort and now had the affection and comfort of music."[9]

These social ties and communal bonds eventually enabled
Brazil's children to organize themselves for a shared political
cause, creating a movement as impactful to them as the US
civil rights movement and the Soweto uprisings were to
oppressed citizens in America and South Africa. In the 1980s
and 1990s, a "soft revolution" underway in Brazil was confronting government authorities and policies—a radical
challenge that had been initiated and led by street children.

The Children's Movement

The National Movement of Street Boys and Girls arose as a popular organization in 1985.[10] The movement, mostly composed of volunteers, was founded with the aim to support children and adolescents in their own struggles for secure rights as citizens and to defend those rights. Instigated by the children themselves, the movement emerged only after many top-down efforts by adults to address their crisis had failed. Rather than drawing up a list of demands, as a group of protesters might, this movement presented itself from the beginning in a positive light. At a time when a new Brazilian constitution was being written, it focused on how street boys and girls could be a productive part of the country's shift to democracy and recommitment to the rights of citizens.

The Catholic Church had pioneered the charitable approach of rescuing or "salvaging" homeless and abused children. Individual children benefited from this aid, but it did little to address the real problems at the roots of their situation. In fact, during the 1970s, when charity was the dominant source of aid, the number of street children increased—perhaps because these programs made street life easier and drew more children into dependence on service providers. The alternative to charity-oriented solutions are development-oriented ones: activities that build children's capacities to function effectively in both family and society and enable them to realize more of their potential. Lacking the kind of program that can help young participants strengthen their connections with family, school, and the community, no amount of goodwill can deliver positive, lasting impacts. It also takes lobbying and advocacy to make the voices of street children heard, and bring about changes in policies and laws that affect their lives. NGO programs hoping to increase their impact with more sustainable solutions should network and cooperate with municipalities and local services on initiatives geared to the developmental needs of vulnerable groups.

Yet the charitable approach looked good compared with the reformatories: the dreaded government facilities maintained from 1964 to 1990 by FUNABEM (short for Fundação Nacional do Bem-Estar do Menor, which translates to the innocuous-sounding National Foundation for Child Welfare, or Well-Being).[11] The people charged with running these had built such a toxic institutional culture that the reformatories were deeply distrusted and despised by children and their advocates.

By the 1980s, outside of church charity and government indifference, a mushrooming number of NGOs were pursuing the philanthropic approach. These groups were staffed by salaried professional administrators and social workers. Unfortunately, many of these organizations seemed ever more self-serving, rather than truly invested in the welfare of children. The need to keep getting funding and maintain their staffs created incentives to expand the numbers of the needy. After all, if there were no street children, they would have no reason to exist.

The National Movement of Street Boys and Girls was completely different. It did not have a charitable attitude, nor was its purpose to "rescue" street children. It was a low-key, informal movement that did not seek grants or revenue streams. The movement originated when groups of street children began organizing events that reflected an awareness of themselves as political activists. Some adults acted as mentors and facilitators, but children were the leaders. The adults involved were progressive, perhaps even radical. The point was that children were taking a stand and making a political decision of their own, rather than waiting to be saved. Rescuing the poor was not going to stop police brutality, clean up FUNABEM reformatories, or control sexual exploitation and drug dealing. Nor would it shut down the death squads.

Within a short time, word of these groups spread, and a national movement was formed, made up of scores of local grassroots organizations. In 1988, busloads of street children from all over the country converged on the National Congress in Brasilia, which was beginning work in earnest on the new national Constitution. They wanted to shine a light on police brutality and assert their rights to be protected and to be heard. The children handled themselves well, with minimal adult guidance. They asked for a special audience with the Congress to present their concerns, and were granted it.

A documentary video made for UNICEF, *Raised Voices*, shows the children, some barely teenagers, testifying to lawmakers. It is obvious that something exceptional was going on.[12] These really were children, and they really were leading a political movement. They were talking directly, face to face, to their representatives in Congress, and determined to bring about change. The movement spearheaded the ultimately successful effort to include special children's rights in the Constitution. Two years later, in 1990, these rights were legislated as the Child and Adolescent Statute (*Estatuto da Criança e do Adolescente*).[13] The statute radically reformed the legal status of children and redefined the responsibilities of the state and civil society. In particular, it states: "It is the duty of the family, society and the state to assure with absolute priority the rights of children and adolescents to life, health, food, education, leisure, occupational training, culture, dignity, respect, freedom, and family and community life, and in addition to protect them from all forms of negligence, discrimination, exploitation, violence, cruelty and oppression."[14]

To decentralize and broaden participation in policy and budget decisions, the statute mandated the creation of Children's Rights Councils (*Conselhos de Direitos*) and Guardianship Councils (*Conselhos Tutelares*) for each of the country's 5,560 municipalities. The fifteen-member Children's Rights Councils are made up of state employees responsible for implementing the statute. The Guardianship Councils, each composed of five elected members, are responsible for monitoring compliance with the statute while serving as advocates for vulnerable children within their communities and providing referrals to needed services. These are unpaid positions.

One problem that proved complex within the National Movement of Street Boys and Girls had to do with its own leadership. Children co-managed the movement's local branches, with some adult assistance. But how could children participate as equals if they knew less and were less skilled than the adults who were helping them? There had to be a learning process. Benedito Rodrigues dos Santos, one of the movement's adult organizers, described the challenge:

> The process of training and organizing boys and girls is entirely new. The very path is created in the making. . . . Available parameters are from other experiences which are almost totally from the world of adults. Following this path implies walking a tightrope: not belittling children, believing in their potential, and capacity for participating and organizing, without transforming them into mini-adults; providing minimal organizational references without imposing models. The challenges must be overcome as the movement matures.[15]

Despite these problems, by the early 1990s the movement had succeeded in creating throughout the entire country a kind of informal but permanent workshop on the implementation of the statute.

Children's Rights in Action

São Paulo is the locomotive that pulls the Brazilian economy. It is the largest and wealthiest city in the country. Consequently, it is also a magnet for street children. By the 1990s, a range of services targeted the city's homeless boys and girls; the prevailing strategy was to intervene where they lived rather than resort to institutional solutions. As in Rio, most such programs operated in the central districts of São Paulo and offered a combination of outreach and immediate rescue services, such as identifying children who needed HIV testing or treating drug overdose cases. Prevention programs were not as common. The active organizations were far too busy with "downstream" interventions in acute situations to deal with whatever was going on "upstream"—in the poor neighborhoods on the city's periphery where most of the young homeless population came from.

There were, however, a few programs emerging in these upstream communities. One such "sender" neighborhood offered, extraordinarily, a circus training program. Dozens of children, mostly between the ages of seven and fourteen, were learning to walk tightropes, juggle, and perform as clowns. The instructors' talent and enthusiasm inspired the growing competence and confidence of these young trainees. The program was open to all children living in the neighborhood. Attendance rates were high, and not many children dropped out.

After the program was established, many benefits became evident. The teachers and facilitators at these successful programs saw it as their job to develop their young charges as citizens securely attached to their communities. And being part of a full-fledged big top, just like the one on the outskirts of São Paulo, boosted the respect and dignity of the child. Even the rate of child abuse in the community was reduced. Parents and other adults seemed to value the children's newfound competence. The model of the circus skills training was fresh and compelling, and apparently effective.[16]

But how was Brazil's Child and Adolescent Statute being implemented in those places where it was most desperately needed? As a measure of its disadvantages, life expectancy in the northeast region of Brazil was seventeen years shorter than in the south. Quality of life in southern cities like Rio, São Paulo, and Porto Alegre was equivalent to many European cities, while the northeast region was one of the poorest parts of South America.

Our first visit to the northeast was to Fortaleza in 1996, a port city of 1.8 million that was struggling to implement the Guardianship Councils and Children's Rights Councils required by the new law. The municipality had meticulously documented the size and scope of the problem of street children but provided relatively few services and programs for them. The gracious, bespectacled chief executive officer of the Child Rights Council said that Fortaleza had six thousand street children and that more than six hundred nongovernmental organizations were working with them. That amounts to one organization for every ten street children! But, said the official, many of these organizations were inefficient or downright shady, and so much of the municipal Children's Rights Council's time was taken up in monitoring them, rather than investing directly in services.

Guardianship Councils are the most localized units in the government's decentralized structure of accountability for the statute. In Fortaleza, where there should be at least nine such councils based on population size, there was only one. The reasons were not clear. At Council sessions, one heard one complaint after another but not much about actual services for children. It appeared that in this city, the zeal and determination of the movement had been bleached out by administrative woes.

Nevertheless, there were some bright spots—for example, the Restaurant for Street Youth. This project trained street children in all aspects of running a restaurant, from cleaning tables and washing dishes to cooking and accounting. The restaurant appeared very successful; the youth seemed highly engaged and conscientious. Another impressive effort was a community center in a suburb with a large population of street children. To improve local conditions, the municipality had encouraged a skills development program that included classes in sewing, computing, and martial arts, as well as academic subjects for children who needed extra help. Such programs, with their successful characteristics—designed to boost self-efficacy and collective efficacy—would inform our neighborhood research in Chicago, and later our work in Tanzania.

Lessons Learned

One of the last places we visited in Brazil was a farm about thirty kilometers south of Recife, very near the smaller city of Jaboatão. The farm was a rehabilitation center, run by a Spanish priest, that UNICEF regarded as a model worth replicating. When we arrived, nothing suggested that anyone was expecting us. At last, one young resident emerged. His name was Williames. We surmised that he was about ten, possibly eleven; he did not know how old he was.

Streetwise on the one hand, innocent and playful on the other, Williames's smile invited us to come closer. As a group of other boys gathered, older and domineering, Martinha introduced us by explaining our work on gang violence and guns in Chicago. This proved to be a clever way to place us in a context that made our presence understandable, even fascinating, to these street children.

The older boys kept pointing to Williames. They wanted him to pull up his shirt. When he did so, we saw the huge scar covering the entire center of his chest and abdomen. At the age of eight or so, Williames had crashed as an "airplane": a runner engaged by drug dealers to inconspicuously move merchandise from the favela into the city center. He had been shot and left for dead. He was now useless to the drug dealers, and, in a manner of speaking, retired to this farm. The other boys laughed at him, but not disrespectfully. They gave him space to tell his story and to show off his scar.

We wondered: Was Williames actually *retired*, or was he being *rehabilitated*? "Retiring" a child indicates low expectations, or no better ideas, for their future. This isolated farm was quite unlike other programs we visited. Some of those were merely shelters, a place to sleep and obtain a meal. Others, run by the Brazilian Center for Children and Adolescents (*Fundação Centro Brasileiro para Infância e Adolescência*), were government-funded residential schools and juvenile detention centers created under a new authority after the 1990 statutes did away with the harsh, prison-like FUNABEM institutions. But it turned out that the farm where Williames now lived was considered by UNICEF to be a more ambitious and progressive environment for homeless children.

We suspected that Williames had never before been asked to show visitors around. It was quite clear that he enjoyed serving as our guide or, better yet, our agent. He was learning to make goat cheese. He took us to his favorite goat and put his arm around her neck. There was something palpably hopeful in this picture. Goats are affectionate and simple creatures. They don't demand much. They have a lot to give. Using our magical Polaroid camera, we snapped photos, one for him and his goat to keep, and the other for us.

Despite being closely monitored by the others, our guide never stopped smiling. His wide smile, eye-to-eye contact, and direct and engaging use of speech and gestures indicated that his early socialization had been well preserved. Despite his short, intensely violent career, Williames had survived and remained a nice boy. Someone had once loved him. Had he slipped away, pulled by the excitement of the streets? Or had he been pushed into trafficking to earn money for his family? Like Liliana, he was a victim of late deprivation. Relative poverty, drugs, guns, and desperation had overtaken what may have been a reasonably secure early childhood. Removed from the danger and exploitation of life on the streets, in this setting where mutual respect and security were the norm, Williames's early development might well serve as a foundation for his rehabilitation.

Before we left, Williames pulled from his pocket a little book to show us: *The Rights of the Child*. Through Martinha, we asked, "Do you know what this means?" We were completely unprepared for his explanation, which did not come across as practiced: "I also have obligations," he said. We asked him what those might be. Williames, who was not only a charming guide and apprentice in the art of making goat cheese, answered: "To respect the teacher and not break the school windows." He was a citizen, as well.

After our experience with the movement—and with Chicago and Romania always in the back of our minds—we returned home with a wonderful, though controversial, idea: children are capable of being social agents and active citizens. But as we related the stories of the Brazilian movement, and of Brazilian adults nurturing the process of children becoming active citizens, we were met at first with incredulity: "Isn't that the place where they kill children on the streets?" A few sympathetic listeners credited us with being boldly idealistic but assured us that there was nothing practical about child rights. One particularly shocking comment from a colleague was that "the problem with American children is that they have *too many* rights." Perhaps this was the prevailing attitude that kept the United States from ratifying the Convention on the Rights of the Child. Within a few months of our return, it had become clear to us that for most US citizens, Brazil might just as well be Mars. Yet we were changed, and we knew we were on to something significant for all children, everywhere.

In Brazil, the statute that Williames shared with us had spread widely among children. On more than one occasion, we met street or institutionalized children who would show us their pocket-sized copies. Every child we asked about rights had a cogent answer. Even though the government systems to protect and promote the rights of children were weighed down by bureaucracy, the Movement of Street Boys and Girls had pervaded popular thinking.

Despite this hopeful and progressive climate, the latest official tally by Brazil indicates that there remain over twenty-three thousand children who regularly sleep on its streets. The number who work on the streets and return home each night remains impossible to know.

As we developed the Young Citizens program, it was especially important for us to understand the Child Rights and Guardianship Councils as legislated models of community-based, rights-informed care and protection for children. Did these entities of local, decentralized government generate and maintain high levels of collective efficacy for children? Between 1997 and 2004, there was considerable, but uneven, expansion of both types of councils.[17] More affluent municipalities, located in the south of Brazil, were more likely to have councils than poorer municipalities in the northeast (60 percent versus 8 percent). There are two major unanswered questions about the Constitutional reforms. The first is how the statute has improved the lives of Brazilian children, During the era of the child rights legislation there have been impressive changes in infant mortality, school attendance, educational achievement, and family income. But it is difficult to attribute these improvements to the legislation because of the confounding of the geographic distribution of Councils and family wealth (and associated assets). This bias brings up the second question: How does the public regard the Councils?[18]

Just as Romania left an indelible mark on our understanding of what a society can do to thwart development in the first years of life, Brazil did the same with regard to development in late childhood and adolescence. Yet in Brazil, we believed that progress was possible. If we were to return to Romania, we would expect that children who had been abandoned as infants would not be as smiling, engaged, or animated as the children we met on the streets of Brazil. It is difficult to imagine children who spent their early years in institutions organizing and leading a social, political movement. In Brazil, an imperfect democracy, children had created their own path to citizenship.

Romania taught us how important it is for communities to be monitors and advocates for their youngest and most vulnerable members. By persuading society to acknowledge both the dangers of neglecting children and the power and progress generated by valued, organized children, Brazil proved that young citizens were essential to winning a world worth living in, for all people.

By bringing back these lessons to the Chicago project and its discovery of neighborhood collective efficacy for children, we were poised to launch the next phase of our research. If fostering the well-being of children is dependent on the social context of a nurturing community, we were better prepared to address a vital question: How can collective efficacy be created?

PART II

Voice

4

Wishes of the Community

After the power of language had been acquired, and the
wishes of the community could be expressed, the common
opinion of how each member ought to act for the public good,
would naturally become in a paramount degree the guide to
action.

—CHARLES DARWIN

How will children secure their rights without first voicing
their concerns, and hearing others do the same? How will
adults learn the wisdom of children—and the error of their
own ways—without younger people daring to speak up? What
would it mean for society if children had the confidence to
question, to protest, to demand change? Read the quote from
Charles Darwin above. Would he have counted children as
"members" of the community, with the "power of language"
and "wishes" to be expressed?

When children are allowed to vocalize their thoughts, fears,
concerns—and hopes and flights of imagination—they take a
step toward making the world align better with their own lives
and needs, whether what they need is community safety in
Chicago, political representation in Brazil, or nurturing and

social contact in Romania. In this chapter we recount our first explorations, with young people, of a new way of relating to and communicating with children. The idea was to create a level playing field between adults and children where everyone's perspectives would be valued as we worked toward consensus on an issue selected as important to the group. We wanted to find a way for children and adults to talk to each other as citizens.

In Part I we saw Nurture as essential to a child's capacity for citizenship; this is something that must be provided to children by caring adults. Now we move to three elements that children can claim and develop for themselves. Voice is the first step, followed by Choice and Action, for children's transformation from disenfranchised into active citizens. In Chicago, we talked directly to residents to get at what made their neighborhoods tick; children's concerns were filtered through adult perspectives. In Romania, we found voice in an unexpected form, by monitoring the hormones of those unable to speak for themselves. In Brazil, we saw the power of children speaking in unison, and causing their society to make positive legislative changes. Now, coming full circle back to Chicago, we were prepared to create a space within the project for children. Our research assistants were eager to help enlist children to speak up for themselves, so they could better their own lives and those of their communities. We began by recruiting a small group of teenagers to join the research team to pursue a bilateral learning experience—they would learn social science research methods from us, and we would learn about how they thought about the problems and challenges of growing up in Chicago's neighborhoods. As paid interns in the Chicago project, they could work full-time for the summer months with an option of continuing during later parts of the year.

Voice was integral to the Young Citizens program from the outset. The program encouraged children to present their own perspectives, and, at the same time, to listen to those of others: to arrive at that "common opinion," as Darwin wrote, about how to achieve the "public good." In Chicago and Cambridge, we will show, adolescents eagerly and skillfully participated in prolonged deliberation as they selected and tackled pervasive problems in their communities and schools.

Unexpected Questions, Unexpected Answers

Only a few years after the original Chicago project began in 1993, it expanded, having secured two new grants. The first grant funded our efforts to improve ways of measuring children's exposure to violence.[1] The second grant allowed us to take up the challenge of engaging more directly with children's voices.[2] The project recruited a diverse group of six adolescents from high crime, underserved neighborhoods in Chicago. Among them was Deandre, who began this book with his earnest question and excited surprise that the UN Convention on the Rights of the Child, not to mention the US Bill of Rights, applied to him. Although he was only thirteen years old, he was an important member of the group.

Soon after their recruitment, the group was invited to participate in what may have been the first conference in the United States to address children's rights since the United Nations Convention on the Rights of the Child was ratified.[3] On stage at St. Xavier University, an attractive campus in the southwest corridor of Chicago, the two of us were joined by six young citizens and the adult facilitator from the Chicago project (Billy Brooks). Before an audience of students, parents, lawyers, educators, social scientists, philosophers, and college administrators, our nine-member group conducted an hour-long, probing discussion of personal experiences with violence. Maya introduced the group and offered background on "participation rights" as a category included in the UN Convention. Those rights, viewed as fundamental to child citizenship, are to have an opinion, to be listened to, to assemble in groups, to receive information, and to have a say in decisions that impact one's life. The children, with their captivating sincerity and composure, made a compelling case for the exercise of their participatory rights.

From the audience's keen interest and questions, including from the president of the college, it was obvious that we, as a group of adults and children, were achieving something important. The principles of respect and mutual understanding were in evidence. The children themselves highlighted these principles. For example, despite frequently meeting with us in the two months leading up to the conference, Deandre could not believe that we adults seriously regarded him as our equal. Listen to what he said at the office in one of the earlier sessions: "It's easy for you to say we are equals, but think of me, a black child, saying to you, 'we are equals.' At first, I didn't feel comfortable because of the whole Harvard thing. I didn't see why they would want to talk with me. I stuck it out and talked about violence and how it affected me and then I started to see that they wanted to know more about my experiences . . . and then I felt at ease to tell them my thoughts."

Deandre spoke with the same authority on stage as he did in the office. As always, he paid close attention and was responsive to what others in the group had to say. No one could doubt that he felt himself to be an equal contributor to the group's deliberation regardless of his relative youth.

This was a unique experience on both sides. The children had been selected because they lived in neighborhoods that were dominated by gang activities and violent events that seemed normative. But they had never before been tapped to give an account of how they experienced the unpredictability of living in such neighborhoods. Neither had the adult audience been exposed to such a penetrating discussion driven by adolescents. How did this happen? How did they prepare to participate with such initiative and confidence?

On stage, the children were asked to share their own experiences of violence. As adult researchers in a late stage of designing a new measure of children's exposure to violence, we were especially listening for questions or topics they might bring up that we had not considered. And indeed, when asked directly, the children did share fears and violations that the adults had not expected—such as their fears of walking through a public park that was perceived to be "gang turf," or of being stopped by the police for "no reason." By speaking out, they were seizing the opportunity to value their own perceptions and make their opinions known.

Another surprise for the adults in the room was talk of metal detectors. The students talked about how these devices, intended to keep weapons out of school, were violating their bodily integrity. Jeanette told about the time that a friend of hers came through a detector at the school door and it mysteriously went off. Everyone knew she was not the type of young person to have a weapon, but the security guards patted her down. Then they used a scanner wand to isolate the problem area. It beeped as they waved it close to her chest, and when they repeated the motion it beeped again. After ordering her to take off her blouse—in front of everyone—they discovered the culprit: the metal underwire in her bra. To embarrass the girl like this, Jeanette declared, was a violent act—and young people were putting up with humiliations like this all the time.

The stories went on. We researchers had failed to think of some important things, all of which might go under the category of structural violence. The very social institutions designed by adults to keep children safe and develop their capacities were actually harming these young people in many ways—from schools stocked with metal detectors, security guards, and uncaring teachers to police forces quick to harass and push young people around for no apparent reason.

Human Rights for Children

The idea of codifying child rights is not new. It predates even the United Nations. The League of Nations adopted the Declaration of the Rights of the Child in 1924, and the United Nations General Assembly unanimously supported an expanded version of this declaration in 1959. The General Assembly proclaimed 1979 the International Year of the Child and appointed a working group to draft a more comprehensive declaration. It was this effort that culminated in the adoption of the Convention on the Rights of the Child in 1989.[4] Over the next decade, as member after member ratified it, it became the most universally endorsed human rights treaty of all time. As mentioned in the Introduction, the United States remains the only UN member not to ratify this UN convention.

The first internationally ratified human rights treaty came after World War II, soon after the founding of the United Nations, in the form of the sweeping Universal Declaration of Human Rights endorsed by the UN General Assembly on December 10, 1948.[5] It includes articles specifying the political rights to freedom of thought, conscience, and religion (Article 18); freedom of opinion and expression, including the right to seek, receive, and impart information (Article 19); and the right to peaceful assembly and association (Article 20). Its Preamble opens with the foundational statement that the "recognition of the inherent dignity and of the equal and inalienable rights of all members of the human family is the foundation of freedom, justice and peace in the world." It further asserts a shared faith by the peoples of the United Nations "in the dignity and worth of the human person and in the equal rights of men and women." A reasonable reading is that this treaty covers children, as it covers "all members of the human family," and that they are not excluded by the "men and women" clause in the later gender equity clause. It did, however, require another forty years for children to be provided their own treaty to make certain of their rights— given the ambiguity of "all members of the human family."

The UN Convention on the Rights of the Child proved crucial to the Young Citizens program, both in shaping its research goals and in informing the children's understanding of themselves. Examples of the "participatory rights" it outlines were shown through actions of children in different settings. These represent only six of fifty-four articles but are by far the most unconventional; they mark a contrast with other articles' basic protections of and provisions for those under eighteen years of age. Yet these six rights categories are remarkably similar to the political rights included in the earlier Universal Declaration of Human Rights. These six entitle children to the opportunity to be heard in any judicial and administrative proceedings affecting them (Article 12); freedom of expression (Article 13); freedom of thought, conscience, and religion (Article 14); freedom of associations and peaceful assembly (Article 15); protection of privacy (Article 16); and access to information from diverse sources (Article 17). Collectively, these rights are foundational to the Young Citizens program. We will keep referring back to them in what follows.

Setting the Stage

The St. Xavier conference was a high-visibility moment for the program. But it was only the beginning of the contributions our six newly recruited adolescents would make as young citizens. Afterward, they immersed themselves in the research, working together as junior social scientists in a dialogue group. Their purpose was to gain a more thorough understanding of how Chicago youths experienced fear and insecurity. In their quest, they would challenge the boundaries of conventional wisdom, establish new pathways to community improvement, and devise new strategies for energizing children.

Early on, the children's perspectives undermined some of the certainties of social scientists and political theorists. Note that the study's focus was on exposure to violence, and these were children who lived in neighborhoods where street gangs, drug trafficking, easy access to guns, and police brutality were the norm. Yet it quickly became clear that their major concerns centered on daily living conditions. This was unexpected— although, to be sure, the UN Convention also declares, in Article 27, that every child has the right to an adequate standard of living.[6] Its effect on the research was to expand a narrow view of violence, and bring a "capability approach" to bear on challenges in human development from a child's perspective (as will be discussed in Chapter 7).

The young citizens' discussions were provocative, compassionate, and eye-opening. One important lesson we learned was that dialogue, which comes naturally to children and draws them in, is an invaluable tool for research and understanding.

The children valued their dialogue. By the time we held our fifth session, there was a sense of satisfaction and discovery in the group.

They were impressed with themselves and justifiably so, as a group of young Americans of diverse descent—African, Mexican, Polish, and Irish—freely sharing experiences. The group was surprised that children of a wide range of ethnicities could easily become so open and engaged with each other.

One of their discoveries was the maturity of their own language and reasoning. "We were people of different backgrounds and ages with opinions different from my own," wrote one of the group, Linda, in the group's newsletter, "and I managed to let my ideas be heard without feeling insecure or intimidated about anything. . . . I learned how to argue in a good way, instead of getting nasty with anyone." To discover that capacity within oneself is powerful and empowering. Linda went on: "During the conference I was hoping that my message was getting across and that I was making myself clear and after the conference the people there gave me compliments and they themselves let me know I did a good job and I felt happy for what I had done." There you have the satisfaction. As Deandre put it, "dialogue is a mature way of talking." He should know; he matured more than anyone else over the next two years. Jeanette was one of the older youths, still with us when she turned eighteen; we watched her cross from childhood into adulthood. She had this to say: "The more you dialogue, the easier it becomes and after a while you can dialogue with anyone off the street about any topic that comes out of your head. It is supposed to be fun and educational and if you are comfortable it will be." It was a revelation to the group's members that children could talk like this, let alone with adults. Their confidence took off.

As these young citizens matured, their dialogue focused on the relevance to their lives of the UN Convention on the Rights of the Child. From its forty-plus articles, they unanimously chose to prioritize Article 27, focused on standards of living, in their discussions and research. This meant they wanted to consider what living conditions were "adequate for the child's physical, mental, spiritual, moral, and social development."

What was needed now was a method for cultivating collective efficacy. But where to begin? We needed a well-established social theory by which to evaluate communities, one that allowed for a deeper analysis of the social mechanisms through which trust and reciprocity are generated and maintained. Only then could we determine how a community functioned, and how then to encourage better functioning.

The work of the German sociologist and philosopher Jürgen Habermas caught our attention in the mid-1990s. His scholarship may be dense, but his conclusions are disarmingly simple. Habermas's principal idea focuses on *communication* as preparation for *action.*[7] He argues that when members of a community come together to identify and freely discuss their common problems, their discussion is not "just words" but rather the first step toward consensual, rational, shared social action. Thus, Habermas argues everyday democracy is based on the unique human capacity for language. But this must be understood as ordinary, mundane language that coordinates our routine social interactions. In these terms, language is to be judged not so much by what it says, but by what it does.

By this measure, the young citizens of the Chicago project should be praised. Their language revealed previously concealed threats to their well-being, prepared them for greater participation and independence, and created new communities and visions of solidarities they—and we—had never imagined.

The group over that first summer demonstrated that, beyond a doubt, they could contribute to sustained, probing dialogue. For the second summer of the Chicago Young Citizens Project, the group was composed of ten youths. The four veterans from the first year and six new members spent the first several days earnestly working on a mission statement to focus their thinking and actions for the next two months. Here is what they came up with: "Our mission is to establish young people as citizens. . . . We are a representative few who will work through dialogue and scientific strategies to justify human rights for children. We will also learn how to apply our findings to enable the flourishing of all children and the betterment of our city."

One long exercise for the group was to read, discuss, and understand the details of Article 27.[8] It specifies that parents or guardians have the main responsibility for securing adequate living conditions for their children. It adds, however, that states are obliged to provide assistance and support, "particularly with regard to nutrition, clothing and housing," within their governments' means. Thinking beyond these material needs, these young citizens provided their perspective on how fear and insecurity affect living conditions. Fear and insecurity were pervasive and profound influences in the lives of all the youth who worked with us, cutting across the ethnic and class divisions that spatially and politically separated them.

The group's most significant deliberation was devoted to arriving at a consensus on its own theory of the social universe of childhood. Authority was a vital element of it, the group agreed, and there were different types of authority figures. The ones who mattered most were parents, teachers, and police. But the authority that adults commanded in their lives could be either positive or negative; either way, this authority was the main driver of the standard of living they experienced as children.

The group decided to conduct a survey to measure conditions against a standard of adequacy. Thus, the young citizens developed a survey instrument—a standardized set of questions that each of them could use to interview other young people in their communities. The instrument opened with some context-sharing: "We are a group of teenagers from different neighborhoods across the city of Chicago who have come together this summer to dialogue about our rights and responsibilities as young citizens. We have worked together with concerned adults about how children and adults can effectively collaborate to improve the lives of children. We would like to ask you some questions about your views on certain topics. First, we need some basic information about you, so we can see how your answers differ by age, neighborhood and so forth." During their final weeks of summer, they would synthesize their responses and the whole project would come together.

It took a couple of weeks of work to decide where to go and how to gain access to children of varying ages. In the end, the group decided to go to the Chicago Park District since many children throughout the city spent time in its programs during the summer. In Chicago's parks the group could expect to find a lot of children, many of whom would likely agree to answer the survey questions. The Chicago Parks District granted permission to the group to hand out questionnaires during camp activities, and was helpful in other ways in providing a secure base for the young citizens to interview a diverse group of other young people across the city.

Once the basic information (on the respondent's grade level, neighborhood, ethnic identity, and so forth) was collected, twenty-one questions followed. To facilitate statistical analysis, responses were coded according to whether the answer indicated "a lot" or "about average" or "very little or none." Respondents also had the option to say, "I don't know." The questions called for responses regarding the three major authority figures in the children's lives: parents, teachers, and police:

> How caring are the following authority figures toward you?
>
> How caring are the following authority figures toward your neighborhood?
>
> How much respect do the following authority figures give you?
>
> How much freedom do the following authority figures give you to state your opinion?
>
> How much privacy do the following authority figures give you?
>
> How quickly do you think the following authority figures respond to your emotional needs?
>
> How safe do you feel around the following authority figures?

The survey yielded impressive results. With project researchers providing statistical assistance, the group's analysis discovered a surprise in the question on ethnicity. We, the adult scientists, had emphasized the importance of gathering information on race, ethnicity, and family structure, and these had, of course, been collected for the larger Chicago project survey. But this bit of advice did not resonate with the young citizens. They reluctantly agreed to include questions on race and ethnicity but predicted that age and gender would turn out to be much more important. The data eventually proved them right: there was little variation in survey answers by race or ethnicity, but the degree of caring, respect, and protection children obtained from all authority figures declined as the children got older—and the slope of this decline was greater for males than for females. As boys aged, they consistently reported that adults showed less interest in them and less respect for their rights. For them, this was a major challenge to their well-being and development.

It was a result that the adults might not have noticed without the keen participation of these children. The young citizens had shown us, again, that when we listen to children and encourage them to listen to others, discoveries can take place that point to important areas for change. The voices of children are not simply worthy in their own right or in some abstract way—they are instrumental to progress. We cannot learn how to improve a community without understanding it, and we cannot understand a community without listening to what its children have to say.

A celebratory dinner was arranged at the end of the program. Parents were invited, and everyone dressed up for the occasion. There was an excited buzz in the air as parents got to meet other young citizens and their parents. The young citizens simulated one of their sessions for the guests. They read notes from a newsletter they had produced some weeks earlier for the Chicago project's archives, describing their deliberation experiences over the summer. Finally, they took questions from their guests and posed some of their own.

One guest at the celebration asked one of the children if he had learned anything surprising from listening to the others. On the one hand, he replied, "Not really. The things I am going through, they are going through." On the other hand, that in itself was eye-opening: "I would think that the police wouldn't mess with James as much, being a white guy. The way they do James is not *new*, because I hear and see it all the time. Him being a different *race* shocked me—the police messing with white boys like James say they do. Working with people from a different race brought my self-esteem up higher. It showed me that no other race would be better than my race. I learned that I have a lot in common with them."

Asked what they had to say about their rights, the whole group knew the substance of the participation rights. One of the group, Percy, began with "the right to an opinion—because in public housing, my experience with adults has been their way or no way. They don't listen to my opinion even if I might have been right at the time. They say, 'stay in a child's place.' Another one is protection from drugs and drug abuse. I am basing my information on where I am at. Every day when I go home I see drugs and more drugs. The young people know everything about drugs; they know how much a dime bag costs. They know very little about school. They are wasting their lives."

A tender moment took place when Paco introduced his mother to Deandre's mother. It was clear from the way Paco's mother approached Deandre's mother that she had something important to convey. For months, Paco's mother had had something weighing on her mind: a story Deandre had brought up in one of the sessions, a story about moving from an African American neighborhood to a more mixed one with Latino and African American people. Deandre's new neighborhood was near one in which Paco had grown up. Soon after Deandre's family moved in, a rowdy pair of Latino brothers had thrown several eggs near the front door of Deandre's house. Paco's mother apologized to Deandre's mother, saying she was embarrassed by such hostilities. "I have been waiting to welcome you to our neighborhood for a long time," she said.

Knowing how his mother felt, Deandre then attempted to smooth things over by suggesting that the event was not racially motivated; after all, he pointed out, those boys were known to harass everyone, even their own relatives. Deandre's mother was gracious, but her facial expression conveyed a mild rebuke to Deandre that he was being naive. Yet the connection made between these two mothers was genuine. They went on to have an engaging conversation about their shared community. Neighborly dialogue like this can create and maintain collective efficacy. And often, children, with their more flexible minds, are able to lead their parents to such mutuality.

More than twenty years have passed since that celebratory gathering, and we have stayed in touch with Deandre and gotten to know him well. We have seen his mother, too, from time to time, and together listened intently to his war stories about life in an artillery brigade in Afghanistan. Returning home in 2007, he entered Triton College with the goal of becoming a police officer. Learning he would likely be assigned to his old neighborhood as an undercover officer, a role he could not accept, he looked for another path toward stability and security. A new professional focus on business, and later transportation, helped him make a series of life-course decisions: to marry, to become a parent, to establish a home, and to inspire a next generation of young citizens.

Our most recent rendezvous was to have dinner not far from our old office building, not only with Deandre but also Percy, another veteran of the program. There was a lot of catching up to do, between our reporting on nearly completing the Young Citizens project in Tanzania, and Percy's determination to pursue a doctorate degree in mathematics.

Percy told a story we hadn't heard back in the 1990s about how he became interested in going to college and got in the habit of studying hard to make it happen. He had grown up in the notorious Robert Taylor Homes in Chicago's South Side. As a young man in the Homes, he had been involved in recreation programs there. The attitude of the counselors, he said, was that the kids who passed through the programs could only expect to become "statistics." These children were off the street while they were in a program, but that wouldn't go on indefinitely; their counselors did not or could not imagine vibrant and varied futures for them. Percy recalled learning about the UN Convention on the Rights of the Child, and starting to think of himself as a citizen through the deliberation sessions. As his expectations for his own future began to expand, he became more daring: "Why not be anyone I want to be?" he remembered thinking. "Then I saw it—I am going to become an Einstein! To do that I will need to major in mathematics."

We knew that he had gone to Malcolm X College for two years for his first degree and then on to Chicago State for his bachelor's and master's degrees. For the last few years he had been a math tutor in Chicago schools, hoping to resume his graduate studies after saving some money. While working during his undergraduate years, he had saved enough to buy his mother a home on the far South Side of Chicago. This was just prior to the demolition of the twenty-eight high-rise buildings of the Taylor Homes.

Before taking off in different directions we all agreed to check in with Paco, who had become a classical guitarist. It has been an inspiration to maintain contact with him over the years and watch him bloom as a performer. After several years of switching colleges and career goals, he had an epiphany: his passion for the guitar could be his professional foundation. After finishing his undergraduate degree in education at Northeastern Illinois University, he was chosen for internships at Lincoln Center in New York City for two consecutive summers. He always tells us that learning to deliberate as a young citizen had a profound effect on him. He describes how he uses deliberation in his own classrooms, now that he is a music instructor. His final recital to mark the completion of his Master of Arts degree at Northwestern University was a duet of guitarist and narrator, combining the words of a Spanish poet with music. Discourse—voices in relationship, informing, respecting, and framing each other—was even prominent in his music.

Asking Questions, Raising Voices

In the summer of 1999, we brought what we had learned in the original Chicago citizen program to a new city: Cambridge, Massachusetts. We recruited six youth, ages fourteen through seventeen, from Cambridge Rindge and Latin High School as interns for a six-week period. As members of the Cambridge Young Citizens Project, their responsibility was to develop a method of applying children's rights concepts to health promotion. (This project planted seeds that later bore additional fruit in the Young Citizens program in Tanzania). Brian Chan, a Harvard undergraduate who had helped facilitate the first installment of the Chicago program, remained for the summer to assist as a facilitator with this new group.

On the first day of work, the most important idea to get across was that the students were encouraged and even obligated to conduct themselves as equals: equals with each other and equals with adults, starting with the two of us. To clarify this expectation, we shared a diagram outlining the "ladder of participation," a group tool for self-assessing collaboration adapted by Roger Hart for use with children.[9] The ladder has eight rungs, with the three lowest actually representing nonparticipation and five highest representing ascending degrees of participation. Starting with the bottom, the lowest three rungs are labeled *manipulation, decoration,* and *tokenism.* These are ways that children may be pulled into participatory settings only to give the appearance that they are true participants. Preschoolers at a protest are being manipulated, for example, if they have been promised cookies to wave signs that they do not themselves understand. The ways children might actively participate in an adult-led group climb from *assigned* to *consulted* to *adult-initiated with shared decisions with children.* The top two rungs of the ladder are participation that is *child-initiated and directed,* and, most impressively, participation that is *child-initiated, with shared decisions with adults.* Our group spent time parsing the distinction between these two top rungs. All agreed that it was a higher form of participation to share decisions with adults than to have adults acting only as sounding boards or resources to child-initiated projects. What they were saying was that they preferred having these older people fully committed to, but not in full control of, their pursuits.

With the ladder as a tool for defining and monitoring the desired quality of participation, the young citizens then proceeded to produce their own mission statement: "Our mission is to explore the diverse issues of importance to young people, examining both their positive and negative experiences. Through our explorations, we hope to increase awareness of rights of youth for ourselves personally and for all youths and adults. We want to make positive changes in the lives of youth, but more importantly, we want to show how changes can be made. Ultimately, we would like to produce something real, which will give us a feeling of accomplishment."

The next step was to introduce the text of the UN Convention on the Rights of the Child and begin a dialogue on the relevance of this document to them, living as they did in a relatively secure and progressive urban environment. First, they reflected on the participatory rights guaranteed to children, discussing how the ladder of participation was itself a micro example of how children's participatory rights might work at a macro level. The next, more challenging task was to examine how an understanding of the children's rights could help them realize their mission, "to explore issues of importance to young people . . . to show how changes can be made."

The project grew and changed with them in unexpected but ultimately fruitful directions. Having crafted a mission statement and considered the UN Convention on the Rights of the Child, they sought out a major theme to guide their project, one that could inform their lives and those of their peers, and prove worthy of exploration and study. They settled on expressions like "well-being" and "quality of life" to kick off a dialogue that ran for several days. Whatever the focus of their project ended up being, it had to be readily comprehensible and meaningful to a young person growing up in Cambridge and attending public high school. Gangs and drugs were considered, but they affected subgroups, not the majority of students. When the topic of *detachment* came up, the group immediately wanted to explore it in detail. It was a broad term, diffuse and difficult to define, but it seemed relevant and widespread, although experienced in different ways by different individuals. How to target an elusive concept like detachment? One aspect of it seemed to capture its essence—that a detached person was someone who had lost affiliation with others. Detachment is like being outside looking at the crowd on the inside.

The group tapped its three adult members for ideas about what methods might best be used to assess detachment. In response, we adults started a session by giving a primer on social science research design. We had recently adopted the Delphi method in a separate project, working with a group of adults who were also deliberating on well-being. This method, originally developed by RAND Corporation researchers in the 1950s as a way of arriving at a consensus opinion among experts, now typically involves an internet-based exchange of ideas and opinions by a dedicated group committed to achieving a consensus.[10] Despite the novelty of the technology application, the young citizens were not impressed. We then suggested that they do a traditional survey of the student population, showing them the survey designed by the Chicago group. Again, there was little or no enthusiasm. To make matters worse, the young people complained that we organizers were slipping down the ladder of participation, changing the project from one of child leadership—or at least participation—into something else. They were irritated. This was what typically happened with adults. How sincere were we about equality?

The young citizens envisioned a more appealing method to gather information that could reach a large audience of their peers and that would not come across as being academic—something like a video. The problem with that idea was that none of the adults had ever made a high-quality video, and the group had already agreed that its work would be first-rate: rigorously done and skillfully presented. "So, if you can't help us, why don't you help us find someone who can?" they asked. Here we were teetering on the top rung of the ladder about to fall off—but we found a volunteer video producer just in time in Barbara Gullahorn Holecek, an award-winning documentary producer for PBS, *Nova*, and WGBH Boston.

Having reestablished themselves as equals, the young citizens began discussing how they would make a video on the theme of detachment, one that would be well-executed and appealing. They deliberated every day for a week on every aspect of detachment. Was it always bad? Was it a way of coping with stress? Did detached people ever "reattach"? And on it went. Deliberation is the best quality of deliberative citizenship, but it can also make projects take longer—or grow in unexpected ways.

While discussing other matters, the topic of racism and racial segregation came up. The young citizens regarded these together as a clear violation of child rights. Racism was not supposed to be prominent in the famously "liberal" community of Cambridge; but anyone visiting their high school would not fail to notice the separation of racial groups in classroom seating arrangements, lunch tables, and extracurricular activities. What was this? Self-segregation seemed like a strange term, but maybe it was an apt way of describing something that was real, poorly understood, and potentially harmful. Did the students and their peers really want or need to self-segregate? Were these habits of self-segregation compensating for something school officials or parents were not doing? Leaving "detachment" behind, they decided to seek out more information on self-segregation.

Over the next week the young citizens managed to achieve four things. First, they interviewed each other about their individual attitudes toward race and ethnic differences. Then they went back through the UN Convention's articles to see how racism had been addressed in the context of child rights. Next, they collectively read Beverly Tatum's *Why Are All the Black Kids Sitting Together in the Cafeteria?*[11] Finally, they met with a professor at the Harvard Graduate School of Education and discussed his studies on the effect of self-segregation on achievement.

Time was running out. The students were now beyond the halfway mark of their six-week internship and were only just beginning to reach a consensus on what they wanted to do. Nevertheless, because they had already planned to recruit a representative mix of students by social class and ethnic background for their video, they were able to secure ten volunteers quickly. They assembled a sequence of open-ended questions to guide the interview process. The students conducted interviews in pairs, with one person posing the questions and the other videotaping. In a little over a week, they completed and recorded nine interviews. With the guidance of the television producer and technical support from a community television station, the students then spent a week editing their video.

The job was done. They had produced a twenty-minute video called "Chillin" which explored self-segregation at a public high school in a progressive community. It was assuredly a high-quality production, and the interviews were sincere and provocative. One interviewee, who made statements some considered inflammatory, even chose to sit behind a semi-transparent drape to conceal his identity. The video opens with scenes of high school activity and mingling groups of students, set to music. The young citizens introduce their program and state that the video's purpose is not just to explore "why we divide ourselves by race" but also to ask: "Does it offend us? Does it affect our well-being?"

An African American girl worries about the consequences of clumping with people from your own race: "What will happen when you grow up and your boss is white? You're screwed." The boy behind the curtain, dubbed the Mystery Man, makes an observation that, if you came on Parents' Night, you might think the school was 95 percent white. This angers one of the young citizens, who hears in Mystery Man's observation a negative insinuation about African American parents. Some interviewees say self-segregation is ingrained, but reversible. Others think the problem is getting worse. Some blame teachers for placing students in categories, or for only caring about their paychecks. The video ends with a statement that this production "was an exercise in citizenship." The viewer is left with the sense that the range of points of view has been explored responsibly and honestly.

But the young citizens did not feel they had gone far enough. Nine students could not possibly reflect the range of attitudes about this complicated and revealing topic of self-segregation. Their plan was to show the video to small groups of students and then to conduct exercises in dialogue and deliberation with them, just as they themselves had during the internship, as a way of building on the experience. "Are we not obligated to do a survey of the whole student body?" one of the young citizens asked the group during their final session. Time was up, but the job was not really complete.

What happened next surprised us: The young citizens volunteered to extend their commitment. With the support of facilitator Brian Chan, they created a survey based on the questions they used to guide their interviews. Over ninety students completed the questionnaire. They informed the

school administration of "Chillin" while the new survey responses were coming in, and they charted out a plan for
disseminating the results of their work.

Good news followed: it turned out that the school was
already revising its "house system," which divided up a student
body of two thousand into smaller "schools." At that time, the
"houses" were not created randomly. They aggregated students
based on achievement, interests, and choice. The new system
would assign students to houses strictly randomly. The young
citizens' exploration of self-segregation supported this decision
and, indeed, legitimized it. This was a thrilling validation of
the Young Citizens program as a whole, supporting a positive
change in the students' own world.

We found these young citizens deeply inspiring. They left
us more convinced than ever that young people in their teens
could contribute significantly not only to research, but to real
change. The lengthy and probing dialogue sessions, the
relevance of the child rights platform, and the desire to take
some sort of shared action put us on a new, hopeful track. We
began compiling a more formal version of the curriculum we
had employed in Cambridge and Chicago—a complete manual
of the principles of rights, health promotion, collective efficacy,
and deliberative citizenship. This would constitute a how-to
guide for building young citizenship—even in a very different
part of the world.

Toward Tanzania

Over the three years of the Chicago and Cambridge Young
Citizens programs, we planted seeds of a new vision of youth,
a new way of promoting their well-being. Late childhood is
often stigmatized by society, which tends to cast adolescents

as people whose criteria for making decisions are questionable and whose lifestyles are deficient. When we sometimes saw a lack of healthy respect and communication, our sense was that teens were not being given sufficient settings for expressing their views in a constructive manner, even in response to events that directly affected them. We were changing that.

Chicago and Cambridge presented us with two very different groups of young people, but both, despite minimal prior experience in deliberation, succeeded in accessing relevant literature on the topic, engaging us and one another in sustained critical and rational argumentation, reaching mutual understanding about a chosen issue, and arriving at a consensus action plan. These projects were compelling proof of concept that children should contribute as citizens.

In an egalitarian and critical setting, these young citizens had become knowledgeable and persuasive agents of change in their communities and schools. The procedures their groups developed effectively promoted trust, perspective-taking, mutual understanding, and shared social action.[12] In fact, they were confirmed as effective when we applied them again, in work with two other Cambridge groups made up of middle-school-aged children.

These Young Citizens program groups had developed a sense of community, the skill of trusting others, a practice of collective deliberation, and more. Having watched them do this, we now had an approach for building collective efficacy in children. It had to be done *with* children and *through* them, not on their behalf by well-meaning adults. This is because children must strengthen and refine their own skills in talking, reasoning, deliberating, reaching consensus, planning, and coordinating actions with other children *and* with adults. Surrounded and guided by adults who believed in children's potential (and rights), these young people, soon to be adults, discovered that they could become worthy citizens and effective promoters of their schools' and communities' welfare. We had encouraged them to raise their voices and to recognize what it means to be heard.

The work encouraged us to go farther: this time to Tanzania to confront the HIV / AIDS epidemic and the profound impact it was having on children, family integrity, and the whole fabric of society across sub-Saharan Africa.[13]

5

Big Ideas in Small Places

Where, after all, do universal human rights begin? In small places, close to home—so close and so small that they cannot be seen on any maps of the world. Yet they are the world of the individual person; the neighborhood he lives in; the school or college he attends; the factory, farm, or office where he works. Such are the places where every man, woman, and child seek equal justice, equal opportunity, equal dignity without discrimination. Without concerted citizen action to uphold them close to home, we shall look in vain for progress in the larger world.

—ELEANOR ROOSEVELT

Young citizens, we have spent our careers discovering, can be grown and nurtured anywhere. We began in Chicago and made stops in Romania, Brazil, and Cambridge before taking everything we had learned and putting it to work in Tanzania. At the beginning of this millennium, we challenged the gloomy and distorted characterization of Africa as a dying continent paralyzed by HIV stigma and harboring legions of orphaned and vulnerable children. After engaging in site visits with local government authorities, nongovernmental organizations, HIV consortiums, street children projects, and orphanages, we had a sense of guarded optimism. Equipped with insights and research from around the world, we broadened our expectation that adolescents, local residents, and elected leaders could act together to confront HIV. We reasoned that young people who had been trained in deliberative citizenship and provided with basic scientific knowledge could catalyze their communities to confront the devastating pandemic.

Here, at last, was a chance to put the full scope of the Young Citizens program into action. From Chicago we had learned about collective efficacy—how neighborly actions toward children make communities thrive, and how to encourage community members, especially children, to engage in informed and rational discourse about serious local challenges such as violence. From Romania we had learned the importance of social contact and interaction in the first years of life—that the social potential of our species can only be realized if adequate social contact and reciprocity are a consistent feature of infants' nurturance. Without the formation and stabilization of these early social capacities, becoming a citizen at any age will be denied. From Brazil, we had learned how older children who have established basic social-emotional-cognitive capacities in the first years of life can maintain meaningful relationships with peers (and trusted adults) even in the absence of family and community support—relationships that not only allow them to survive on the street but to speak up about their experiences and aspirations.

In Tanzania in 2003, massive numbers of children were susceptible to the loss of parents, a threat dangerously exacerbated by community denial and stigmatization of HIV / AIDS.[1] We believed that the children themselves, with the right support, could establish the confidence and competence to inspire their communities to become knowledgeable about the facts of HIV. In Tanzania we encouraged local citizens to consider the potential of an innovative program involving young citizens to help solve major health challenges. This chapter presents a picture of the Young Citizens experiment, which consisted of a scripted curriculum embedded in a rigorous evaluation framework. This was a big step to take and was in marked contrast to the small, intimate groups we ran in Chicago and Cambridge. We worried it might prove that we had been overly optimistic in our expectations of children's social capacities and interests.

MKOMBOZI CENTRE for Street Children, Moshi, Tanzania, 2003. There are eight boys: George, Ally, Brusel, Zakayo, Anthony, Gabriel, Abel, and, of course, Mandela. (How could there be eight boys gathered in any part of Africa and not have at least one named Mandela?) They are darting around the grounds of the shelter where they are temporary occupants, their hands gesturing briskly toward the sky as if they were flying kites. But nothing can be seen above. The sky is clear, devoid of visible flying objects. It is difficult to estimate ages because some of this group seem likely to have been undernourished and therefore growth retarded. But there is nothing malnourished about their enthusiasm.

Norris Kamo, a Harvard student who spent two summers with the project before and after his first year in medical school, has prepared a manual on GPS technology for the group. He and Samwel, a Tanzanian facilitator, together have run several sessions with these boys on issues of trust and perspective-taking. And now the boys are calculating their velocity with GPS units. One of them asks: "But how are the satellites fed?" Norris explains. Turning the pages of his manual from a picture showing the global pathways of satellites to another picture of the radio signals emitted, he explains that the satellite is like a cell phone. While satellites receive their energy from the sun, the GPS receiver units have batteries. "Both the sender and receiver must have energy."

"This was a good day," Samwel says. "Are you young citizens ready to go into town with both your cameras and GPS units?" The response is enthusiastic. "Ndiyo, kabisa," they exclaim—yes, absolutely. Norris nods and smiles. "Tomorrow let's start at the market in Bondeni."

The next morning the facilitator introduces the boys to the street leader for the market neighborhood. This is a striking event for these boys, who have reputations as petty thieves and street urchins. The boys explain their GPS project and ask for permission to take pictures. Pleasantly surprised by the boys' confident manner, the street leader escorts them to a corner of the market, where the market's manager sits under a brightly colored canopy. The boys must explain their project again. The manager looks perplexed but, taking his cues from the street leader, says it is alright as long as he can accompany the boys to see exactly what they are doing.

The boys walk around in two groups of four, with an air of authority in their gaits; after all, they are street boys. They are taking pictures of certain things that they notice, things that are either good for health or bad for health. They record the GPS coordinates for each picture, giving them two sources of information: image and location. Pointing to dozens of melons lying uncovered on the ground, the boys complain that these melons are getting contaminated by dirt that contains fecal matter. Click. Their next photo shows a yellow-tinged pool of stagnant water in a ditch outside the health center adjacent to the market: "Look, they are letting mosquitos breed right outside the clinic, so you can get malaria on your way to see the doctor."

Norris, Maya, and I are worried about the third photo, but we are relieved to learn that they had received official permission. This one shows a green, gated playing field, lined with large trees, at the police training academy. The boys had arrived at a consensus that this might be the healthiest place in all of the municipality of Moshi and the place they most enjoy. Through the fence that kept them out, it certainly looked like the most inviting space to play soccer and just run around. And now they could say exactly where it was situated on the globe.

In the space of a week they have begun to act like local citizens and to think like cosmopolitan, even global, citizens.

Counting on Tanzania

Our idea in Tanzania was to conduct an experiment in which children would be guided through a coordinated series of activities designed to promote the skills associated with deliberative citizenship. The young people would be encouraged to raise their voices, listen to one another, and use facts and reason in their arguments. They would learn about their personal health as well as their communal health and then put that knowledge to work in all their decision making. And they would be coached on how to work together to channel their concerns and decisions into the wider body of society, to show their peers, neighbors, parents, and teachers how to take action.

Our challenge was to enable young Tanzanians to avoid the pessimism, charity, and helplessness conveyed by the expression "orphans and vulnerable children." If given the opportunity, they could, we believed, become skilled, confident, and proactive citizens, even in the face of a serious epidemic and chronic poverty.

Could the Tanzanian young citizens learn about the biology of HIV infection and its social transmission? Would elders object to children talking about this stigmatized disease? Meanwhile, Tanzania requires students to take a Primary School Leaving Examination at the end of Standard 7, and only those who pass receive certificates qualifying them for public secondary school. Would parents and teachers cooperate, or would they worry about participation distracting the children from schoolwork and preparing for that dreaded exam? Would boys miss soccer matches? Would girls have too many household chores to attend regularly?

The project would present many challenges involving logistics, personnel, and organizational management. But the children themselves never wavered. Their energy and commitment—to confront rather than succumb to the raging HIV pandemic threatening the populations of much of sub-Saharan Africa—were educational and inspiring. They proved to us once again that children are more than capable of being citizens.

Two expectations underlay this dramatic experiment. The first was that children would benefit from becoming more confident of their own capacity to communicate rationally and respectfully with others. The second was that children, after becoming more confident, would be integrated into their society as informed, responsible agents. These two expectations—respectful communication and inclusion—are at the heart of what it means to be a citizen. And we believe every child should get to experience being an active citizen.

With our objectives and expectations established, we began, much as we had for the Chicago project, by creating a new organizational structure, one with the scientific, ethical, and administrative capacities required to run a large-scale research project effectively. We named the organization Child Health and Social Ecology, which was instantly converted to an acronym, CHASE. The young citizens usually referred to it by its diminutive, "chasi." CHASE's primary responsibility was to develop a Young Citizens curriculum and then to test its merits, so it could be shared with the world.

How did we get this program off the ground? We drew on the life philosophy we had embraced a decade earlier while directing our massive study in Chicago: Do whatever it takes. Yet the Moshi project was even more demanding than the Chicago project, and we were not getting any younger. Repeatedly making the eighteen-thousand-mile round trip, spending weeks or months at a time training and supervising a Tanzanian staff, toggling between two languages, Swahili and English—all required mental and physical endurance. Time management could be cruel. Tanzanians live by two clocks—the official timekeeping of the East Africa time zone three hours past Greenwich mean time, but also the traditional Swahili time pegged to the rising and setting of the sun. Although we spent years going and coming, there was a lingering uncertainty about when exactly events would begin. We always felt as if we were on the brink of a personnel crisis or at an administrative impasse. But we never doubted our purpose.

We selected Moshi Municipality, in the Kilimanjaro region of northern Tanzania, as the site. We were familiar with this region, which we had first visited in 1974 to see the newly founded Kilimanjaro Christian Medical Centre (which would later become our research partner for the CHASE project). During a second visit, in 1986, we had climbed Mount

Kilimanjaro with our twelve- and eighteen-year-old daughters. Working in Moshi, every glimpse of that nineteen-thousand-foot mountain served as a reminder to do whatever it took.

Moshi, a midsized municipality of 150,000 people, sits at the foot of Mount Kilimanjaro, the highest point in all of Africa. When the cloud cover lifts, the mountain is visible from every location in the city. Moshi is located on a major highway between Dar es Salaam (the nation's capital) and Arusha, which serves as a tourist destination for Kilimanjaro climbers and visitors to the nearby Serengeti and Ngorongoro Crater National Parks. This location placed Moshi directly along the route of the HIV epidemic that was sweeping across the eastern and southern regions of the African continent.

We were inclined to choose Tanzania as the most suitable setting for a project because of our twenty-five-year history in visiting this country and appreciating its post-colonial struggles. The fact that it had an accessible, decentralized, local government structure was also germane. We were proposing to focus the Young Citizens program on upper-level primary school students, and were aware that Tanzanian schools were well-balanced in terms of gender through age fourteen. After that point, with the transition to secondary school, the student population skews towards males.

Over this month-long trip we visited three cities in different regions of the country and considered whether it would be best to base the study in just one of these cities or if two would better reflect the complexity of the epidemic. We quickly realized that the scale of the program we were planning would be too demanding to push beyond a single location. With Moshi being the preferred site, we officially began in 2003, with full support from the US National Institutes of Health for a seven-year period. Our intent was to create opportunities for reciprocal interaction between children and their residential communities in response to the HIV / AIDS crisis. If successful, the program would integrate children as equal, active participants in the civil and political activities of their local communities.

The research unit we created was located in a large, centrally located building in the center of Moshi. We had generous office space with satisfactory infrastructure and large windows that pointed northward toward Mount Kilimanjaro. Its magnificent peak, Kibo, could tell us every day: "whatever it takes." The CHASE staff was composed of an experienced postgraduate research director, twelve Tanzania research assistants, and three administrators. The research assistants were divided into six college graduates serving as lead facilitators and six secondary school graduates as assistant facilitators. There were two drivers, each equipped with a four-wheel-drive Toyota hardtop. With many students attending schools outside their residential neighborhoods, the drivers' primary responsibility was to transport students to and from our weekly sessions in their communities.

The grant from the National Institute of Mental Health was awarded to Harvard Medical School. Harvard in turn created a subcontract with Kilimanjaro Christian Medical School (also in Moshi) to cover all expenses connected with the research project. This included staff salaries and benefits, rent, insurance, and transportation costs. We also, as scientific directors, maintained staff in our Harvard offices, who together with the staff in Moshi collaborated on all administrative and research responsibilities. These included tasks such as obtaining ethical clearances, preparing documentation of the curriculum, and resolving logistical issues related to the collection and analysis of survey data for our health and community surveys.

Fortunately, Tanzania had already made considerable progress in its political and human services decentralization policies. To promote participatory governance, significant amounts of decision-making and service delivery had been delegated down to the local level. The country had been divided into small jurisdictions, each with around four thousand citizens. Democratically elected leaders at all levels facilitated both the formal workings of local government and the informal organization of civil society. The existence of these geopolitical units was ideal for configuring the CHASE program. Having a health infrastructure based on geopolitical units provided a child-friendly scale for a community-based activity like the Young Citizens program.

The execution of this social experiment required close attention to details and consistent monitoring of community partnerships, as well as the administration of surveys and the implementation of a complex and innovative intervention. The Young Citizens program was conducted in fifteen *mitaa*. (As the smallest geopolitical unit in Tanzania's local government structure, *mtaa* means "street unit" or "neighborhood"; the plural is *mitaa*.) Another fifteen matched mitaa served as comparisons. The research program was organized into four phases: pre-intervention, intervention, post-intervention, and sustained.

In Moshi, we rolled out a unique program of thematic modules inspired by our research in Chicago, Cambridge, and Brazil and informed by Romania's cautionary experience with voicelessness and vulnerability. Each module covered and enacted a vital step in the generation of inspired and informed young citizens. The development of the curriculum began by

Table 5.1   Structure of Intervention Modules

Module 1	Aims to promote the formation of group identity and trust among adolescents and introduce concepts of deliberation, critical thinking, assuming the perspectives of others, and preference ranking to reach mutual understanding about health issues. (5 sessions)
Module 2	Educates adolescents about their potential for active citizenship by introducing them to their local leaders and coaching them to acquire skill and confidence in observation, mapping, and interview techniques to plan and organize shared social action to build HIV / AIDS competence in their communities. (4 sessions)
Module 3	Introduces adolescents to detailed biological, behavioral, and social knowledge about social transmission of disease, especially malaria and HIV / AIDS. Through deliberation and dramatization, adolescents learn the microbiology of these highly prevalent diseases and the social circumstances leading to their acquisition, diagnosis, and treatment. Adolescents receive health promotion certificates following successful learning and performing of dramatic sequences. (5 weeks)
Module 4	Represents an extended period of interaction with the community, through scheduled and facilitated HIV / AIDS weekly or semiweekly performances in their mtaa. As the adolescents become increasingly skilled in presenting the social context and microbiology of HIV / AIDS in public spaces, fellow citizens engage in active public dialogue about prevention strategies, stigma reduction, and family issues. (14 sessions)

Source: Mary Carlson and Felton Earls, "A Health Promotion Curriculum for Adolescent Young Citizens: Deliberation and Public Action for HIV / AIDS–Competent Communities," *American Journal of Orthopsychiatry* 81, no. 4 (2011): 453–460.

considering the Child to Child program, a London-based child rights agency administered by the Institute of Education.[2] We had learned about this program through UNICEF and were pleased to learn that it had been used in Kenya and Tanzania. Evidently, that program's child-centered approach had proved acceptable to children, families, and communities in the region. Given the theoretical guidance that informed the Young Citizens program, our aim was to design a more detailed and standardized curriculum than could be provided by the Child to Child program. The foundation for our approach was to create modules that reflected the principles of communicative action theory and a capabilities approach.[3] Yet, we benefited from a formal consultation with one of that program's regional directors during our planning period. Our modules were designed to guide children in working together in a participatory and deliberative manner, recognizing their own rights, and believing in their own competence as child citizens. The goal was to mobilize them to take informed social action to address health challenges.

How to Become Young Citizens

The first two modules of the Young Citizens program are designed to enhance children's voices. In Module One, a group of children ages ten to fourteen, all from the same neighborhood, is randomly selected, and they begin to work together. The second module directs this newly formed group to introduce itself to, and gain the support of, the neighborhood's adult authorities; this is to prepare the group for community reconnaissance. The first module unifies their individual voices. In the second module, this unified voice begins to address the community.

The first module, Group Formation, takes as its initial task educating the children about how collections of people—like classrooms, neighborhoods, or nations—are organized, and how they can function in egalitarian, non-hierarchical ways. In Tanzania, group formation was accomplished across five sessions, each two hours long, which immersed the children in topics related to group structure and deliberative citizenship. These sessions were held in classrooms in the local primary school after school and on weekends.

The sessions' concepts and activities themselves were designed to help the group develop its own egalitarian structure. The group worked to build trust. Members intently took each other's perspectives into account. They practiced using explicit communication and reasoned discourse. And they took shared social action. These four steps are essential for developing children's competence in group work and confidence in their ability to engage in rational argumentation, or deliberation. All this work laid a solid foundation for the action they would choose to take, because—again, recalling Habermas's theory of communicative action—deliberation is not just talk. Rather, such reasoned discourse is the necessary prerequisite and catalyst for action.[4]

Among other topics, the group was introduced in the first session to *social-ecological thinking,* in which the development of a child is seen as situated in circumstances that range from proximal (the family) to distal (the national government), as described by Urie Bronfenbrenner.[5] Bronfenbrenner, one of the most influential child psychologists of the twentieth century, developed and continually refined an elaborate and comprehensive theory to account for all the environmental inputs needed to safeguard the healthy development of children, from infancy to adolescence.

The group also learned how the Young Citizens curriculum planned to achieve egalitarian group dynamics and mutual respect among children and adult facilitators. As they studied group structure diagrams (not charts), members were asked to compare hierarchical versus egalitarian groups. In the beginning, some participants expressed a preference for the hierarchical manner: in school, for example, the teacher did the work and asked the questions, allowing students to take it easy. This was soon to change.

During this first module, children made progress in hearing and reflecting on different perspectives, showing respect for the perspectives of others, and displaying their capacity to argue with others and to support their arguments with facts. The concepts of social skills and communicative skills were introduced, along with activities to promote effective deliberative citizenship.[6] This contributed to their increasing comfort and competence with this communication style, which enabled effective and egalitarian social interactions.

The first module used a number of games and organized activities to encourage the basics of deliberative citizenship. The most basic concept of all was rationality, defined as "giving reasons." When the children began giving reasons for their statements, the frequency of the Swahili term *kwa sababu* (because) increased notably. A basic assertion of causality, it was a simple indicator of their increased proficiency in rational thinking. As they learned how to argue their positions, the young citizens also learned how to give and take criticism. They focused more on evaluating the evidence given for a point of view, rather than criticizing or praising the speaker. By the end of Module One, the children had begun to establish an egalitarian and cohesive group structure and had understood the meaning of citizenship as it applied to their lives.

The fifteen groups then moved to the second module, Understanding Our Community. It showed children how to explore and engage with their neighborhoods by walking the boundaries of the mtaa, meeting with their elected local representatives, and using interviews and mapping to learn about the demographic makeup of their schools and homes. The story we related above of the Mkombozi boys using GPS and GIS technology came from this second module.

Module Two is designed to offer children, over the course of four sessions, a set of new concepts about citizenship and new ways to approach and understand their communities. One key concept is cooperative learning, which the children demonstrate by volunteering for important responsibilities such as timekeeper, map tracker, and materials manager. At the same time, they develop skills in survey interviewing, geographic mapping, and photography—all as ways of documenting the health status of their communities. These skills help them understand the health of all their neighbors, as well as the multigenerational relationships that support or undermine good health. It is important that these sessions be active, interesting, and fun—as they clearly were in Tanzania, judging by the engagement of the children.

The young citizens spent time in the community going on neighborhood walks with their facilitators and with community leaders. They learned the geographical boundaries and administrative responsibilities of their neighborhoods as governmental (structural) units. They learned to summarize the information they collected in the community, and they mapped features of the neighborhood that affected health either positively or negatively, as the Mkombozi boys had done in the initial pilot project.

The children's interaction with neighborhood leaders was the highlight of this stage, especially as they planned and executed the neighborhood walks. Together, they observed the social and physical context in which residents lived, and reflected on the health implications of community members' activities and experiences in various places and at different times of day.

The young citizens created skits depicting noteworthy conditions they observed in their communities. Following the guidelines of *what, where, when,* and *why,* these brief performances sought to portray, rather than simply describe, important issues or dilemmas that had emerged from their forays into the community and their group dialogue. Doing the skits in their neighborhoods allowed each of the groups to experience citizenship as a practice rather than an abstract concept—and helped everyone imagine possible transformations from an unhealthy to a healthy scenario. We discussed what actions might reduce the risk of poor health.

The results of their community activities were shared with their elected local leader after being practiced in schoolyards with parents and teachers. It was especially gratifying to observe the young citizens in the company of their community leader, acting with a real, earned sense of purpose, dignity, and legitimacy. On one walk, young citizens ventured into a community of the municipality that was unplanned (meaning very poor) yet politically active and a small group of them noticed piles of broken branches and other decaying vegetation along the footpath to a house. They walked to the front door, introduced themselves as "young citizens," and asked the resident, who was not familiar with any of them, if he would please see that this *takataka* (Swahili for trash) was properly discarded. The facilitators had wondered if they should restrain the children, but when the resident saw the community leader standing with the rest of the group beyond his fence, he responded positively to the polite and earnest manner in which he had been approached as a fellow citizen. He came out into the yard to say he understood and would take care of it soon. This type of interaction occurred often; with an adult present, the residents would allow themselves to trust and listen to the young citizens.

After they had performed their initial skits for the community, the children were increasingly recognized as political agents. Importantly, this gave them confidence that the community drama they were to perform in public places would draw attentive crowds. These were the transition into Module Three (Health and Our Community) and Module Four (Making Community Assessments and Taking Community Action), which we will describe in later chapters, given Part III's focus on Choice, and Part IV's focus on Action.

The Tanzania Young Citizens program amounted to a grand social experiment involving over seven hundred parents and children, which rewarded us with many rich encounters with particular children and also advanced our scientific mission to study broad populations of children. The scientific stance with its rigorous, objective perspective is what allows us to claim that we know something. We credit the more informal, personal experiences, however, with allowing us to ask the right questions.

The Curriculum

As noted already, the Young Citizens curriculum is divided into four modules for a total of twenty-eight sessions. In Tanzania, these played out from April through September of 2005. Each session was organized around one or more themes and related activities, described in a detailed script. Each session script was introduced by a standard agenda, which contained the time slots for a review of the previous session, an introduction to the current agenda and objectives, activities, a snack break, time for reflections, and a preview of the next session's objectives. The cooperative roles played by the young citizens required them to assume joint responsibility for specific session duties. The investigators and supervisory staff collaborated to develop the sessions based on the underlying theory guiding the Young Citizens program and the evaluation of previous session reports from all fifteen mtaa groups. In other words, the roughly thirty sessions were not completely scripted before the program began; they took into account the progress and problems encountered the week before.

We achieved quality control by carefully selecting, training, and supervising our team members and by requiring standardized, detailed reports of all sessions and team meetings. As important in the making of a successful project was our on-site presence. This required regular visits to Moshi with the length of stay determined by the specific needs and tasks the team encountered. We made four to five trips a year from Boston to Moshi, each lasting from three to six weeks. Quality assurance was achieved through weekly monitoring by trained and independent observers. They ensured fidelity to method by observing classroom-based sessions, using a checklist to note adherence to the session script and the sequencing and timing of themes and activities, and flagging any indications of age or gender bias in implementation.

The curriculum thus had a "rolling" format that provided flexibility. Facilitators submitted detailed session reports by the following day so that the research teams in Cambridge and Moshi could review all fifteen mtaa groups' reports. For the next week's session, the research team would reach a consensus based on the modal progress of all fifteen intervention groups.

148   Voice

Given that we had carefully established the general structure of modules, selections of session details were made through deliberations by the Moshi and Cambridge research staff and the scientific directors. Future sessions were designed to anticipate the next topics, with content bridging from previous sessions, and feature discussions and activities of durations that fit within a two-hour period.

The Experiment

Historically, the practice of medicine was based on trial-and-error empiricism. If a treatment seemed to work in the hands of one doctor, it might be adopted by others, based on the reputation and persuasive skills of the first doctor. All of this changed radically in 1910 when the Carnegie Foundation published an influential study authored by Abraham Flexner.[7] The Flexner Report advised deep changes in the structure and content of medical education. Doctors were to be trained in scientific thinking. Students should henceforth enter medical training with an expectation that the methods and treatments they learned to apply would be scientifically evaluated in terms of their efficacy. This expectation led to the standard use of the randomized trial to test all medicines for safety and effectiveness—a rigorous approach that subsequently influenced the behavioral and social sciences. Especially in the past thirty years, these too have adopted the reasoning, methodology, and standards of controlled experimentation which randomly divides a population of subjects into some who will receive a given treatment and others who will not.

The design for testing the safety and effectiveness of the Young Citizens program is a cluster randomized controlled trial, in which the units of analysis are neighborhoods (clusters). Children and their families are included as members of a neighborhood. This design accounts for the multiple ways in which personal factors, family influences, and neighborhood environments shape a child's destiny. The complexities involved in such multilevel designs required that we add a statistician to the team.

Before the Experiment

It was imperative at the outset of the Tanzania project to establish a relationship with local officials and community leaders. In a series of structured sessions, the project staff and ward officers of the municipality shared facts and discussed perceptions about improving children's health and well-being, anticipating likely challenges and resources needed. The goal was for these authorities to understand the ideas behind the project and the research design proposed, and to appreciate the value of cultivating citizenship in children. We organized open houses for parents and community members to meet the research staff and discuss the project.

It was also essential to obtain ethical clearance for the research plan from several sources, including our medical school (Harvard), a local medical school in Tanzania (Kilimanjaro Christian Medical College), local and national public health authorities in Tanzania, and the community itself. One of our concerns was that community elders might consider it inappropriate to engage children as young as age ten in a project that dealt with a stigmatized, sexually transmitted disease, or in any activity that would interfere with their studying for the dreaded Standard 7 exam, the qualifying exam for secondary school.

For a cluster randomized controlled trial to be successful, it had to be large enough to detect differences between the intervention and comparison neighborhoods. This meant we needed to determine how neighborhoods differed with respect to demographic and social factors prior to introducing the Young Citizens program. We carried out a baseline community survey across the entire municipality, which included sixty neighborhoods. The basic survey was borrowed from the community survey measure used in the Chicago project and adapted to fit the organization and social climate of Moshi.

We selected half of these neighborhoods for the experiment and, predicting that intervention neighborhoods would enjoy a moderate degree of benefit, designated fifteen neighborhoods as the treatment group, leaving another fifteen in the comparison group.[8] Mindful of the possible diffusion of effects from intervention to adjacent neighborhoods, we made choices such that the thirty neighborhoods outside the experimental design were positioned as buffer zones.

We also did a second and completely separate baseline assessment, this time focusing on the health and behavior of the children who would be asked to volunteer for the experiment (with their parents' consent). Twenty-four children ages ten to fourteen were randomly selected from each of the thirty experiment neighborhoods, the households of which had recently been mapped using geographic information systems tools. GIS mapping overlays site-specific data onto displays of spatial geography, making it possible to visualize phenomena, label features, and spot patterns in a physical area. This project preceded the availability of satellite-based mapping, but we were able to obtain recent digitized aerial photographs of Moshi from the National Bureau of Statistics of Tanzania, which we used to construct and illustrate the spatial configuration of intervention, comparison, and unassigned mitaa.

After the random selection, we made some corrections to ensure gender balance and spatial representation within the geopolitical boundaries of a neighborhood. The adolescents and their primary caregivers were assessed independently using parallel structured interviews. These assessments included sections on growth, pubertal development, sexuality, schooling, family relations, worries, mental health, and self-efficacy. An important distinction exists between self-efficacy and the more popular term *self-esteem*. The former is clearly understood as the child's confidence in his or her competence regarding a specific area of functioning, while the latter has a more diffuse meaning making it more subject to biased interpretation and unreliable to measure.

The community survey and health assessment provided a baseline against which the impact of the treatment (the Young Citizens curriculum) would be measured. After this assessment was done, we formed matched pairs of neighborhoods, with fifteen randomly assigned to the Young Citizens curriculum group and fifteen to the comparison group. The purpose of matched pairs is to minimize differences in social and economic factors that characterize communities.

During the Experiment

As described above, the scripted Young Citizens curriculum was given to twenty-four children in each of the fifteen intervention communities. An equal number of children in the comparison mitaa waited to learn if the intervention proved effective, in which case it would be repeated in their neighborhoods. Meanwhile, the comparison group carried on their daily lives without contact with the CHASE staff.

Unlike the more informal agenda for the Young Citizens sessions in the early groups in Chicago and Cambridge, the randomized controlled design we employed in Moshi required that a detailed, scripted curriculum be pretested and adapted to the local sites prior to launching the trial. This requirement stemmed from several concerns. Such experimental designs by their nature involve multiple individuals, or if it is a "cluster" trial, multiple communities as in this program. To guarantee a certain uniformity of treatment from one individual or group to the next, there must be a formula that describes the behavioral "treatment": in this case, the curriculum scripts. In a drug treatment trial, a chemical formula defines the entity being tested. In our experiment, the behavioral equivalent of the drug was a scripted curriculum of objectives, games, demonstrations, and topics for discussion. Each script included a schedule specifying the content and duration of each feature. This ensured greatest possible uniformity of treatment across all fifteen neighborhood groups; it also made it possible to repeat this same design with fidelity in other locations. To be certain that the scripts are well suited for this kind of administration, a "rolling" curriculum design routine was used as described above.

An essential requirement was to ensure that children were not being harmed in any way by this novel intervention. For this purpose, an independent Data Safety and Monitoring Board composed of scientists and members of the community was established to observe sessions and to collect information on possible adverse events that might be caused by participation, such as an increase in a child's punishment by parents or teachers. It was also valuable for us to know what parents and community leaders thought of the program's integrity.

After the Experiment

At the end of the twenty-eight-week experiment, the research staff organized a post-intervention community survey by recruiting and randomly selecting a new cross-sectional sample of adult residents in the comparison and intervention neighborhoods. We needed a new sample to account for changes in neighborhood composition that might reflect patterns of in- or out-migration of residents. Interviewers who were unaware of the random allocation were employed as data collectors. The community interviews repeated many of the baseline survey's questions, with special attention directed to the protection and support of children and to adult perceptions of children's knowledge and skills as community health agents.

Once the post-intervention community survey was completed, a post-intervention health assessment was also conducted with the children and their caregivers in both the intervention and comparison mitaa. Most of the content of this assessment was identical to the first health assessment, given the need for statistical analysis of differences before and after exposure to the intervention. In what ways did the young citizens change? When we compared the intervention and comparison neighborhoods, we confirmed that the differences were small to moderate in size, but statistically significant. Relative to children in the comparison groups, children in the intervention groups showed higher self-perceptions of deliberative efficacy, communicative efficacy, and emotional control.

Deliberative efficacy was assessed by having children rate their own capacities in a variety of respects, including:

- I know how to express my opinions to other children my age.
- I know how to make my ideas understood when other children disagree with me.
- I know how to use talking and reasoning to solve problems I have with other children.

- I know that other children will value me even if they disagree with my opinions.
- I know how to express my opinions to adults.

The structure for assessing communicative efficacy was similar but had the children reflect on their efficacy with adults:

- I know how to ask for assistance from adults to solve any problems.
- I know how to have adults listen to me.
- I know how to ask adults for advice about sexually transmitted diseases.
- I know how to talk to adults about what troubles me.
- I know how to express those thoughts and feelings that are important to me.

To self-assess their level of emotional control, the children rated their strengths in these additional areas:

- I know how to manage my feelings.
- I know how to be a good friend.
- I know how to recognize my strengths and talents.
- I know how to understand and accept myself.

The fact that averages were higher for children in the intervention group on the first two of these scales was not surprising given the emphasis placed on speech and language by the theory and practice of the Young Citizens program. The intervention group's self-assessments on emotional control were not predicted to be significantly different than the comparison group's, but in hindsight reflected the camaraderie of the group. The responses in two other areas—regarding academic efficacy (for example, in response to a statement that "I know that if I study hard I can be good at math") and peer resistance (for example, "I know I can say no to alcohol")— showed no difference between the intervention and comparison groups. Had differences been significant on these, they would indicate that the intervention had effects beyond its intended goals.

The statistical models used to analyze these results indicated how widely shared these positive results were among all participating children. It is important to emphasize that the benefits for individual young citizens of participating in the four modules' activities were consistent across gender, age, and social class categories; enhancements of deliberative efficacy, communicative efficacy, and emotional control were universally experienced across all fifteen intervention groups. The models adjusted the scale scores to reflect differences attributable to the child's status at baseline. They also included neighborhood features such as population density, average years of residence, and proportions of residents who were gainfully employed, homeowners, acquainted with the neighborhood leader, and had attained certain education benchmarks (primary school, secondary school, and university graduation).

The first rollout of a comprehensive Young Citizens program had begun. Some of the effects were obvious: increased confidence, more vocalized opinions, and greater reliance on deliberative debate and argument. Some, however, were not yet clear and would await later analysis: whether the program had changed the children's relationship to the community, whether adults viewed them as equals, and whether these trained young citizens could instigate change from the ground up. As we will see in Chapters 8 and 9, these latter benefits would follow.

PART III

Choice

6

Reaching Mutual Understanding

Since moralities are tailored to suit the fragility of human
beings individuated through socialization, they must always
solve two tasks at once. They must emphasize the inviolability
of the individual by postulating equal respect for the dignity
of each individual. But they must also protect the web of the
intersubjective relations of mutual recognition by which these
individuals survive as members of a community.

—JÜRGEN HABERMAS

To make change, people must decide what actions to take.
In cases where a change will affect only themselves, individuals may reflect simply on their own preferences to
make such decisions. But if their choices have consequences
for the lives of others, methods of social choice are required.
Social choices can be made either by communicating with
others to reach informal understanding or by aggregating
private choices to reach a sanctioned formal choice, as by
voting.

With this chapter, we move from "voice" to "choice" in our
consideration of how children can contribute to their communities as young citizens. Before we begin to investigate how
Tanzania's young citizens came to understand one another and

choose a course of collective action, our story takes us back to an earlier moment, in Chicago, and two groups of adults learning to listen to each other and work together for the good of their children and their community. This group's need was to agree on actions that would affect the lives of infants and young children who had not themselves attained the communicative and rational capacities to make choices for their own well-being. The adults' experience presents an excellent case of Jürgen Habermas's theory of communicative action and the practical procedures it implies for discourse ethics.

The Chicago project had yielded a new way to gauge collective efficacy in a community using objectively measurable factors, and to rigorously assess its protective and health-promoting impact. We wanted to know more about the relationship between collective efficacy and child well-being, and also about how neighborhoods could gain more of it. In search of social theory to clarify how collective efficacy is generated in neighborhoods, Maya spent a good chunk of 1993 in the catacombs of Harvard's Pusey Library; in that pre-Google era, randomly pulling books off the shelf was a plausible search strategy. This is how we became aware of the work of Jürgen Habermas, whose name has already come up in prior chapters.

Born in 1929 in Germany, Habermas came of age during the time of the Second World War, amid revelations of genocide on a massive scale and widespread misery driven by political extremism. Wanting no society ever again to endure such catastrophe, he devoted his career to providing a stronger intellectual basis for the pursuit of fairness, equality, and individual rights. Themes of rationality and communication dominate his extensive writings, which are suffused with the expectation that rational argumentation and critical discussion will prevail when human beings work toward the goal of mutual understanding. Habermas posits that democratic life prospers only when citizens have the capability and freedom to debate matters of public importance in ordinary language, and to reach informed consensus—again, in ordinary language— about actions to take.[1]

Habermas's core observation is that the informal aspects of community life bring inhabitants of a place together to identify and freely discuss their common problems, and that these discussions result in consensual and rational political action. This is what he calls deliberative democracy. His argument is that this mundane form of democracy is based on the unique human capacity for language. Language is to be judged not so much by what it says, but by what it does.

Having freshly arrived back from Romania, we had decided to engage parents in Chicago who were concerned about the quality of out-of-home care available for their young children. This was in the wake of major welfare reform in the United States, when the imposition of new work requirements had parents scrambling for scarce daycare resources. The Chicago project had revealed that nearly half of all three- and four-year old children were enrolled in daycare of one kind or another, whether licensed or unlicensed, in-home or facility-based. How did this non-parental, out-of-home experience operate, and how did it contribute to or threaten the children's well-being? Having the scientific authority to explore this challenging issue, the ongoing Chicago project obtained the needed funding and permission from local and state-governing bodies.

The project engaged two separate groups whose goals were identical—both wanted their children to thrive—but saw them arrive at very different plans of action. While they were

presented by the project with the same opportunities to engage in dialogue sessions about childcare quality, their widely
divergent paths to improving their communities were driven
by their distinctive approaches to democratic deliberation and
decision-making.

El Valor: Child Rights and Stress Test

The project's extended engagement on the question of
childcare began at an excellent, multiservice, early childhood
center located in a Mexican American neighborhood. This
early-childhood program was administered under the auspices
of the El Valor Center—its name featuring the Spanish word
for *courage*. The group engagement began with a presentation
about the stress hormone cortisol and a discussion of the pros
and cons of using it as an indicator of abuse or deprivation.
Staff members at the center were concerned that certain
children might be experiencing abuse in their homes, but they
could not of course cite any incidents seen with their own eyes.
They were uncertain about approaching families to discuss the
problems. The question the group took up was this: What
additional information might the measurement of cortisol
provide about children's exposure to abuse or neglect?

The support for the project came in 1996 from a research
grant awarded to Maya by the National Science Foundation's
Ethics and Value Study Section. The stated goal of the research
was to document how extended deliberative communication
between research scientists and a community-based organization's director, selected staff, and parents could lead to a
new approach to engaging human subjects in research. For the
children of the many recent immigrant families that used El
Valor, the topic of value and salience was the child rights

framework presented in the UN Convention on the Rights of the Child, much more than the idea of a novel stress-evaluation method based on measuring cortisol in saliva samples.

The plan was to design a collaborative approach by which practitioners, parents, and researchers could reach consensus on applying new technologies and discursive ethical procedures in ways appropriate to specific communities' needs and desires. This approach featured a series of discourse sessions in which caretakers and service providers would exercise their participation rights through dialogue; together, they would deliberate about the ethical implications of measuring cortisol in children. They would also learn about the conception of rights promoted by the UN Convention on the Rights of the Child and evaluate its importance.

Applying Habermas's theory to these deliberations, we designed the sessions to incorporate two of its central principles— first, the principle of *discourse ethics,* with its call for practical, participatory deliberation, and second, the principle of *universalization* which says any norm established must be accepted by all those affected by "the consequences and the side effects." Discourse ethics differs from the majority of moral theories, which are based on monological as opposed to dialogical processes. Habermas's theory of discourse ethics is grounded in a pragmatic purpose: to use communication among parties with different perspectives to arrive at common solutions to normative problems.[2]

Over the course of eight months, a group consisting of five staff members, two parents, and the two of us met for two-hour sessions twice a month. The group exchanged information and points of view, in conversation and in writing, about potential risks and benefits of using cortisol measurements to assess children's stress. Participants expressed a variety of opinions and perspectives about how this technique might be used to monitor the effectiveness of social services and to evaluate the appropriateness of institutional care settings. They also discussed the principles and articles of the UN Convention on the Rights of the Child, noting that Mexico was in the process of ratifying it and that UNICEF had a strong presence there, assisting the government in crafting rights-based policies for that country's children. Because this was our first venture in engaging families and childcare professionals in a discourse ethics format, we thought it prudent to share at the outset our recent experiences with these two topics.

The group endorsed the concept of children as rightsholders entitled to the protections, provisions, and participation stated in the UN Convention's principles and articles. In contrast, the group consensus was to reject the use of cortisol to flag possible abuse of a child who appeared distressed. Staff members were concerned: if they were to ask permission from families to take cortisol samples from a child and found high levels, how might they use this information? Would they encourage a family to seek diagnostic home visits? What judgment would be conveyed? The testing might well create suspicion and dissolve trust between the family and program. In some ways, a cortisol test might even interfere with a family's accepting assistance when it was needed. One staff member described a recent example of approaching a father who was suspected of some level of abuse, beginning with the simple overture "Mr. Lopez, let's talk." The staff felt that honest, direct, probing dialogue with parents was best: the kind of dialogue they had been using in our sessions.

From a scientific perspective, we shared with the group our own knowledge that the new cortisol assay methods certainly did not yet have a level of reliability and validity that would warrant their being used as a basis for referring a family to social services. What if the cortisol test yielded a high rate of false positives, indicating that children were suffering abuse when they were not? Or false negatives, failing to detect children who were being abused?

With regard to the value of the UN Convention on the Rights of the Child, and its relevance to the staff's obligations to care for children in the program, the group was persuaded that the rights approach offered a new and important basis for setting ethical and legal standards for caregivers. Deliberations focused especially on the concept of participatory rights, and how that part of the treaty resonated with the importance this group placed on having enough choices in high-quality early childhood education and care. Members of the group also noted that, because the UN treaty had been ratified by nearly all its member states, its definition of children's rights applied to children of many different nationalities and could be considered universal.

The National Science Foundation's funding of the project included a special allowance to engage an experienced bio-ethicist to evaluate the theory and ethical nature of our delib-erative approach and practices. After attending some sessions and reviewing transcripts of them all, Bruce Jennings of the bioethics research institute the Hastings Center concluded that the project met what he considered to be the ethical standards of discourse ethics. By the second meeting, the group had established an atmosphere of mutual trust and respect. All participants felt comfortable enough to exchange personal stories about their children, their own childhoods, raising families, and developing self-confidence in the context of Amer-ican society. "Doctor Carlson directed the meetings in a way that did not stifle or unduly direct the conversations," Jennings noted, "and the participants felt trusting and comfortable enough to speak out without falling into hierarchical small group patterns of communication." This provided important reassurance to the National Science Foundation regarding our understanding and application of Habermas's theories. It was also a sign to us that we had chosen an important ethical approach and our application of it was consistent with its stated examples.

This was an exploratory project meant to extend the minimal standards required by ethical review committees for engaging children in research. The traditional approach requires that a parent or legal guardian provide written consent for a child to participate, based on an adult understanding of the risks and benefits of participation. In some states and some circumstances, children as young as sixteen can give their own consent. It is also sometimes the case that children must give their "assent," explicitly affirming that they agree with their adult guardians' consent. But it is not well established at what age and in what circumstances this simple endorsement of an adult's decision should be required. We had in mind to establish a much strengthened ethical process, in which researchers would go well beyond their traditional approach and involve parents, and in some instances children themselves, as more active agents—not only in making decisions about participation, but in evaluating the benefits or hazards of the research methods and goals.[3]

In his formal evaluation of the project, Jennings called it "modestly encouraging but not definitive." Although the scope of the project was limited, he said, it might "lay the groundwork for a more inclusive and extensive project at El Valor or elsewhere" about the "theme of parental responsibility and debilitating stress among children." His assessment continued:

> One original contribution this project made, compared to other similar projects with which I am familiar, is the notion that a locally based service facility, such as El Valor, can be one definition of the community. It can serve to define one civic space that a diverse group of individuals share. This project reinforced the proposition that civic deliberation works best when grounded in tangible, everyday concerns that are immediately meaningful in the participants' lives. Instead, the most substantive ethical issues readily come alive in the direct comprehensible experience of individuals in virtue of their simply being parents or citizens, concerned, affected human beings. This project demonstrated that admirably.

This strict oversight was a great benefit of the National Science Foundation's funding. For the first time in our work, ethical thinking and talking took primacy over scientific reasoning as a driver of decisions and actions. The El Valor group, by willingly engaging in discourse to critically address the details and implications of two novel areas of scientific inquiry, demonstrated how the exercise of choice could become an integral part of our research. It also created an opportunity for parents, childcare professionals, and administrators to share their perspectives on both topics with academics, and achieve group consensus.

And Jennings was right, of course: El Valor was "laying the groundwork for a more inclusive and extensive project." That would take the form of the Young Citizens programs in Chicago, Cambridge, and Tanzania.

Families Struggling to Make a Difference

The success of the El Valor group's protracted dialogue in reaching an unforced and reasoned consensus on new and controversial issues put wind in our sails. But the challenge of defining and achieving high-quality childcare for disadvantaged families did not go away. It loomed larger than ever after a major change in social welfare policy for disadvantaged families—by which cash payments to dependent children would be replaced by work requirements for single mothers—was debated and eventually passed by Congress and signed into law by President Clinton. The Personal Responsibility and Work Opportunity Reconciliation Act of 1996 replaced Aid for Families with Dependent Children (AFDC), which had been in place since the Social Security Act of 1935, with Temporary Assistance for Needy Families (TANF). Among many other changes, this new policy required heads of households receiving benefits to work part-time or participate in job training, whether or not they were single parents of young children. New subsidies were created to help with the high cost of childcare during these hours away from home.[4]

Many of these disadvantaged families, however, feared for the safety and well-being of their children, given that quality out-of-home care was already in short supply. Beyond cost and quality issues, existing options did not provide much schedule flexibility. Yet the kinds of low-paying jobs that were accessible to most former AFDC recipients featured irregular hours and days of work. The greatest concerns centered on the youngest children, especially in states that had not made special provisions for households with newborns. As one activist group summed things up, "Six states have policies that require parents to work when an infant is one day old. Another 11 states require parents to work when an infant reaches three months."[5]

TANF affected poor Latino and African American mothers alike, but long-established residential patterns and ethnic self-segregation kept them from sharing stories of the common challenges they faced. In 1996, we decided to form a new dialogue group to explore the common human experiences that should connect these strangers living in adjacent Chicago neighborhoods yet for all practical matters apart.[6] The point of their deliberations would be to define as closely as possible what mothers collectively considered to be the minimum acceptable standards of quality for out-of-home childcare. We expected that, in the course of using the sessions to articulate what they would and would not accept, these mothers would express a strong sense of agency and experience the value of deliberative citizenship. With the legislation covering infants and young children in vulnerable social and economic conditions still evolving, their insights could be valuable input. As many of them worried about having to compromise their children's health and development to qualify for government support, they were acutely concerned that there must be protections for children and families.

Through community childcare programs known to Chicago project staff, we recruited a group of ten mothers, half of them African American and the other half Mexican American. To participate, they had to have a child between the ages of two and five, be directly affected by the new legislation, and be committed to long-term membership in our dialogue group.

Once again, we did our best to close the gap between researchers and participants by respecting the agency of the families for whom TANF had been fashioned. Our intention was to collaborate with these families to present the results of our group's dialogue to state and federal authorities. In addition to the ten mothers, Tony, Maya, and Jackie Robinson (an experienced group facilitator from the Chicago project) were usually present; if we were not in town on a meeting date, we participated on speakerphone.

We met at a Head Start Center on the South Side once a month. Each session lasted two to three hours, during which time the participants' children played together in groups supervised by the center's caregivers or by young citizens. In the first two sessions, by discussing the program's egalitarian stance and by relating personal stories, we devoted special attention to establishing reciprocal trust and respect among our membership. We then presented two approaches to measuring the quality of out-of-home childcare. One was a questionnaire that evaluated quality from the perspective of the parent (the Child Care Quality Rating System). The other was a well-established observational measure used by outside raters (the Early Childhood Environment Rating Scale produced by researchers at the University of North Carolina).[7] Because these two approaches gauge different aspects of children's and parents' experiences with childcare facilities, their measures are not highly correlated. For example, flexibility in scheduling and routines was highly valued by parents, given their need to work variable hours; but the observational measure did not consider that such convenience for mother's schedules might be experienced by young children as unpredictable and disruptive. Giving more information to parents should increase their investment in and awareness of their children's experiences in childcare arrangements.

The mothers soon formed a stable association, and indeed continued to meet for nineteen months, seven months longer than initially planned. They named the group "Families Struggling to Make a Difference." Among them, true friendships, respect, and understanding developed. Participants met members of the Chicago Young Citizens and El Valor groups on several occasions and contributed to a television documentary made for the Discovery Channel.[8]

Families Struggling to Make a Difference diverged from El Valor in a striking way. As these mothers moved through the deliberation process—first building trust, then taking perspective, and then reaching mutual understanding—they eventually heard about our ongoing research on the collection of stress hormone in institutionally-reared infants in Romania. Immediately they asked why we had not informed them about this work earlier. We explained that our collaboration with the El Valor group had led us to believe that cortisol testing would not be acceptable to parents. Moreover, this situation was very different from El Valor, where staff were concerned that parents might have something to hide. Here, the parents were committed to probing the enormous issue of quality substitute childcare and eager to help identify and represent their children's stresses. There had seemed to be no cause to bring up the measurement of cortisol in a group whose members had made effective use of their voices in initial meetings.

The group felt otherwise. Its members reached a strong and immediate consensus that having more information was better. A biological indicator of chronic stress might be a useful way to validate both their children's and their own experience of chronic and severe stress. Maya tried to redirect the line of thinking away from the idea of measuring stress hormone in these mothers and children, saying she wasn't doing that type of work anymore. But the group persisted, explaining how, if they could show how stressed their lives were, it might put to rest the demeaning stereotypes that depicted them as "welfare queens" and "the undeserving poor." They hated being seen as freeloaders when they knew themselves to be dignified women committed to providing good lives for their children, despite the extraordinary difficulties of their own lives as children and now parents. Having this biological indicator—this *science*—on their side could only help. As one mother asserted after hearing about the method used to assay hormone presence in spit samples, "when they measure my stress level, it will break that thing."

They also wanted to inform policy debates by revealing the psychological and biological harm they were enduring as young parents living in the midst of chronic urban violence and now being forced by new welfare policies both to find jobs and to line up adequate childcare. This could be a forceful new theme in the national debate surrounding the transition from welfare to workfare. Perhaps these women could bring their personal experiences to bear on the creation of a more humane social policy discourse. As someone who, as a student of social policy at the Kennedy School, had been dismayed to watch this new welfare policy gaining support, Maya found it difficult to resist this argument.

The group then determined that it would be valuable for each member to share her *lifeworld* (to invoke an important Habermasian concept) with the others by telling the story of her family, including, if she wished, photographs. Exchanging these would help the women comprehend what allowed them, as individuals and as a group, to carry on.[9] As they worked on their profiles, their eagerness to have their cortisol levels measured only grew. Having profiles of stories and photos combined with documented cortisol levels would make them more rational and informed authorities on their own and each other's lives. They wanted to be heard by policymakers who were announcing, preparing for, and celebrating TANF as if it were an unalloyed good. Two of their stories especially stood out, not because they depicted exceptional circumstances but because they poignantly captured features common to these women's lifeworlds.[10] The first included a street scene labeled "Murals on the Viaduct down the Street from ES's House and Roberto's." It began by explaining the artwork:

> This one was made mainly to stop the killings in the neighborhood. Too many kids were dying. They did that because too many kids were dying at the hands of gang bangers. Was supposed to tell him to stop doing what they're doing. Don't be out in the streets taking innocent lives. Because there's lots of kids that died in that neighborhood. Ever since they put that up, I haven't heard anything going on any more like shootings or fighting. They were about thirty kids involved in doing the mural. It took kids to stop the violence.
>
> This is a picture of my sister, the one that got shot and killed. And this picture of my sister, makes me see the pain my mother goes through. My sister's birthday passed this Monday. It was Monday. She would have been nineteen. It was a block away from the house, a block away on the corner. She was running to go into a building, and then she lifted her hands up, they shot her, and the bullet went all the way through and took her heart—her heart in the process.
>
> What got me more involved was when my son got shot. Roberto, he's the one who got shot in the face. It was just that it's on the other side, you can't see it. He got shot when he was five years old. Basically, after he got shot was when they decided they were going to do the mural. They were shooting at one another, and it happened again in the crossfire. Ever since that, he says I'm never going to join the gangs—I don't like gangs. A lesson well taught. The wrong way but well taught so actually, as painful as it may be—there was some good that came out of that.

The second profile includes a photo referred to as "SJ's Family at the Park."

Before I even had kids, when I was pregnant with my first daughter, I had the same exact experience, except it was my cousin who got shot by a young man—who was my daughter's father. . . . And I knew they'd had conflicts the day before, because the boy wanted his gym shoes. Back then it was the gym shoes, and they were taking gym shoes and jackets. So, my cousin didn't give it up to him. But he took the boy over there, and the boy pulled out a revolver and shot him in the head.

And all the time, from the process of them finding the body, and what I hate most of all was, reading the newspaper one day, and it was the Chicago Defender— they said they were playing Russian roulette. So, I called them, and . . . said, but that was not Russian Roulette. And I said whoever wrote that article needs to get their facts correct. I said, you can't believe what other young people say on the street. You can't believe people that supposedly be witnesses, because it's not about that. I said, if you don't know the facts, don't try writing up your little articles because the information is not accurate.

And he was dead. And you know the other thing I thought, well, he was my family. We see each other, all of us. There's somebody getting married or somebody dying. And we have a really, really large family and we had made it a vow not to do this anymore, where we visit people when it's not just these occasions. So far, it's been good, but you still don't see everybody. We had over—just family members, not including friends—over fifteen hundred people to the church, and they could feed and seat all of us. Some of us was outside, some of us was on the balcony. But it shouldn't have to come to that, before you're able to see your relatives. So, I can understand exactly what ES's family goes through with her sister.

So, my daughter, I had my daughter four months later her name was Patrice. Patrick was his name. So, you know she got his name, you know about him since she knows my friend and my cousin were crazy, they just used to talk about each other all the time so that's how her name came to exist.

This is a picture of all of us, mother, daughter NP, and son. And I would say he's my boyfriend, he's not a husband, but he's a boyfriend but we've been together for ten years.

All these pictures are taken at that park because we always go to the park doesn't matter if it's cold. The purpose of my taking these pictures is because there's no trash in the park, on the playground area. It's beautiful scenery as you all can see. Well, the skies was changing and stuff, but they have friends and have fun, we don't have to worry about no shooting, but they don't have to worry about the violence or somebody's coming over to knock them off of things. It's—our area is totally different from where Englewood is.

That's one of my favorites because my daughter . . . she's like a tomboy, then she enjoys climbing trees. And they always play together, figure out who's who—she's actually a tomboy, she's the one who runs the fastest, jumps the highest and climbs the farthest.

We followed through on the group's request for us to measure cortisol in themselves and their children. The group was informed about the science of stress physiology and the recommended saliva collection technique for measuring cortisol. Our colleague Michael Meaney, whose seminal work on touch deprivation had so powerfully influenced our work, was in town during a week that the mother's group met. He offered to come by to discuss cortisol with them in the context of their stressful life circumstances. It was hard to imagine anyone better prepared to discuss this topic, especially as it related to the lives of these women and their preschool-age children.

We planned for the first collection to capture the diurnal variation from waking to bedtime, as in the Romanian study. (It was not feasible to examine stress responses, which would have meant staging stressful situations in their home settings.) The mothers would be in complete control of the procedures. They collected samples before eating upon rising, and again at bedtime on four consecutive days: two weekend days and two weekdays. The sampling plan allowed for different sleep cycles and meal times, and included a verification strategy: every day, a mother had to call into a designated phone line at the Chicago Project office and leave a message reporting her name and the times at which family members had cortisol samples taken. All samples were sent to Meaney's laboratory in Montreal to be assayed.

Each mother was given a diary and detailed instructions describing the standard procedure for sampling salivary cortisol by the filter paper method.[11] Each woman received a plastic fishing tackle box with color-coded labels and divided compartments; this contained the filter paper strips for themselves and their children, organized by day of week and time of day. We wanted to make collection easy for mothers to incorporate into their working and bedtime routines. They were instructed to take their children's and their own sample immediately upon waking, prior to brushing teeth, drinking milk or juice, smoking, or eating breakfast. The saturated strips were returned to the tackle box and the time noted. Following the evening collection, mothers recorded in the diary who cared for each child at home, in childcare, and in school, along with any unusual experiences that occurred during the day. When the samples were returned to the project

offices, the mothers were asked to complete a short questionnaire about the level of predictability and perceived control
they had experienced over the last month.

We describe this complex data collection procedure because
it was possible that the mothers did not know what they were
getting themselves into when they asserted their enthusiasm
for measuring the stress hormone. Remarkably, most followed
the data collection script precisely. Eight of the ten mothers
turned in the box of strips having completed the protocols
completely and accurately.

In fact, this data collection went so well that the mothers
agreed to perform a second round during an organized, day-
long, Saturday retreat of the group. While the mothers met in
their deliberation group, the children could engage in supervised play at the daycare center where the mothers usually
met; twenty-five children came along with their mothers.
The mothers collected their own and their children's saliva at
hourly intervals between 9 AM and 5 PM.

Each mother was the owner of her family's information,
which was treated as privileged and confidential data. With
our guidance, the mothers interpreted for themselves what the
results meant. We can report, however, that while there was
significant variability across individuals, the levels for both
adults and children were extraordinarily higher at all times of
day than would be expected in the general population. The
cortisol levels of these mothers and children exceeded those
of prior groups who used the same methods and assays. At a
conference where Maya presented a paper in 1999, another
study using the same hormone measures was also shared. Its
research population was made up of Army Special Forces
soldiers participating in mock training sessions; as their daily
samples were being taken, they were experiencing helicopter

drops into "enemy territory," eventual capture, and interroga-
tion for long hours by "enemy guerrilla forces."[12] Yet their
hormone levels were noticeably lower than those of Chicago
mothers and children.

As the mothers continued meeting, they decided to add to
their original name, Families Struggling to Make a Difference.
They added "$8.50 and Up," turning the group's full name into
"Families Struggling to Make a Difference: $8.50 and Up." The
reference to hourly pay well above the current minimum wage
signaled their aspiration to go beyond "struggling." Rather
than presenting themselves as women who were overwhelmed,
they would adopt a more assertive stance and advocate that
the kinds of jobs they were likely to find start paying a living
wage.

Having decided to present this demand directly to federal
and local authorities, the group got just such an opportunity
when the director of the National Institute of Mental Health,
Steve Hyman, planned a visit to the Chicago project. We
thought it important to introduce Hyman to these mothers,
whose tight-knit group was an example of the network of
activities spawned by that larger project. They were keen to
inform policymakers about the merits of their deliberative
citizenship exercises and about the data they had collected on
themselves. They related the stories of friends and family who
had been disabled by criminal violence or lost their lives.
Hyman brought up the crisis intervention team model that
had been put in place, by which officers with specialized
mental health training were added to the police force; he asked
the group's members how effective these teams had been in
covering their neighborhoods. Their response was abrupt:
there was no such team. "You're looking at the team," one of
the mothers informed him. "We are it."

These Chicago mothers impressed Hyman with the knowledge they had acquired about the biology of stress and the initiative they took to measure cortisol in themselves and their children. The deliberation process had successfully enhanced their capacity to understand and act on their needs and concerns. The group recognized Hyman's authority as a scientist and administrator, and he in turn recognized the authority of a deliberative group of parent-citizens resolved to make life better for their children.

Researchers or Fellow Citizens?

One lesson from these two groups is that ordinary citizens see value in group experiences that are grounded in sincerity, talking, and critical thinking. At the same time, we cannot emphasize enough the value we derived from these two groups (and the Chicago and Cambridge Young Citizens groups). Our knowledge as scientists was important input to the dialogue and deliberation, but in many ways we were the ones being educated as people allowed us into their everyday lives.

We were certainly not in control of the distinctly different decisions made by the El Valor and $8.50 and Up groups. If anything, we went into this project expecting the service providers to be the more enthusiastic group regarding the potential value of cortisol analysis. The mothers, we thought, might have had their fill of social scientists dropping into tough neighborhoods and documenting the obvious, then abruptly leaving residents in the same desperate condition in which they found them. To have impact, we would have to commit to being legitimate and coequal agents in the process of group decision-making, gaining consensus, and reaching mutual understanding. We should participate as fellow citizens more than as advisors, experts, or advocates.

One of the Latina mothers commented that, when traveling on the train or bus around the city, she had wondered what it would be like to have an African American mother as a friend. The group satisfied this desire and in doing so created the basis for Habermas's chief concern to be answered: collective deliberation could be used to solve social problems even in the context of the pluralism that characterizes modern cities.

The group achieved its stability and actions despite terrible setbacks in members' lives, serious forms of deprivation, and daily levels of uncontrollable stress, all undermining these mothers' capacities to think about the future. Of course, there was variability in just how overwhelming life was or had been for them, but every member was affected to some extent by serious adversity. They learned how a group like theirs, especially when its dialogue is extended over months, could (and must) provide emotional support. Without blunting the group's social and political objectives, it was essential that this responsibility of its members also be recognized and discharged.

These two efforts, El Valor and Families Struggling to Make a Difference: $8.50 and Up, strengthened our belief in deliberation and informed decision-making as the keys to meeting ethical standards of discourse. Instead of coming in with traditional, top-down "problem-solving" approaches, these efforts involved working with communities to make choices about action. That led to greater engagement and also opened up new avenues of exploration.

Could the same powers of deliberation and choice be made available to children—younger and older ones alike? They could be, we were convinced after the Chicago and Cambridge

Young Citizens programs, if children learned to use the key that unlocked them: voice. They could make use of, as Habermas called it, language that does. In Tanzania, we would discover that citizens as young as age ten could be capable of innovative approaches to decision-making and public engagement, of educating and inspiring their communities, and of increasing the solidarity and collective competence of the community as a whole.

7

Promoting Human Capability

In noting the nature of human lives, we have reason to be interested not only in the various things we succeed in doing, but also in the freedoms that we actually have to choose between different kinds of lives. The freedom to choose our lives can make a significant contribution to our well-being, but going beyond the perspective of well-being, the freedom itself may be seen as important. Being able to reason and choose is a significant aspect of human life.

—AMARTYA SEN

The idea of having the freedom to choose between different kinds of lives should appeal to most readers; indeed, the ability to determine one's own future is among the most cherished goals of adult life. But how might high school students, primary school students, or even preschoolers respond to the idea of choice in their young lives? At what age does it make sense for children to *choose* what they want to be or what they want to do in life? Children are often asked by adults making conversation: What do you want to be when you grow up? The typical replies to that question are familiar: sports star, ballerina, nurse, farmer, teacher, and so on. But why not ask children of all ages: What do you want to be and to do *now,* and over the next few years of your life?

Choices—true choices—are few and far between in a child's life. Many adults discount children's abilities to make choices about their own lives and believe it is foolhardy at best to take seriously their perspectives and reasoning in public deliberations. Yet democracy rests on the principle that, as one group of eminent political scientists puts it, "political participation affords citizens in a democracy an opportunity to communicate information to government officials about their concerns and preferences." The concept of young citizenship asserts that children's perspectives and insights are valuable input to public decisions.[1]

In Chicago and Cambridge, we saw how young citizens, by sharing crucial information about their experiences with violence and self-segregation, could enrich the understanding of the adults in their midst. In Chapter 3, we saw how Brazil's young street-dwellers organized a national movement to demand that their country recognize the limitations presented to them and dangers they faced as they simply sought to survive. They lobbied for provision, protection, and participation rights, expanding their ability to choose better lives for themselves and, in the process, for all children in their society.

This chapter's epigraph, taken from Amartya Sen's *The Idea of Justice,* points to a pillar of the capability approach: the importance to well-being of having the freedom to reason and to choose what kind of life to live. Note the emphasis Sen places on *being able* to reason or choose. This is why it is crucial to incorporate the capability approach into the science of human development: building the ability or capacity to do this is essential to progress. And this is what drew us to the tragic circumstances of Romania's institutionalized infants and Brazil's marginalized older children living on the streets. Exploring these extremes of early social deprivation yields insight about what is required to engage and maintain the basic social and cognitive abilities of infants and older children. In this chapter, we return to those environs to learn more about what human capability failures can teach us about the process of capability achievement—and how varying opportunities and choices make a difference to capability achievement in childhood.

Choices matter. A key component of the Young Citizens program is to provide children with opportunities to make informed and reasoned choices as participants in deliberation about issues of common interest to their communities. The capability approach provides an entirely different perspective on choice than the communicative approaches presented in earlier chapters, where deliberative groups seek consensual agreement as resolution. Capability is often understood as applying to individuals more than to groups, as in a person's freedom to choose among different kinds of lives. Our own view began there, but evolved to emphasize capabilities for discussion with other people. A chosen life would be composed of a set of basic states that one would value "being" and a set of basic activities that a person would value "doing." Together, these would constitute a life worth living.

Referring again to our choice of epigraph, we assume that Sen refers to adults' ability to reason and to choose among the beings and doings that are available to them, in the context of the opportunities and resources available at different times of their lives. If we shift the focus to children's ability to reason and choose, we must think of how that ability emerges over the course of their development, beginning at birth, and what types of opportunities and resources they encounter in their first two decades. At each stage of neural and behavioral development, a child's ability to choose is either expanded or diminished contingent upon past opportunities and achieved abilities. After *voicing* their concerns in community groups, children can better understand the *choices* before them of what to do and how to be. They can consider what types of opportunities they require to achieve their goals, and what kind of *action* to take to improve well-being for themselves and as agents in their community. This concern for the choices expressed by individuals (Sen) and deliberative choices achieved by groups (Habermas) is the basis of the Young Citizens approach.

Origins of Sen's Capability Approach

Amartya Sen was born in 1933 on the campus of Patha Bhavana, a primary and secondary school he would later attend, in Santiniketan, West Bengal, India. The school was founded in 1901 by Rabindranath Tagore, the poet, short story writer, playwright, and novelist. After Tagore won the 1913 Nobel Prize in Literature, the campus was expanded, in 1921, to establish Visva-Bharati University. Sen's maternal grandfather taught Sanskrit and Indian cultural history at the university, and his mother received her education there, as well. Sen himself won the Nobel Memorial Prize in Economic Sciences in 1998. In an autobiographical sketch posted on the Nobel Prize website, Sen attributes his persistent optimism and love of learning to his early years of progressive education in Santiniketan, where cultural diversity was celebrated in an idyllic setting of open-air classrooms, gardens, and sculptures.[2] Yet, even as a child, Sen could not escape the tumultuous events of the World War II era in India, when so many lives were lost to starvation and to violence. The slow-motion collapse of the British Empire led to the Bengal Famine of 1943 and the catastrophic 1947 partition of Bengal between India and Pakistan, resulting in sectarian violence that killed or displaced tens of millions of people.

Sen earned an undergraduate degree in economics from Presidency College in India and doctorate degrees in economics and in political philosophy from Cambridge University. His academic career, like his education, involved many transitions between India and the UK and eventually to the United States, initially through visiting professorships and eventually, in 1988, in residence at Harvard University. He returned to England from 1998 to 2003 as Master of Trinity College in Cambridge, only to return to Harvard in 2004. Sen says he has returned to India and Santiniketan at least once a year since he first left for the United Kingdom in 1953.

Firmly committed to the importance of education to human welfare, Sen has had a remarkably influential career. His work and public persona exemplify a deep commitment to scholarship and moral solutions to human deprivation and inequalities. It was in his first tenure at Harvard (1988–1997) that he deeply explored his interest in democracy and human inequality. Sen had first introduced the concept of *capability* to address human inequalities in 1979 in his remarks in the Tanner Lectures on Human Values, published the following year with the provocative title *Equality of What?* In those remarks, he defends the importance of equality in the ability to lead a good life. At the same time, he expresses concern about theories that placed income or wealth at the center of debates over equality, and by doing so relegated other vital equalities—in freedom, choice, opportunity, and welfare—to the periphery. In Sen's capability approach, "poverty" is understood as deprivation in the capability to live a good life, and "development" is understood as capability expansion. As an example, consider a qualifying exam for entrance to a college of one's choice. Passing it is a form of enrichment because it offers capability expansion; failing would be a capability deprivation.

We first met Sen at Harvard University's Center for Population and Development Studies, where he spoke about the recent release of the premier Human Development Report in 1990 by the United Nations Development Program, which introduced the groundbreaking Human Development Index.[3] By gauging the relative development of nations according to measurable aspects of human well-being, the index marks an important contrast to traditional scorecards based on measures of economic output, such as Gross Domestic Product. The report's statement of the fundamental value of human development strongly echoes the fundamental principles of Sen's capability approach:

> People are the real wealth of a nation. The basic objective of development is to create an enabling environment for people to enjoy long, healthy and creative lives. This may appear to be a simple truth. But it is often forgotten in the immediate concern with the accumulation of commodities and financial wealth. . . . Human development is a process of enlarging people's choices. The most critical of these wide-ranging choices are to live a long and healthy life, to be educated and to have access to the resources needed for a decent standard of living.

We introduced ourselves to Sen after the seminar and conversed about our shared interests in human development. This encounter subsequently led Maya, who already had plans to enter the Mid-Career Master's Program at Harvard's Kennedy School in 1991, to ask Sen to supervise her independent study in the Economics Department at Harvard College. This was a unique opportunity to integrate her previous research on brain and behavioral development in primates with his extensive scholarship on human development, equity, and capability. There was potential here for work with major relevance to social policy for children.

Health Promotion as Capability

In Chapter 1, we noted the official name of our Chicago project: the Project on Human Development in Chicago Neighborhoods. Now, here was Sen, coming from the field of economics, using the term *human development* in the same sense that we used it in public health. The only real difference was the level of social organization in focus. In Chicago we were interested in the health and welfare of children at a city level, spanning hundreds of neighborhoods, while the Human Development Index tracked human welfare at the national and regional levels.

Public health is a discipline devoted to pragmatic problem-solving; it seeks to understand the origins of pathologies of the body and the mind. It defines "health" in the broadest of terms. This was recognized by the World Health Organization (WHO) as far back as 1946. "Health is a state of complete physical, mental and social well-being," asserts the preamble to WHO's Constitution, "and not merely the absence of disease or infirmity." That definition was refined in two follow-up meetings.[4] First, in its Alma-Ata Declaration of 1978, WHO declared that primary health care was dependent on the community as a support system. The designation of health as a human right was also advanced at that meeting. Next, in 1986, WHO put forth its Ottawa Charter for Health Promotion defining health in "as a positive concept emphasizing social and personal resources, as well as physical capacities. Therefore, health promotion is not just the responsibility of the health sector but goes beyond healthy lifestyles to well-being." This expanding definition made it clear that, beyond having a "health sector" in its economy, a community or government was responsible for providing citizens with "a secure foundation in a supportive environment, access to information, life skills and opportunities for making healthy choices."

Collective efficacy, as explored in our Chicago project, offers a good example of what comes from this comprehensive and positive view of health. In Chicago, input from the academic disciplines of sociology, developmental psychology, statistics, and law, along with the professional disciplines of criminology, pediatrics, and child psychiatry, coalesced under the umbrella of "public health." It took this synthesis to produce a scientific breakthrough: the discovery of collective efficacy as an important determinant of children's mental, behavioral, and physical health. This is consistent with the idea that health promotion should enable people to assume control over the determinants of their own health. As an outstanding example consider the importance of physical exercise and proper nutrition to preventing cardiac disease. These have long been recognized to promote health and fitness generally, but adherence to them is controlled more by the motivation of individuals and the resources available in their communities than by the top-down advice of doctors. Our argument is that children should not be excluded from this sense of control. They benefit personally from choosing healthy habits (for example, by experiencing less asthma, obesity, and bullying) and they can also function as health agents influencing others (for example, through anti-smoking, gun control, and climate change campaigns). This definition of health is at the core of the Young Citizens program.[5]

Details of Sen's Capability Approach

The capability approach is a moral framework; it claims that the freedom to achieve well-being is of fundamental moral significance, and also that freedom to choose is itself of significant value to one's well-being. The capability approach to evaluating human development is based on the freedom and ability to choose a life worth living, and therefore represents a much needed and unique contribution to the realm of welfare economics. It reflects Sen's interdisciplinary training and career-long commitment to bridging the fields of economics and analytical philosophy to challenge the dominant paradigm of neoclassical economics with its impoverished theoretical foundations.

To understand his choice of terminology and abstract characterizations of how well-being or a valued life can be achieved, it is important to define and provide examples of what Sen refers to as *functionings*, what he means by *capabilities*, and what constitutes *effective freedom* to choose among valued "beings and doings." But we first must note that this innovative approach is meant to correct for the shortcomings of the two conventional types of models, which Sen has criticized extensively as inadequate to address the achievement of well-being: the utilitarian models, which frame well-being as a mental state akin to happiness or enjoyment of preferences; and the resources models, which propose commodities or primary goods as the ends of rather than means to achieving well-being. *Capability* in his thinking is to be understood as the genuine opportunities that individuals have to do and be what they have reason to value. The capability approach is not intended to describe or explain how a life of well-being or ill-being has come about but rather to help conceptualize the role of human choice in achieving and maintaining valued doings and beings.

Sen's model proposes that one measure human *functionings,* defined as "beings and doings"—the various states people may be in and the activities they may undertake. Examples of "beings" would include basic states such as being well-nourished or undernourished, and more complex states such as being respected or disrespected in a community. Examples of human "doings" include basic activities such as riding a bike, and complex activities such as caring for a child. It is not required of functionings that they be desired or considered socially acceptable to others; they refer to the presence or absence of beings and doings valued by the individual in question.

Capabilities refers to the set of valuable functionings to which a person has access, and therefore the effective freedom to choose between different combinations of functionings. This may also be seen as the freedom one has to choose between different kinds of lives that one has reason to value. Sen makes an important distinction between functionings (as latent capacities present and valued by a person) and what he refers to as "capabilities" (in the plural, although they are sometimes referred to as a single "capability set" in the capability literature). Capabilities or capability sets allow an analysis to focus on combinations of functionings related to particular aspects of life—for example, capabilities for health, literacy, or citizenship. Capability sets are defined as alternative collections of functionings and the resources and opportunities required to realize a valued lifestyle. These may be bundles of *available alternative* functionings or, when a person actually chooses them, bundles of *achieved* functionings. Either can serve as the basis for assessing personal achievement, or assessing the equity and efficiency of social policies. As capabilities reflect a person's real opportunities or positive freedom of choice to achieve a desired lifestyle, Sen argues that "acting freely" and "being able to choose" are as important to the pursuit of a good life as whatever combination of potential functionings is realized.

A frequent misunderstanding in the literature concerns the use of the term *freedom* with respect to the capability approach. Especially in his later work, Amartya Sen often equates capabilities with freedoms, without always specifying in more detail what kind of freedom he is referring to. Yet this equation can easily be misunderstood since, as Sen himself acknowledges, there are many kinds of freedom (some valuable, some detrimental, and some trivial) and freedom means very different things to different people. *Capability* refers to the set of valuable functionings to which a person has effective access. An individual's capability therefore can represent the effective freedom that an individual has to choose among the different functionings combinations they have reason to value. But to achieve capability sets, there are certain "conversion factors" required—elements that enable people to convert available, but latent, resources and capability sets according to their needs. Having access to certain resources as well as freedom to choose allows them to convert their potential functionings into achieved functionings. To say it is a substantive freedom that one can choose among alternative sets of functioning does not require that a choice actually be exercised. It only needs to exist as an option, as a latent choice. Capability, as freedom, is seen as having both an intrinsic value (because it contains latent possibility) and an instrumental value (because exercising free choice realizes that potential).[6]

Applications of Capability Approach

Maya completed her studies at the Kennedy School and with Sen at Harvard College, and it was in the following year that we became inspired by the recent accomplishments of UNICEF. The organization had done much to advance the endorsement of the UN Convention on the Rights of the Child. Beyond that, it was assembling a comprehensive approach, covering research funding and policy advocacy, to the problem of children growing up in "especially difficult circumstances." UNICEF's role was to channel funds and technical support to related work being carried out on the local level, often in collaboration with other parties. As these projects matured, UNICEF would use its first-rate publication platform to highlight local results and suggest their applicability to others working in similar conditions around the world. UNICEF's approach inspired us to think about applying the capability model to study the development of children in extreme conditions. These are settings where the mechanisms and indicators of deprivation are pronounced, but our emphasis would be on successful human development—that is, capability achievement possible in these settings rather than the prevailing deprivation or capability failure.

Around the same time, we were also considering the implications of capability as an alternative framework for crime prevention in the Chicago Project.[7] Whereas a conventional approach would focus on preventing criminal acts at the point of action, a capability-based approach would emphasize health promotion as a means of deterring crime and violence over a lifetime. To do this research work appropriately, we realized we would have to broaden our understanding of the ethical implications of working with families and children living in extreme environments, whether in Romania, Brazil, or Chicago. While we acknowledged the near-universal significance of the Convention on the Rights of the Child, we recalled Sen's message that rights, while necessary, were not sufficient. We had heard him say it ourselves: "Rights is an incomplete approach."

With this perspective on human rights, our challenge was to complete a framework that could address both capability achievement and capability failure (or deprivation) of children growing up in "especially difficult circumstances." This framework, which would guide any research and practice we conducted, had to integrate universal law and developmental sciences, be equity sensitive, and involve governance since it is governments that ratify UN conventions, enact legislation, and enforce the rule of law. Our decision to work with institutionalized infants in Romania and street children in Brazil allowed us to design research to explore the utility of the capability approach to human development, in addition to other research themes that traced the etiology of these massive failures in national social policy for families and children.

Institutionalized Infants in Romania

Think back to Chapter 2 and consider the capability achievement in the home-reared creşă children versus the capability failure in the leagăn-reared (institutionalized) infants. The development of a leagăn-reared infant stands in sharp contrast to that of a home-reared child who attends the creşă on weekdays. One key conversion factor for the leagăn-reared infants is their age at admission to the institutional environment; another is the quality of care provided by their poorly trained, detached caregivers. Standard conditions are bleak in the leagăne (and presumably also in most infant nurseries in the maternity homes where these abandoned infants would have lived until they were delivered to the leagăne). In them, roughly twenty infants are assigned to each caretaker, whose duties are understood to be essentially custodial. In family settings, there are commonly adequate nursing and reciprocal social interactions to promote sufficient nutrition and tactile contact, and such achieved functionings as physical growth and socialization are commonly present. In the family setting, then, there is capability achievement as opposed to capability failure. By contrast, the leagăne-reared children, although provided with adequate caloric input and medical services, experience severe social neglect and this results in pronounced growth retardation and lifelong behavioral deficits (as described in Chapter 2).

Most infants, we know, demonstrate from birth the capacity to nurse to achieve nourishment from breast or bottle. This "nursing capability set" is composed of multiple functionings, to use Sen's terminology. The rooting reflex present in newborns causes the infant to automatically turn its face in the direction of the stimulus when a cheek or lip is touched, and accompany this turn with sucking movements. Although this movement is reflexive in the newborn, a fair degree of nursing attention is needed from a mother or caregiver to make positional and temporal adjustments during feeding. The rooting reflex is coordinated with two other reflexes: sucking, and opening and closing the esophagus to swallow when milk is ingested. All three components (or functionings) must be present for the nursing capability set for adequate nursing to be achieved.

The rooting reflex (really a chain of reflexes) disappears after three to four months, as nursing becomes guided by sight. Bottle-fed, touch-deprived infants are often found excessively sucking their fingers as a substitute for the breast or bottle access. Such non-nutritive sucking is seen as capability failure since social reciprocity is lacking. This type of capability failure demonstrates the primacy of social reciprocity in all stages of infancy and early child development. Human beings cannot raise themselves alone.

Conversely, the access to a nursing capability set marked by adequate socialization illustrates that social reciprocity between infant and caretaker is critical for normal development. Soon after birth, infants display a strong interest in objects, but they don't pay special attention to eyes or faces until around four months of age. Infants' first smiles are reflexive and non-social, and these occur for about eight weeks. Social smiling, associated with self-control, starts between the sixth and eighth weeks. This is an emerging social capacity that requires social reciprocation to be maintained. In alliance with a responsive caregiver, an infant is capable of making purposeful vocalizations as early as three months of age, which become more frequent when answered by simultaneous smiling, clucking, and touching. Early social communication made up of eye contact, smiling, and vocalization progresses from reflex to reciprocity and finally to self-control. This progression is the essential developmental process of emerging and reciprocated social capability.[8]

Abandoned infants who were admitted to Romanian institutions before six months of age and then remained in such neglectful conditions up through two years of age typically had stunted physical growth and enduring social and communicative deficits because their deprivations lasted throughout the critical period for socialization. As these infants' early social and motor capacities came more under their own control, but remained unreciprocated, the infants developed enduring abnormal, self-directed movements. Examples include eye-poking, gaze avoidance, muteness, ritualized finger movements, self-clasping, repetitive jumping, swaying, and head-banging, many of which can persist throughout adulthood. These infants create a deeply disturbing image of sameness. They have developed atypically but along eerily similar lines. For them, the absence of reciprocity has led to communicative capability failure.

Street Children in Brazil

In Romania we studied early social deprivation; in Brazil we considered late social deprivation. To understand the consequences of late social deprivation for the achievement of other forms of later-developing social and cognitive capability sets, we considered two brothers from a favela, living amidst the sprawling slums that make up the periphery of Rio. Both of the boys, one twelve years old and the other fifteen, had worked from a young age in the informal economy of the central city. They were among Rio's large population of "working children." The younger brother was one of those referred to as *on* the street. He attended school, lived at home, and worked each day for several hours, after school and on the weekends. His older brother was *of* the streets, meaning he lived with other children away from any real home, sleeping in a large public square surrounding a downtown cathedral. Ever since the boys' family had arrived in Rio as migrants from northeastern Brazil, they had endured the stress of living in poverty, in crowded slums, and with poor infrastructure.

The brothers illustrate different relationships to two capability sets that have major significance to their life course at this age: *personal security* and *orientation toward the future.* Both are major preoccupations of adolescence. Personal security is determined by three functionings: *nourishment, intimacy,* and *physical comfort.* The younger brother put himself at risk by selling small objects on the street to supplement his family's income, but had personal, social, and environmental conversion factors and access to resources that allowed him to choose and maintain personal security. He ate meals with his family and enjoyed the company of his parents. He chose to remain at home and attend school. He avoided the temptation to join his older brother as a child *of* the street. He achieved "personal security," but it was unclear that he would maintain it as he aged.

But perhaps he knew what his older brother's life had been like since leaving home a few years back. He might have seen enough to not want that life for himself. It began when his brother dropped out of school, failed to find steady work, and formed friendships with other boys *of* the street. The older brother began to use drugs and inhalants, get his meals by begging, theft, or scavenging, submit to sex work, and sleep on stone steps or park benches. Shelters for street children sometimes provided temporary protection and security. As a resource they could avert a crisis, but they did not offer a secure and reliable base to achieve comfort, warmth, and acceptance. The older brother's dismal social and environmental conversion factors and lack of resources combined to create *personal insecurity* and *capability failure.* Despite believing that his family might allow him to return home, we might say he chose the streets.

Choosing what one wants to be and do is the paramount objective of adolescence. Teenagers are expected to begin charting their paths toward social and economic self-sufficiency. The components of the younger brother's capability set encompassed the resources required to become a productive adult: access to a structure of adult relationships (parents, teachers, and neighbors), peer attachments (classmates, teammates), and industrious activities (school, the arts, and sports). Together with the resources he obtained through his occasional street vending, he had expectations that collectively guided him toward a realistic set of skills for future roles in the economy, family, and community. He was achieving and maintaining the functioning of *future orientation.*

In the past, the older brother had applied his industriousness to those same activities. But his efforts to find income subsequently turned his industry toward pimps and drug dealers. His free time was spent playing video games. His peer attachments shifted from those around the cathedral to the gangs from the favelas, which fulfilled his needs for income and for belonging—but were much more dangerous. The adults in his life were older gang members and shelter workers, and of course the police, whom he avoided. His access to resources might have improved, and he maintained social contact, but his environmental and social conversion factors became increasingly dangerous and illegal. He appeared to develop a fatalistic orientation.

The more time that children spend being *of* the streets—seeing others killed by cars, vigilantes, and drug overdoses—the more they come to see life as uncontrollable and fleeting. They stop seeing how it could improve. Shelters might have occasionally rescued the older brother from acute threats, but they offered little guidance or long-term planning. His sense of his future was hijacked by the bitter reality that his greatest immediate desire was to survive for another day. Such a shift to a fatalistic orientation can only be seen as a capability failure, characterized by a paucity of valued beings and doings. The street and shelter workers who encounter these adolescents by the hundreds each day know that most of them could still choose other options. But returning home to parents and neighbors—after becoming dependent on drugs, exposed to street crime, and convinced of the immutability of their marginal status—is unlikely. What does choice look like to a child who is socialized, but marginalized, when he thinks of home?

Deliberative Capability Diagram

Working with children in extremely difficult circumstances was preparation to work with all children. After all, we were interested in citizenship, a status to be granted to members of a community without regard to the deprivations they might have experienced growing up. Regarding citizenship as a developmental process implied that children could acquire social and communicative skills that would boost their confidence in acting as responsible members in their communities. To be sure, the profound degree of neglect and social deprivation experienced by infants raised in institutions could not provide the foundation for the emergence of capabilities to act as a citizen. But we believed that the great majority of the world's children did possess the competences to be thoughtfully engaged members in their local political and social settings.

The central concern of our charter as researchers is to encounter children in different circumstances and to precisely recognize and define these skills. Just as an educator might work to identify the skills that go into learning to read or write, we are asking about the origins and emergence of competences that establish confidence in expressing one's opinions, the use of reason to solve interpersonal problems, engagement with peers and citizens of all ages in a community, and genuine a concern for the well-being of others. It is with this purpose in mind that we undertook to build a bridge from Habermas's theory of communicative action to Sen's capability approach to human development. From this melding of ideas, we defined deliberative capability and ways to measure it as a fundamental contribution to democratic principles and shared social actions. Table 7.1 illustrates a composite of capacities and opportunities that must be present for deliberative capability to emerge in childhood. When we return to the Tanzanian Young Citizens program in Chapter 8, this abstract concept will come to life in dramatic fashion.

We used the approach above in the conditions of extreme social deprivation and capability failure we found in Romania and Brazil. A statement by Sen's astute colleague, Ingrid Robeyns, clarifies how the capability approach can be used to conceptualize complex behavioral and social phenomena: "The capability approach is a normative theory, rather than an explanatory theory: in other words, it is not a theory that will *explain* poverty, inequality, or well-being, but rather a theory that helps us to conceptualize these notions. Nevertheless, the notions of functionings and capabilities in themselves can be employed as elements in explanations of social phenomena, or one can use these notions in descriptions of poverty, inequality, quality of life, and social change."[9]

With this firmly in mind, the diagram was crafted to capture the complexity of components and conditions of three capability sets: communicative, cognitive, and emotional / motivational. We propose that these three capability sets

Table 7.1 Deliberative Capabilities

POTENTIAL CAPABILITY SETS (functionings—f)	ACTUAL OPPORTUNITIES / FREEDOMS / RESOURCES	ACHIEVED FUNCTIONINGS Actual "Doings and Beings" (Functionings—F)
COMMUNICATIVE CAPABILITY SETS		
f1) Expressive	Time and space to convey ideas	F1) Ability to articulate or express an idea or emotion
	Shared signals and meanings	
f2) Receptive	Time and space to receive ideas	F2) Ability to register, accept, reject, or consider new ideas or suggestions
	Attention and openness to receive ideas	
COGNITIVE CAPABILITY SETS		
f3) Critical thinking	Open climate to objective judgment	F3) Ability for rational argumentation
f4) Perspective-taking	Exposure to various points of view	F4) Ability to understand ideas of others
f5) Comprehension	Access to clarity and detail of concepts	F5) Ability for deep understanding
f6) Decision-making	Sufficient space, time, and mutual respect of resolve positions of others	F6) Ability to compare / contrast / decide / choose
EMOTIONAL / MOTIVATIONAL CAPABILITY SETS		
f7) Trust	Context that promotes reliable and predictable exchanges with others	F7) Ability to recognize reliability in oneself or others
f8) Confidence	Climate of certainty and reliability of self, others, or circumstances	F8) Ability to recognize certainty or predictability in events, oneself, or others
f9) Agency	Context that permits or enables action	F9) Ability to act deliberately or intervene
f10) Intentionality	Conditions conducive to thinking and acting with a sense of purpose	F10) Ability to act with objectives, resolve, aspiration

taken together define the deliberative capability, which is a dominant characteristic of becoming and being a deliberative citizen. Recall, as described in Chapter 5, that these are the same characteristics measured as the outcomes of the Young Citizens program. In the rigorous evaluation of its impact, these were the aspects of communicative and deliberative efficacy tracked in the program participants as well as in their local communities.

The *communicative capability set* is the first component of being a deliberative citizen. The expressive functionings of language require the space and the time for conversation and discourse to enhance one's ability to articulate one's opinions, values, and ideas. The receptive functionings of language depend on there being at least two individuals prepared to be responsive speakers and attentive listeners to a variety of points of view. This type of reciprocal exchange creates the opportunity to be sincere and open to the experiences of others.

The *cognitive capability set*, the second component, includes the functionings of critical thinking and perspective-taking. As we will argue further below, critical thinking requires the skillful application of the six steps of information processing, which allow a person to argue and be persuasive in deliberative exchanges. For perspective-taking to mature, exposure to varied points of view is required. By blending critical thinking and perspective-taking, citizens improve their comprehension of events and relationships in their community.

The *emotional/motivational capability set* is the third component of deliberative citizenship. The basic functionings here are trust, confidence, agency, and intentionality. Developing trust in others and confidence in oneself is conditioned by a history of reliable exchanges with familiar group members, and a climate of relative certainty that members can achieve valued goals in life. These functionings of individuals are necessary for the transmission of trust and personal confidence from older to younger members of the community.

The functioning of agency is the willingness to become actively involved in pursuit of the common good by acting on behalf of others. Intentionality is people's purposeful, voluntary action. These two components indicate a citizen's willingness to intervene in public affairs. To achieve these motivations as a capability set, the child needs exposure to an environment where these attitudes and behaviors are accepted and encouraged. It is in this sense that the early deprivation witnessed in the leagãne in Romania and the late deprivation in the streets of Brazil are experiences that undermine the achievement of citizenship.

Introducing Critical Thinking

Because choice is so closely aligned with and dependent on the capacity to reason, it is essential for human beings to acquire critical thinking skills.[10] Such skills are vital for making informed, legitimate decisions. We end this chapter with the importance of introducing the young citizens to critical thinking as a formal procedure. As the curriculum moves from voice to choice and action, the use of reasoning skills should bolster their efficacy (or capability) as community health agents.

In this part of the program, the children are presented with the six steps of critical thinking, which, they are told, will help them evaluate a chosen approach. The steps are knowledge, comprehension, analysis, synthesis, application, and evaluation. They are asked to articulate the meaning of each of these steps in their own words or with examples from their daily experiences. In addition, they are encouraged to think about how these steps relate to what they are learning or already know from daily experience.

Here are a few examples from Tanzania of the young citizens' comments for each of the steps, selected to illustrate the spontaneous grasp they had of the idea, rather than the accuracy of the classification.

KNOWLEDGE: *basic information that can often be memorized without understanding.*

Oswald: To know an answer for a given mathematical problem but you do not know exactly how to get the answer.

Goodluck: You might also know that, that is a bulb and gives light, but you do not know how it ends up giving light.

COMPREHENSION: *an individual's ability to understand an idea or concept.*

Ayubu: I believe that if you don't eat you will die.

Jonas: If you want to buy a pen from the shop you must have money.

ANALYSIS: *asking why and how things are the way they are; scrutinizing a concept or idea in greater depth; and breaking down concepts into parts to gain a greater understanding.*

Frank: Soil erosion is caused by cutting trees, burning of forests, and floods.

Nasra: The problem of car accidents near our school is because of high speed, lack of speed bumps, and houses too close to the road.

SYNTHESIS: *ability to put parts together to form a coherent or unique new whole; sometimes results in the creation of possible solutions to problems.*

Sara: A potter gets clay soil and mixes it with water and then combines it together to make something out of it, like a pot or something.

Winfrida: You may have wheat flour, cooking oil, and eggs, mix them together, and then you put this in a frying pan to make chapati.

APPLICATION: *using knowledge and comprehension of a concept in a new context.*

Paulina: I know the watch always helps us to know the time.

Frank: We are using water for drinking, washing, and cleaning our houses.

EVALUATION: *analyzing the effectiveness of an action. How well did we achieve our goal?*

Selemani: Why so many students didn't pass their examination this year, is because they were not reading or listening to teachers and parents.

Nasra: Last year we harvested very few sacks of maize because of low rainfall.

Critical thinking is all about the kind of systematic and scientific questioning that allows people to generate informed reasons for the types of projects they have chosen and to determine the most effective ways to achieve their goals.

Among its many advantages, critical thinking helped the Tanzanian group understand and respect the perspectives of others, as deliberation encouraged participants to share perspectives in the process of rational exchanges that questioned views and evidence. Systematic critical discourse helped the group to evaluate knowledge gained in sessions about HIV transmission, diagnosis, and treatment as well as how these factual issues were dealt with in the macroworld. The application of their critical thinking skills assisted the young citizens in making choices about the design, content, and production of their newsletter in Module 3 of the program, and in Module 4 it allowed them to jointly craft their community engagement action plan in response to the challenges of the HIV epidemic. Facilitators constantly reminded the young citizens that they should keep the six steps of critical thinking in mind whenever they had decisions to make in any setting.

It is difficult to believe that we have covered so much ground on the topics of critical thinking, citizenship, and democracy and never referred to a person whose philosophy has contributed so much to our ideas: John Dewey. We thank John and Evelyn Dewey especially for their wise 1915 statement that defines our work so well: "If we train our children to take orders, to do things simply because they are told to, and fail to give them confidence to act and think for themselves, we are putting an almost insurmountable obstacle in the way of overcoming the present defects of our system and of establishing the truth of democratic ideals."[11]

One might wonder why we quote the Deweys in closing this chapter on Amartya's Sen capability approach. In part they come to mind because Sen's childhood mentor, Rabindranath Tagore, was considered the father of progressive education in India, just as John Dewey was in the United States.[12] We must save the last word for Sen, however, so we end this chapter as we began—with the final line of its epigraph: *Being able to reason and choose is a significant aspect of human life.*

PART IV

Action

8

Educating Our Community

Development brings freedom, provided it is the development
of people. But people cannot be developed: they can only
develop themselves. . . . He develops himself by what he
does: he develops himself by making his own decisions, by
increasing his understanding of what he is doing, and why; by
increasing his own knowledge and ability, and by his own full
participation—as an equal—in the life of the community he
lives in.

—JULIUS NYERERE

A s children achieve strong voices and enhance their capacity to make rational choices, they are better prepared
to take the final step: they can plan shared action to tangibly
improve the welfare of their communities. We saw children
acting as pioneering agents of change in the street children's
movement in Brazil and in the bold actions of the Chicago and
Cambridge young citizens. Might the young citizens of
Tanzania prove that, as children even as young as ten, they also
could become change agents—and in situations of major
health peril and limited resources? In the epigraph above,
Tanzania's first and longtime president Julius Nyerere asserts
that people "can only develop themselves" and that they do so

by reflectively taking actions and making decisions as full, equal participants in their communities. Is that true for children, as well?

Place affects the opportunities children have to develop the skills of citizenship. Tanzania has a favorable social climate for the development of democratic citizenship, and Nyerere aspired to see his fellow citizens educated as a means to achieving Tanzanian self-reliance. But the nation has faced serious challenges and major setbacks in translating this ideal into reality during its postcolonial advancement. We acquired firsthand knowledge of the country's trials through several visits. On our first to the new nation, in 1974, it was barely ten years old but the two lands that had combined to form it had become unified. Tribalism was giving way to national unity, facilitated by the adoption of a single language, KiSwahili, and by other social and political policies designed to support a cohesive and equitable society. When we visited again in 1986, its economy had faltered. Contributing to its instability were unsuccessful policies, and the country's heavy investment in helping Uganda in its civil war to depose Idi Amin. Yet it remained unified and persevered as a sanctuary and source of support for liberation movements in other newly emerging African nations. On our third visit in 2000, Tanzania's underdevelopment had been compounded by the HIV pandemic, and its economic challenges and health problems were pervasive. It was in this climate that we asked: Could Tanzania's young people take action to respond to the health threat to their nation? How are they included in the life of the nation? Did they have the inclination and ability to make their own decisions through shared discourse, and to become equal participants in community life?

When a new project is introduced in Tanzania, the custom is to call a meeting at which political, religious, and professional groups representing a cross-section of society are briefed on new initiatives. Near the end of a lively question-and-answer period at our initial stakeholder meeting, a tall and distinguished man appearing to be in his seventies rose to comment. His erect stature, white hair, ebony face, and dark, collarless jacket—the type worn by Tanzanian officials since Independence—presented an image of *Mwalimu* himself. The word means "teacher" in Swahili, but *Mwalimu* is also the common and endearing term that citizens of Tanzania use for Nyerere, their first president.

Since the 1960s, President Nyerere has been seen as a teacher, leader, inspiration, and major figure not only for Tanzanians but for all Africans. Nelson Mandela came to play a similar role in the 1990s. Both spent their lifetimes working tirelessly for their countries' liberation and also for peace, progress, and unity for the continent as a whole. The image of this man, looking directly at us with such intensity, was both inspiring and intimidating.

As he fixed his gaze on us, he began to speak in measured, poised English. "Thank you," he began. *Oh no,* we thought, *we should be thanking them for this opportunity.* "Thank you for helping us . . ." he continued, and again our own worries intruded: *please don't let it be that he sees us as coming to help.* And then, for a split second, he paused and smiled before finishing the sentence that would stand as our program's best statement of aspiration: ". . . to be like we used to be." Our apprehension instantly gave way to a sense of camaraderie; this was the most inspirational and respectful comment a Tanzanian could have uttered, and even echoed Nyerere's early text, *Education for Self-Reliance.*[1] "Like we used to be" refers to a period in Tanzanian history, shortly after the country's 1961 liberation from Great Britain, when the new nation enjoyed a sense of collective control and competence in charting a path out of a demoralizing colonial past. It was a superb comment, and it signaled that we were on the right track.

In this chapter we'll drill down into the specifics of the third module of the program we began describing in Chapter 5. This module moves from voice and choice to action, and from the early sessions where adult facilitators closely guided group activities to the later sessions, featuring more balanced leadership organized equitably between young citizens and facilitators. We'll also describe how the program as a whole integrated with the community. Did children engage meaningfully with the curriculum? Could the program be improved, or adapted for other contexts? What effects did the children's actions have? As we share the voices of the children describing how they worked with their communities, note how well the young citizens taught others. It is a reflection of all they learned themselves.

Building HIV-Competent Communities

Recall that, in the first two modules of the Young Citizens curriculum, children in each group familiarize themselves with one another and with the communities in which they live. We designed the modules to progressively build a sense of citizenship that is deliberate, confident, and competent, enabling children's genuine integration into the community. The first two modules prepare participants to understand the information in Module 3 and then, in Module 4, to achieve positive social change by developing their own plan to promote community health. During the facilitator-led sessions of Modules 1 and 2, children acquire new knowledge and experiences. As the curriculum transitions to community sessions early in Module 4, they deepen their comprehension and expand their capacity to think about ways they can affect the health of the community—which they will do later in Module 4.

Module 3 is organized into seven sessions. In Tanzania, five of these were held in the large conference room in Kahawa House, the building where the project had its offices. The remaining two were held in more remote community settings, to ease the children into public settings. The community sessions typically involved twenty to twenty-four children in each group, with an equal number of boys and girls from each of the fifteen intervention neighborhoods. This module happened to fall within the young citizens' short summer vacation, which permitted us to organize daily sessions over a two-week period. Responsibility for the agenda began with the facilitators focused on technical learning but fell more and more on the newly informed and spirited young citizens with each session.

Module 3 began with a detailed introduction to Tanzania's most significant health problems, malaria and HIV / AIDS. The curriculum presented these health conditions as exemplars of health problems young citizens groups could address. An important expectation of participating in the sessions, one that the young citizens themselves helped to create beginning in Module 1, was that freedom of expression would be encouraged, especially through role-playing, skits, and reasoned exchanges of asking questions and stating opinions. The idea was to introduce and contrast the health conditions of, first, malaria, an ancient disease transmitted by mosquitoes and without stigma, and second, HIV / AIDS, a new, heavily stigmatized, sexually transmitted disease. We wanted the children to understand the different ways in which these diseases worked in the human body, their microbiology, the community systems already in place that could be deployed to test for and treat these diseases, and the extent to which their communities understood the science or were misled by myths.

The rationale behind this multifaceted approach to disease—from microbiology to impact on social interactions—was to provide the children with multiple ways to think critically about two illnesses drastically affecting their communities. Young citizens who understood the biological actions of microscopic viruses, we reasoned, could truly understand how HIV transmission, diagnostic testing, and antiviral treatment worked. Such comprehension would allow them to act confidently as knowledgeable health agents in their communities, imparting information, analyzing problems, and using existing social structures to deliver lasting solutions.

Deciding on a strategy to share information about the complicated biology of HIV / AIDS and malaria presented an initial challenge. Biological concepts are typically abstract, complex, and difficult to teach, especially in an informal, participatory setting, and especially to primary school children. We considered digital animations of the biological information, as a means of illustrating how the HIV virus replicates in white blood cells and how the malaria parasite replicates in red cells. But this method, as well as being outside the scope of our abilities and our budget, would have failed to actively engage the young citizens as learners and agents. The alternative approach that emerged involved role-playing and instructional skits performed not on an indoor stage but in popular public spaces, such as marketplaces, bus stops, and or schoolyards, where large numbers of community members regularly congregated. As street performers, young citizens would define the "world" of their actions by laying red ribbon or ropes on the ground to establish a perimeter. Within this small, defined area, traditional grass mats would set the stage for a community action that they would perform, but that other citizens would be invited to enter, too.

Microworld and Macroworld

We arrived at Module 3 prepared to use skits to guide young citizens' own comprehension of HIV, but quickly realized they could in turn use the skits to teach the community. Although we had begun the module sharing information about both HIV and malaria, it did not take long to realize that the children and the community were much more concerned about the threat of the highly stigmatized HIV infection than about malaria, which they knew to be highly prevalent but not stigmatized. When the young citizens presented these two skits to their parents and teachers, it became clear that these adults approved of children portraying the HIV virus in public. With this approval, the group could move ahead, choosing to focus on HIV / AIDS in Module 4 without fear of negative repercussions. Attention to malaria was not completely dropped, however; it was simply postponed to a later stage of the program, described in Chapter 10.

The characters of the HIV skit began life as simple cartoons used by facilitators in teaching. The idea of moving them from the two-dimensional realm into a three-dimensional space of personified biological characters came along the way. So taken were the young citizens with this approach that they soon commandeered that role-playing function, adding voices, personalities, and elaborate actions to dramatize the processes of infection, testing, and treatment. The adoption of skits and role playing came mostly from young citizens themselves. We created rather primitive PowerPoint pages to serve as introductory profiles and factsheets, both to convey information to them and to facilitate participation by others they would invite to join in. We were easily persuaded that performance could be incorporated into the curriculum in a fundamental way.

The setting of the drama playing out on the stage was called the "microworld."[2] This was the human body, in which the protagonists were the white blood cells of the immune system, responsible for protecting the body from foreign invasions of infectious agents. Trying to overcome these soldiers of the immune system was the antagonist: the HIV virus. The progression from HIV infection to the full-blown syndrome of AIDS would be transformed into a narrative depicting the virus entering the body, targeting and multiplying in the white blood cells, and engaging them in combat. A fascinating story could be improvised and performed, with the young citizens using their creativity to shape the characters and dialogue in an anthropomorphic drama from tragedy to resurrection.

A non-biological character, the Joker, served as the neutral, all-knowing master of ceremony, useful to advancing the narrative that the others were developing. With each character's first appearance, the Joker came forward to prompt an explanation of who they were and what their function was. This not only evoked explanatory lines from the immune system characters but also created a moment for a call-and-response exchange with the audience. By cueing the callouts "Who am I?" and "What do I do?" the Joker provided an active learning opportunity for onlookers, who were invited to show what they had learned about the characters rather than just passively watch and be entertained by their story.

By bringing their lesson to life, the young citizens were able to relate to and appreciate biology in a visceral way, and allowed their audiences to do the same.[3] All were more compelled to understand the workings of infection, immune protection, and immune failure. Young citizens took ownership of their characters, inventing and mastering their own personalized but scientifically accurate interpretations. They took responsibility for the costumes that were provided for them, dressing white blood cells in white and the virus in purple, often with small balloons of the same colors attached. These inexpensive and durable costumes and props were appropriately accessible and affordable for a truly community-based program.

The Macrophage, draped in white and having a prominent mouth and large teeth, was always the first to encounter the HIV invader; it took a bite and presented it (as the antigen) to the Commander—a CD4$^+$ T cell, elegantly dressed in silver and wearing a gold cardboard crown. Having perceived the presence of the antigen, the Commander then summoned a hardworking B cell (also in white) to start working on a collection of small cardboard panels designed as locks. These represented the antigen, and it was up to the B cell to use scissors and cut out a key (the antibody) that could fit the locks and thereby disable or destroy the invader. Meanwhile, HIV characters in purple arrived, representing an early stage of the proliferating virus.

The mood shifted after the four initial characters had introduced themselves and their roles in this microworld drama, having been prompted by the Joker to say who they were and what they did. A sense of impending doom descended on the scene as the white blood cells played their assigned roles, trying to fend off the invasion and proliferation of HIV. The virus clearly had the capacity to outnumber the B cell antibodies. Eventually it entered and continued reproducing to the point that it disabled that all-important cell. It was a sad

Table 8.1   Microworld Cast of Characters

Character	Description
HIV virus	I am an HIV virus, the Human Immunodeficiency Virus that leads to AIDS: Acquired Immunodeficiency Syndrome. I can invade your body through unprotected sex, through contact with infected blood, or as an infant through your infected mother at birth or through her milk.
Macrophage	I am a white blood cell, the big eater. I eat foreign bodies such as the HIV virus and malaria parasites. I bite off a piece of the virus to show to the commander ($CD4^+$ or T helper cell).
$CD4^+$ or T helper cell	I am a white blood cell officially known as $CD4^+$ or T helper (T_h) cell. As the commander of the immune system, I give orders to other cells to detect, attack, and destroy germs.
B cell	I am a white blood cell: a B cell. I make antibodies to attack viruses and other foreign bodies. The commander ($CD4^+$ or T helper cell) orders me to make antibodies to neutralize invaders.

moment for the other immune cells, and they gathered around to mourn. With their Commander out of action, these remaining good guys grew confused and fell into disarray. The virus continued its onslaught, taking over the machinery of the immune system by attacking the surviving Commander cells to cause a mortal immune collapse. There would seem to be no happy ending.

But not so fast! Although late to the scene, Dawa (Swahili for *medicine*) then arrived and became the center of attention, dressed in a costume of flowing, colored paper streamers and wrapping a long rope around the Commander, who was still barely standing. Dawa was there to report on a celebratory event. A new medicine had arrived: the anti-retroviral treatment for AIDS, which works by preventing the virus from multiplying within CD4$^+$ T cells. To symbolize its action, which inhibits but does not eliminate the virus, Dawa skillfully tied the rope around the Commander's midsection. As the drug was administered, the Commander slowly resumed strength, but was informed of being completely dependent now on continuing treatment under the doctor's orders. The Commander was warned to comply with the therapeutic regimen, or else the virus's replication would resume and he might not be revived again. This was a treatment, not a cure!

The Joker operated at the boundary line between the interior of the body (the microworld) and the external social environment (the macroworld). The job of this omniscient narrator was to explain transitional moments in the skit and to quiz the audience about the characters, their actions, and the consequences. If a mistake was made at any point, the Joker called out for a "rewind," to back up and perform the narration or action correctly. It was the Joker who announced the victory of the virus and imminent death of the Commander, and then the arrival of the Dawa and the Commander's resurrection.

This drama quickly became a template that could absorb and represent new insights into the biology of HIV infection and the discovery of new therapies. Importantly, by using skits and role-playing to learn and to teach the HIV story, the young citizens reduced societal and personal discomfort in confronting this deadly condition. We were completely unprepared to see the children adding humor to the narrative of each of the characters, even as they portrayed the devastating nature of the virus and its destructive power. In the children's representation, the virus became a cartoon character, and its ability to paralyze people with fear was vastly weakened. The young citizens and their audience members were viewing AIDS in a different, less terrifying context, yet being armed with awareness of its deadly processes and the tools needed to thwart them.

Another crucial benefit of using drama to teach biology was that the young citizens could use the knowledge they gained from acting out events in the microworld to understand the social reality of HIV's impact in the macroworld of the community. For instance, their new understanding of biology allowed them to understand the importance of HIV testing and antiretroviral therapy compliance. In another skit, set in the macroworld, they portrayed a husband who resists his wife's pleas to get tested, and then they role-played different scenarios that could lead to the wife's success or failure to persuade him to do the right thing. Instead of rote-learning a set of guidelines about HIV as a public health problem, the young citizens used their own words and actions to enact their understanding of these concepts, not only to reinforce their own knowledge, but also to teach others in the community.

During Modules 3 and 4, the young citizens became aware of HIV stigma. No one they knew would discuss HIV or AIDS in public. The words were never used at the funerals of victims. Few admitted to being infected. At one community session, a man spontaneously stood up after the skit and addressed the crowd. He said, "I am telling you something I have never told anyone since my diagnosis. I am HIV positive and receiving treatment. Listen to these young people. I wish I had heard someone speak to me like this. I ignored the risks I took in my life and now have a difficult and incurable disease. Listen to them." The audience looked stunned, as if a tornado had passed through town.

After the children learned about HIV / AIDS and practiced their skits, they were comfortable performing and responding to questions from the audience. They invited parents and neighborhood leaders to performances of the skits, either in the schoolyard or outside the municipal offices. Project facilitators awarded certificates designating any young citizen who could skillfully perform every role in the Microworld skit as a "community health agent"—their ability to play a part on either the virus or the immune system side indicated they understood the mechanisms of transmission well enough to be a positive influence on others.

Reminiscent of young citizen groups in Chicago and Cambridge, young citizens in Moshi also conducted a community survey. The purpose was to find out what impact they were having on the health-related knowledge and attitudes of residents in their neighborhoods. A baseline survey was done at the onset in Module 4 and a follow-up survey near the end of that module.

While we had a general idea of how science education and social dramas might develop, the children proved to be much bolder and more creative than we had expected. The young citizens pushed us to a higher level of community engagement and publicly shared scientific knowledge than we had thought feasible. No one we consulted, including community leaders, parents, doctors, and other scientists, anticipated the level of comprehension, humor, empathy, and energy displayed by these children. Given the stigma surrounding HIV / AIDS, most people were gloomy about the prospects of stemming the epidemic. One ward counselor in Moshi we interviewed at the start of the program put it simply to us. The adults, he admitted, had "not done much to solve the problem of this HIV epidemic, so why not give the children a chance?"

By surpassing the expectations of even their most ardent supporters, the young citizens had now reached a point where they had decisions to make. They had gained important knowledge of the biology, testing, and treatment of HIV / AIDS; proved they could gather sizable, enthusiastic, respectful crowds; and earned the endorsements of the local health sector and municipal council. They were now in a position to choose among many options for moving forward and they entered the final weeks of the project's experimental phase. The young citizens were about to realize the possible impact they could have by boosting others' beliefs in their competence, and therefore in the efficacy of their neighborhoods.

Choosing Community Action

Two sessions in the middle of Module 4 were specially designed for each neighborhood group to reflect on the surveys to decide what changes in community knowledge and attitudes they wished to bring about. The purpose of these two sessions was to come up with a strong focus for a community action plan.

The groups had already had some experience in mutually planning action, having worked in Module 3 to agree on how they would summarize their accomplishments as a group in a newsletter. Building on that success, they agreed to work through a series of formal and informal decision-making procedures designed to quickly and transparently generate the widest possible range of possibilities. Of course, they would apply their newly honed critical thinking skills in this process and their routine deliberation methods of seeking consensus.

In preparation for the first of these two sessions, the research team compiled a list of common problems faced by

Moshi citizens at three levels: as individuals, as families, and as communities. Reproduced below is the outline facilitators prepared as a starting point for the young citizens to reason through which topics they would target at what level.

1. Individual

   For the individual already infected:
   What are the signs and symptoms for AIDS?
   What are opportunistic diseases?
   Where and when to go for treatment?
   How to stay healthy?
   How to live with dignity?
   How to deal with stigma?

   For the individual "affected" by having a family member or close friends infected:
   The need for protection, prevention, and regular testing.
   How to deal with illness and death?
   How to deal with loss of economic and social support?
   How to deal with stigma?

2. Family

   The need for testing and treatment for couples, pregnant women, and newborns.
   Information required to maintain the health of a relative living with AIDS.
   Caring for orphans by single parents or in the extended family.
   Stigma directed toward the family as a whole.

3. Community

   Illness and death of productive members.
   Sources of caring for people infected.

Responsibility for the care of orphans.

Availability of community testing centers.

Community monitoring for clinical care and
    medication.

Control of disease transmission within the community
    through vigilant awareness of drug and alcohol abuse
    and commercial sex use, especially in lodging
    establishments.

After the young citizens had gone over this list of issues,
they were encouraged to come up with additional topics. To
facilitate this process, the local group of young citizens was
divided into three subgroups, each assigned to one of the three
population units. The three groups then reassembled, read
through the lists of ideas from each group, and combined
similar topics where this seemed appropriate.

At the second session, facilitators raised more questions to
help the young citizens narrow their focus to a single, vital
topic. For each potential topic, they asked: How much is
known already about this topic? Are there local resources to
contact to gain more information about this topic? How can
we develop an effective community action (using, for example,
drama, newsletters, posters, skits) around this topic?

The method was to use brainstorming techniques to generate questions and then use a simple ranking procedure to
identify the twenty most appealing topics. Presented with
those twenty topics, the young citizens then conducted a bean
vote—using red and white dry beans as ballots—to cut the list
down to five. Each young citizen received five red beans to use
as their "actual" votes and fifteen white beans to use as their
"blank votes." They dropped all these beans into paper bags
representing the twenty different options. It was not permis-

sible to allocate more than one red bean to especially preferred options and every bean had to be allocated. It is a good system for conducting a valid vote quickly while still assuring privacy and resisting social-pressure voting. Once everyone had cast their ballots, the red beans in each bag were counted and the five topics receiving the most votes were listed on a flip chart to enable the next stage: pairwise comparisons.

This next prioritization method requires the group to consider each item with respect to each of the others, pair by pair. Given that five topics had survived the bean voting, there were ten possible combinations for the paired comparisons to be done. An open discussion was prescribed after the results were presented so that individuals could comment on whether these procedures seemed fair and the outcome seemed believable.

After the open discussion, each young citizen received ten red beans and ten white beans, and marked bags were set up for each of the topic pairings. For each pairing, a single red bean was to go into the preferred topic bag, while another single white bean was to go into the non-preferred bag. Only red beans were counted in the end. After the voting, the facilitator counting the beans circled the number of red beans on the paired comparison sheet to determine the total number of votes for each of the five topics. The number circled most often became the group's chosen topic.

In all fifteen neighborhood groups, the scene of these young citizens participating in bean voting was amazing to behold. Children, many as young as ten, approached each voting opportunity in a serious manner, from the first to the twentieth bean! Beans (*maharage*, in Swahili) are an abundant commodity in the Tanzanian diet and a major export crop. In a country that takes democracy and voting so seriously, it seemed to charm the young citizens (as it did all adults present) to bestow upon the lowly bean the dignity of the ballot.

We were present in Moshi during the entire period of the voting and witnessed the genuinely celebratory atmosphere created by these exacting procedures. The young citizens knew that when the facilitators finished tabulating the bean count, they would all discover the topic on which they had chosen to focus their efforts as they tackled HIV in their communities. The facilitators called it out: "stigma" (*unyanyapaa* in Swahili), and the young citizens all erupted into cheering, as if they all were winners. It was interesting that, with all the specificity that was encouraged early on in the process, the focal issue the young citizens would ultimately choose was the most general one—a problem that broadly and deeply affects their fellow citizens at all levels.

We were surprised and heartened, as were the facilitators, to learn that fourteen of the fifteen neighborhood groups had chosen stigma. This level of agreement seemed remarkable across independent, isolated groups; they represented different areas of the municipality and met at different times and locations that week. The fifteenth group had chosen "stigma" as its second choice, opting for "community education" as the first. Many of the other fourteen had chosen "community education" as their second choice. We could not imagine this was a chance occurrence, given the many steps, from brainstorming to ranking to pairwise comparisons, that went into these results—and the fact that these voting procedures were exercised after the children were introduced to the principles of critical thinking. It could only be that these really were the topics most dear to Moshi children's hearts, and probably also to the hearts of their neighbors.

Choice had finally cleared the way for Action.

Evaluating the Intervention

This was the first time the Young Citizens program was mounted in a comprehensive and large-scale manner. Previous efforts had operated at much smaller scale, involving less detailed content for sessions, procedures that were only partially scripted, and only one or two small groups running at a time. The program in Moshi, simultaneously working with fifteen groups of over twenty children each, represented a huge leap.

Beyond the size and scope of the program lay other challenges. The targeted health condition, HIV infection, was highly stigmatized in the community. Although some information about it was taught in primary school, children had seldom been involved in critical exchanges about it, especially with adults. A conservative cultural climate had stymied public discussion of the disease despite its epidemic proportions. The children were also randomly selected—a research design challenge that could well have yielded a sample group much more difficult to engage than a self-selected group of volunteers. And the program timing presented a challenge. Its seven-month span overlapped with major exam periods, school vacations, and a variety of national, religious, and cultural holidays. About 15 percent of participants withdrew from the study for different reasons, some of them moving away from the area, and others going off to boarding schools.

When it came time to evaluate the Young Citizens program two types of information were available. One type was participant-focused, consisting of information relevant to the safety and experience of participation. The other was community-focused, consisting of a post-intervention survey to gauge the collective efficacy of the community. Self-efficacy and collective efficacy are both essential features of the Young

Citizens program. They represent the two levels operating in the formal experiment that was described in Chapter 5. There, we focused on the young citizens' enhanced self-confidence and communicative skills (the personal level). This chapter considers the program's impact at the community level.

Throughout the intervention, not one adverse event stemming from participation in the program was reported. The Data Safety Monitoring Committee, composed of two doctors, a lawyer, a statistician, and a senior community member, had been concerned that parents, teachers, and other adults might complain that children were being disrespectful or disobedient because the intervention encouraged them to be assertive, deliberative, and knowledgeable about health—specifically HIV/AIDS. A perception of disrespect might result in increased use or intensity of physical punishment. Observations by the monitoring committee combined with those of the entire research staff revealed an absence of complaints from either parents or children. The lack of complaints was only partial evidence of the Young Citizens program's safety and acceptance. Other sources of evidence provided more positive indicators of acceptance. One was the level of attendance across thirty weeks of intervention. The overall level of attendance from Modules 1 to 4 was 71.1 percent, with a variation from 56.4 to 83.1 percent across the fifteen neighborhood groups. Attendance increased from Modules 1 to 3 and then declined slightly in Module 4. The period of decline occurred during a time when all school children in Grade 7 (ages thirteen and fourteen) take a mandatory national exam for placement in secondary school.

A satisfactory level of attendance does not prove, however, that children and their caregivers were genuinely and enthusiastically involved. It does not provide a clue as to whether or not children's interests, knowledge, and skills were changing for the better. Since this study was designed as a community health promotion project guided by the actions of children, we also wanted evidence of community leaders' genuine involvement. We believed that, as a structural intervention (one intended to change social norms), the Young Citizens program should produce evidence that communities were adapting positively to its presence. This aspect of community acceptance was satisfied when the program was enthusiastically and formally endorsed by the full Municipal Council.

The children quickly understood and defended the concept of their identity as citizens. We saw them explain to adults the difference between being a student and a citizen. Citizenship, with its rights and responsibilities, was not viewed as a threat to other identities such as student, child, son or daughter, or religious believer. They correctly understood citizenship as a new identity that could and would coexist with others.

For all but one of the fifteen neighborhoods, parent meetings were held during Module 3 to provide caregivers with an opportunity to discuss among themselves and with the investigators their observations and concerns about the project as an organization and the Young Citizens program as an effective way of learning. On average, the meetings were attended by about 65 percent of the children's primary caregivers.

To begin these meetings, the research team provided an overview of some of the common challenges parents face as children transitioned from childhood to adulthood. Our thought was that starting out with generic problems faced by others would make it easier for these parents to discuss their own issues, especially as they might relate to what they perceived to be happening in the Young Citizens program.

The comments of caregivers were uniformly and convincingly positive, highlighting their children's increased levels of responsibility and open communication. Caregivers shared many anecdotes about their children not having to be asked to do chores, giving parents more information about their doings, and showing more concern for the parents' well-being. "What have you done to my child?" one joked. "I don't have to ask him where he is going. Now, he just tells me." What was most interesting about this was that parents pinpointed responsible behavior as a direct outcome of participation, even though the project had been introduced to them as supporting the rights of children.

Assessment of Collective Efficacy

As noted in Chapter 5, the results convincingly show that children in the intervention group believed they had become more competent in deliberating with peers, talking to adults, and having greater control over their feelings, as compared to the children assigned to the waiting comparison group. This result obtained equally for the girls and the boys, equally for the youngest and oldest, and without regard to economic status.

Having shown that the seven-month intervention had enhanced children's self-efficacy in skills related to deliberative citizenship, we examined a more provocative question. It was the one that launched this entire child-as-citizen journey: What role can children play in enhancing *collective* efficacy? To answer this crucial question, we again administered the community survey we had given to adult residents prior to beginning the Young Citizens program, but with one important change: to the post-intervention community survey, we added questions about children's contributions to neighborhood efficacy. Rather than interview the same people, we recruited a fresh sample of randomly selected residents. This would take care of any significant movement of families into or out of the neighborhood. We surveyed roughly forty residents for each of the fifteen intervention and fifteen non-intervention neighborhoods. These twelve hundred adults were interviewed by research assistants who were "blind" to their neighborhood groups.

For each neighborhood, we measured three aspects of collective efficacy. The first was *social control,* which was very much like the focus of the Chicago Project. To gauge social control, we asked questions about willingness to intervene in a variety of neighborhood situations. The responses to each could range from 1 (not likely) to 4 (very likely). The midrange values 2 and 3 were defined as "somewhat unlikely" or" somewhat likely."

> In this neighborhood do you think neighbors would take action to . . .
>
> 1) stop a child from getting in trouble
>
> 2) scold a child who was disrespectful
>
> 3) break up a fight
>
> 4) share water with a neighbor
>
> 5) get food or medicine for someone who was sick

The second aspect of collective efficacy we measured was *neighborhood problems.*

> Do you believe that in this neighborhood . . .
>
> 1) AIDS is getting worse
>
> 2) Robberies are occurring
>
> 3) Groups of teens are causing trouble
>
> 4) Violent arguments are occurring
>
> 5) Rapes are occurring

Finally, to measure what we termed *perceived child efficacy,* we asked about children's status in a positive way.

Do you believe that in this neighborhood . . .

1) children can teach adults some scientific facts about HIV / AIDS

2) children can be as effective as adults in educating the community about HIV / AIDS

3) children can converse freely and openly with adults about HIV / AIDS

4) children can decrease discrimination against HIV-positive people

Each of these bundles of questions was converted to a numerical score for each participant. These scores could vary from four to twenty. Neighborhood scores were calculated by adding up the responses of all participants for each of the thirty neighborhoods. When we subjected these to a rigorous, multilevel statistical analysis, we found only small differences between the intervention and control groups on the first two parameters—that is, social control and neighborhood problems. Perceived child efficacy, however, showed a huge effect favoring the children in the intervention group. This analysis confirmed and validated the many observations we researchers had been making and the parents had been enjoying. On the other hand, the failure to find differences for social control and neighborhood problems implies either that the effectiveness of a child-focused intervention has limited reach in a neighborhood or that it would take more time for children's influence to affect behaviors and attitudes at the level of adult-to-adult interactions. In Chapter 9, we will explore how health fairs organized by the young citizens inspired adults of all ages and both genders to take definitive action to protect their community. This may be taken as evidence in support of the latter interpretation.

At this juncture, we could say that we had completed what we set out to do in the Chicago project. The young citizen's experiment might be the first scientific effort to have created or enhanced collective efficacy for children, and even more surely it was the first to do so through the participation of children in their communities.[4] But, our work in Moshi was not over yet. Based on the results of the randomized trial, along with the observations made on the safety and acceptance of the trial, the staff decided at the end of the treatment groups' last sessions of Module 4 that it was time to extend the Young Citizen's curriculum to the waiting comparison group. After the first intervention's seven months were up, young citizens repeatedly contacted our staff and their local leaders to ask why there were no longer regular sessions in their communities. When the waiting comparison groups got underway, we asked them if they would permit the first intervention groups, who lived in adjacent neighborhoods, to join their sessions in Module 4. To distinguish between the original intervention and comparison groups we adopted the acronyms YC1 and YC2. Having completed the curriculum, the YC1 could now become certified facilitators for YC2 and for new groups to follow.

No Going Back

There are moments when a child manifests a transformation so emphatic that you are forced to imagine that some neural circuit has been switched on, or that a momentary sense of potency signaled "I can do that!" When working with young adolescents, sudden changes may be neural, hormonal, or situational. Most importantly, they can be volitional. Such changes seem to announce, "there is no going back." One day we witnessed a young girl making a robust statement, by her casual actions, about becoming a young citizen—or, as they call themselves in Swahili, *raia chipukizi*—a "sprouting citizen." This child was one of the youngest, smallest, and quietest of the 360 girls in our sample. But on this day at the Njoro primary school, as she prepared for a community session, she made three bounds toward citizenship in a single morning.

Several groups from adjacent neighborhoods had come together to prepare for a special weekend event. The larger group had split up in different classrooms, with some making posters, others rehearsing skits, and some in a room where the drums are stored that young citizens use when they march through communities to spread the word about their events. This early morning there were only two young citizens in the drum room with Maya, one a boy with a drum and the other the small girl, who was sitting near the entry and gently patting a drum between her knees. In walked another prepubescent boy, who glanced at us, then at the seated girl, and then at the other boy. Without a word he reached down and took the drum from the girl and settled himself in a corner chair, where he began to drum. She sat there without uttering a word or even looking in the direction of the drum that had been so rudely snatched away.

As Maya turned to leave, she caught sight of the small girl standing up briskly. Again, without saying a word or making eye contact with the snatcher, she approached him and gently removed the drum from his grasp. She carried it back to her seat, where she began to do some serious tapping. After a few minutes, she abruptly stopped drumming, set the drum aside, and crossed the room. She proceeded to take the drum from the other boy and carried it back to her chair. With both drums between her knees, she spent at least ten minutes beating out an increasingly intricate rhythm.

Later that morning, as Maya moved between classrooms, she chatted with Daniel, a facilitator especially devoted to engaging the young citizens in the role-playing and dramatic activities. When Maya asked how practice was going, he said that it was a great day: one of the younger girls had volunteered to be the skit's Joker for the first time. Furthermore, this child, who one might have thought to be mute, had done a terrific job. Without needing to ask her name, Maya confirmed that she was the same girl who, with her drums, had sprouted right before her eyes earlier that day.

The sprouting girl undoubtedly faced more challenges and some setbacks as she grew up, but she would experience them as a mature citizen, with a growing sense of her own rights and capacities. There was no turning back. She had asserted herself as an individual when she reclaimed her drum, and confirmed her confidence when she successfully took on a role as group spokesperson.

In this phase of the Young Citizens program, everything was coming together. We had built a systematic curriculum and assembled a network of facilitators to give children the tools they needed to confidently organize themselves, the familiarity to explore their communities, and commitment to learn crucial facts about individual and group health. Based on findings that emerged from the post-intervention analyses of the randomized trial of the Young Citizens program, these children were now prepared to take action while fully immersed in the communities they served.

9

Inspiring Our Community

Theatre is a form of knowledge; it should and can also be a
means of transforming society. Theatre can help us build our
future, rather than just waiting for it.

—AUGUSTO BOAL

Only active citizens can build the future. Children are generally not encouraged to think of themselves as citizens because adults generally assume children are not yet capable of reasoned and responsible action. The Young Citizens program radically challenged this assumption by providing children with the space and the encouragement they needed to acquire the stance and the authority of active citizens. Once they had assumed this identity, they were not only personally legitimized; the world around them also recognized and adapted to these new social beings, children as citizens, and so they were publicly legitimized as well. The use of dramatic performance, because it showed their communities what they were capable of, became a dynamic factor in the children's transformation into health agents. Largely due to our discovery of the theatrical methods created by Augusto Boal, drama

contributed as much to the program's success as did the biological and social sciences.

In Module Two of the program (Understanding Our
Community), with support from facilitators and neighborhood
leaders, the young citizens organized themselves and took
their new skills and confidence into their communities. They
mapped, observed, and conducted interviews. These direct
experiences with neighbors provided not only ideas but also a
sense of genuine membership. The fact that they were seen in
the community in the company of elected community leaders,
especially their local street leaders, gave them a new status
with their neighbors; evidently, their activities had the
approval of the municipal government. After an intense period
of training in Module Three (Health and Our Community)
about HIV and malaria, along with two community performances, the young citizens began to see that they could share
what they had learned with the community. It was also possible for them to use a method that facilitators used to teach
them—performing skits—to share their knowledge of HIV
with their neighbors and to use their deliberative skills to
answer questions and engage in discussion.

In this chapter we showcase the young citizens' massive
organizing efforts to educate their neighbors and inspire them
to take action for their health and for that of the community.
These unfolded in the two major activities of Module Four
(Making Community Assessments and Taking Community
Action). Its initial segment focused on building HIV-competent
communities—ones that were prepared to organize and confront the epidemic. Its final section gave the young citizens
their chance to channel this growing confidence and urge for
action. Especially having resoundingly chosen the problem of

stigma as the focus of their community action, they needed to recognize the myths in circulation around this new disease. This misinformation was responsible for much of the stigma, and they would need to dispel it.

Theater as Action

Informational skits and role-playing had proved to be excellent tools for learning and teaching about the "microworld" of HIV / AIDS biology. It was a happy surprise; in the original planning of the curriculum, it had never crossed our minds that drama might play such a facilitating role. Maya was promoting expanded use of it—but at the same time, was quite resistant to the idea of bringing more formal theater techniques into the community actions. When dramatic scripts were written by adults for children to memorize and repeat, she believed, they left no room for the child's view of the world to come through. The acting ended up being timid—and so would the resulting action.

Then we discovered Augusto Boal. Renowned for his activist use of theater since the 1950s in his native Brazil, Boal believed that subjecting people to a monologue to which they had no opportunity to reply was a form of oppression. Audiences at his productions were transformed into active participants, or what Boal called "spect-actors." Specifically, Boal created a method of splitting theatrical experiences into two phases. Participants adopt frozen postures in the initial phase, called "image theater," to represent a social dilemma and a solution. In the next phase, "forum theatre," spectators are invited to join in and intervene with some better solution. In December 2003, Boal led three workshops at Harvard's David Rockefeller Center for Latin American Studies, located in the same block as our home. But his visit to Cambridge overlapped with one of our longer stays in Tanzania, and we were not able to participate. A colleague who knew of our earlier work in Brazil alerted us to his presence. Then, as coincidence would have it, our daughter Tanya invited us to the Cambridge Rindge and Latin School, where she was a history teacher, to witness a dramatic performance he had produced with the entire student body.[1] We were dazzled by how spontaneous and provocative the participants were. But, most of all, it was the blurring of the boundary between actors and audience that enchanted us.

We wondered if, beyond using skits to teach and learn about the biology of the microworld, the children could use Boal's drama techniques to explore HIV's impact on their communities and social interactions in the macroworld. We saw a way to adapt Boal's method to the context of the Young Citizens program, and created the opening exercise for Module Four to introduce the format of "image theater" followed by "forum theater." A skit begins with the character of Chaupele, a young orphan with HIV, living in his uncle's home. A community leader comes to the uncle's house for a meal. The uncle explains to the leader that Chaupele is an unwanted burden on his family, and he yells at Chaupele, telling him to eat at a separate table. The uncle's wife and his son, Godfrey, do not do anything to stop this mistreatment of Chaupele. This scene, depicting a form that stigma can take for orphans begrudgingly cared for by relatives, constituted the image phase of the drama, with program facilitators acting out the scene (rather than presenting a frozen tableau). Next came the forum phase, with young citizens invited to improvise a more humane outcome in Chaupele's situation.

It would prove to be a popular skit. Soon enough, the young citizens were able to act out the initial scene themselves, as well as other dramatizations of stigma, and then invite community members to come forward as "spect-actors" ready to suggest changes or substitute themselves for characters or actions. Everyone, including the audience, was encouraged to take a role and act out the scene to try and guide the scenario toward a positive outcome. Afterward, the children used what was in these sessions to create their own drama of social stigmatization and HIV / AIDS, with the end goal of presenting it to their community.

Our realization that drama could be a powerful tool for making children knowledgeable about HIV, from the microbiological to community level, inspired us to create a dynamic addition to the intervention that helped prepare the young citizens to make a positive impact in their communities by opening minds and inviting collaboration.

Throughout his career as a dramaturgical theorist, producer, and artist, Augusto Boal's core belief was that role-playing made a significant contribution to the quality of life, but that this aspect of our humanity had been invaded and displaced by media and communication technologies. "Theatre is a vocation for all human beings; it is the true nature of humanity," he proclaimed in *The Rainbow of Desire.* How does the human capacity for theatricality inform action? Boal contended that it enables the human being to observe itself, and that, "Observing itself, the human being perceives what it is, discovers what it is not and imagines what it could become." A deep faith in people's ability to improve their lot, regardless of class, gender, and ethnicity, drove him throughout his career. His manifesto, *Theatre of the Oppressed,* is itself not a finished, finely honed product but feels like a work in progress, open to input.[2] It offers a theatrical methodology that practitioners can adapt in various ways to enable audiences and actors together to comprehend their problems and to imagine solutions, whether personal, social, or political. Dramatic expression inspires and awakens citizens to take an active role in imagining and creating brighter prospects.

With Boal's methods in mind, we came to see acting as a method that allows individuals to actively engage in learning, teaching, and critical thinking. Instead of looking at pictures on paper or on a screen, the facilitators and children would themselves animate the concepts that they were being taught and that they were to teach the community. The activation that had been generated largely through dialogue within the young citizen groups and between the young citizens and their community audiences might, with the use of theater, attain a higher level of shared action. Perhaps it really could reduce the stigma associated with HIV—and even bring about collaboration to more effectively incorporate recent scientific and clinical advances in the fight against the oppressive epidemic of AIDS.

Jackson, the Joker

In our Chapter 8 description of the Microworld skit characters, the master of ceremonies figure was named Joker. In fact, this is a name that was given to the character following Boal's lead. Much of Boal's theatrical process requires a neutral party to be at the center of proceedings, usually called the "facilitator" in other participatory theater methodologies. In his own writings, Boal refers to this person as the Joker, in reference to the neutrality of the joker in a deck of playing cards. In this theatrical system the Joker often explains things to the audience or asks actors for their opinions. The intention is to maintain a framework in which audiences can relate to the story even as their improvised contributions alter it.

It is October 2005, and we are at an early session of Module Four. Jackson, playing the Joker, is ready to begin.[3] His guise is a perfect composition of sincerity, innocence, and confidence. He has had no special preparation for this session; like other young citizens, he has learned this role and acquired the information he will share by preparing and participating in less public sessions. Now, as master of ceremony for this session of the community engagement module of the Young Citizens curriculum, Jackson is preparing an audience in the community of Kwa Mtei. These spect-actors will be pulled into skits detailing the processes of HIV infection at a microscopic level and at the level of human social interactions.

Jackson begins with an overview of what is involved in getting tested for HIV. His introduction to the biology of HIV diagnostic testing is accurate and confidently delivered; by now, this kind of event has become typical of Young Citizens groups all over town. What is extraordinary this time is the audience. As well as community members, parents, and neighbors of all ages, it includes the Data Safety and Monitoring Board, first introduced in Chapter 6 as a group of distinguished scientists and doctors. They are here as part of their official responsibility to monitor the safety of the children during the intervention but given their expertise they are also asking questions of the children as tough as they would of their medical colleagues. A medical student serving as a research assistant is filming the meeting, capturing this link between a child's growing capacity for deliberative self-efficacy, as revealed in dramatic expression, and the enhancement of the neighborhood's collective efficacy.

As the Joker, Jackson takes responsibility for logistics and ensures a fair proceeding. Here, the word *fair* means making sure that multiple perspectives will be heard and integrated; the problem will not be solved with implausible ease. The participants must solve the problem in a way that is realistic in the context of their community. The Joker interacts with the audience, but he must maintain neutrality by not endorsing ideas or adding his own to the content of the performance. These are the sole province of the spect-actors.

Creating HIV Competence

Several extremely important research discoveries in the 1980s and 1990s had made this health promotion project possible. The first was the identification of the HIV virus (in 1983–1984) by French and American scientists.[4] This meant that companies could begin to develop tests for antibodies produced in response to the virus. The first test used a blood sample and was known as an enzyme-linked immunosorbent assay, or ELISA. It was approved for use on March 2, 1985.[5] Calls for widespread testing skyrocketed in Tanzania when antiretroviral medicines first became available through the nation's HIV Care and Treatment Plan launched in October 2004.[6] Now, subjecting yourself to a simple and readily available diagnostic procedure not only allowed you to know your status and avoid unwittingly infecting others. It also provided access, if necessary, to a lifesaving treatment for yourself.

The Young Citizens program's first sessions dealing with HIV transmission, testing, and treatment began in June 2005, when effective medicine (*dawa* in KiSwahili) had recently arrived on the scene. Before this access to drugs, an HIV diagnosis was a death sentence that few were motivated to learn about. Now, however, with testing and treatment locally available, the Young Citizens program could offer not only education on prevention but also guidance and hope to citizens of all ages who were already infected or affected.

As we entered full force into the action phase of the Young Citizens program, the theoretical thinking we were steeped in and the practical applications the research team was making (guided, of course, by the curriculum) had converged. The young citizens had become critical thinkers and deliberative citizens. Their neighbors were respectful and interested, and often involved in what they were doing. These accomplishments we could now claim as facts, based on the results of the randomized trial: young citizens had grown measurably in their capacities for deliberative and communicative efficacy, and adults' positive regard for the children in their neighborhoods had risen. But were the children's successes translating to broader outcomes in their neighborhoods? How much closer would they get us to the ultimate goal of raising the HIV / AIDS competence of the community?

The United Nations Institute for Training and Research defines HIV / AIDS competence as having three components. Highly competent communities recognize the biological and social reality of HIV and AIDS; acquire the capacity to respond to HIV and AIDS; and routinely exchange and share knowledge and skills. These beneficial attributes reduce a community's risks and levels of infection and help those individuals living with AIDS to find the support they need to realize their potential.[7]

This idea of an HIV-competent community aligns with the concept of neighborhood collective efficacy. Recall that, in the context of the Chicago Project, this was defined as the presence of strong social ties and the prevailing belief that one's neighbors would take action to preserve security. Collective efficacy operates as a protective factor not only to promote security but more generally to bring about good health. In Chapter 1 we noted our debt to Stanford psychologist Albert

Bandura, a dominant force in developing the theoretical foundations for evaluating collective efficacy. He defines it as "a group's shared belief in its conjoint capability to organize and execute the courses of action required to produce given levels of attainment."[8] Our major goal in working with young citizens was to establish their belief that their voices, choices, and actions mattered in the public discourse about issues that significantly influenced their own well-being. They could organize and execute important actions as part of a multi-generational pursuit of HIV / AIDS competence.

Our approach to building HIV competence was also richly informed by two other major influences. Amartya Sen had defined capability as people's freedom as individuals to choose what they will *do* (including actions they will take in their communities) and will *be* (including identities such as deliberative citizen and health agent). Jürgen Habermas had analyzed the role of reasoned language in coordinating public life and offered a pragmatic approach to advancing social action through mutual understanding. Both had exciting implications for how children could act as citizens in a multi-generational society and proved vital to our imagining how young people might prepare to assume their place.

In *The Structural Transformation of the Public Sphere,* Habermas presents the idea that society has been split in modern times, so that its systems of power and control are no longer connected to the "lifeworld" of the citizenry.[9] People's lifeworld naturally comprises activities in both the private and public spheres. Publicly, they assemble and engage in discourse about problems they face and can address in common, and privately, they communicate, socialize, and connect with one another. Increasingly apart from this lifeworld stand the corporate and state spheres—also referred to by Habermas as the economic and administrative subsystems—which are fashioned to take purposive-rational action in pursuit of money and power. Habermas is deeply concerned that the rise of powerful broadcast media institutions, which have no regard for human connection, has transformed citizens into mere spectators of the systems of power and control, no longer actively engaged in public discourse to shape or constrain them. He concludes his treatise by suggesting that we study ways of rehabilitating the public sphere and thereby the lifeworld. This is exactly what we saw the young citizens in Tanzania preparing to do in their neighborhoods in response to a lethal, biological invasion of their lifeworld.

In Chapter 5, we outlined the full modular structure of the Young Citizens program curriculum at a high level. In Module Four, as described there, the children's focus was on staging dramatic performances in public and engaging their fellow citizens in problem-solving dialogue. At a more detailed level, the breakdown of this final module's content was reflected in the titles of its sessions:

Session 1: Community Assessment and Community Action

Session 2: Making Our Community HIV Competent

Session 3: Assessing the HIV / AIDS Competence of Our Community

Session 4: Interviewing Our Community

Session 5a: Survey Day Preparations

Session 5b: Survey Day 1

Session 6: Reflecting on Our Community Survey

Session 7: Brainstorming Topics for Our Community Action

Session 8: Choosing the Community Action Topic

Session 9: Transferring Power to Young Citizens for Community Sessions

Session 10: Educating the Community About Testing and Treatment

Session 11: Debating Universal Testing with Our Community

Session 12: Addressing Stigma Within Our Community

Session 13: Growing Up with HIV / AIDS All Around You

Session 14: Supporting and Protecting Children In Our Community

Session 15: Reflecting on Community Actions and Survey Day 2

Module Four brought together assessment and action and represented the start of a transfer of responsibility from the program staff and facilitators to the young citizens to plan social action. It also marked a moment when a careful assessment of actions seemed especially important. In their critical thinking exercises in Module Three, the young citizens had learned the importance of evaluation in conjunction with application. It is only through evaluation that one can know whether the application of a principle or procedure has been successful or not. Given that Module Four had the young citizens assuming greater control of session activities and actions, and would be generating a work plan for their efforts to build community competence, they were encouraged early on to build means of assessment into their action plans. Later they would wonder: Did a specific activity they planned and executed to build competence in the community prove effective? Did it turn out to be wholly beneficial or were there unexpected, adverse consequences?

The very first session of Module Four emphasized that assessment (to be obtained by a survey and interviewing neighbors) should accompany action. It provided a stunning example of a historically significant event in Lesotho, a small mountain kingdom in Southern Africa. There, in 2004, Prime Minister Pakalitha Mosisili had decided to make the country only the second in the world—and the first in Africa—to roll out what is known as Universal Voluntary Counseling and Testing. In the article shared, the prime minister is shown mobilizing the population of his home village by being at the front of the line to be tested for HIV / AIDS.

Although the young citizens had been introduced to individual-level voluntary counseling and testing in Module Three, the idea behind a universal campaign was new. It encouraged people, regardless of their expected risk level of having been infected, to volunteer for a blood test for the virus. The ethical standard for the testing had been carefully developed to ensure not only that participation was voluntary but also that test results would remain confidential. To this end, all individuals were provided with counseling, usually in a pre-test session and a post-test session as they learned their HIV status. The idea behind universal testing is that it removes the stigma from testing. When the expectation is that only those individuals who have knowingly engaged in risky behavior will subject themselves to tests, then coming forward amounts to an admission of that behavior. Even arriving at a clinic as a volunteer can lead to a person's being stigmatized. In that case, even the people engaged in risky behavior, some perhaps in denial about it, avoid testing. Meanwhile, many infants and young children born to infected mothers go undiagnosed. Making universal testing the norm gets around this.

In August 2005, the young citizens used the story of Lesotho as the basis for a dramatic script to introduce their communities to the idea of universal voluntary counseling and testing. For Lesotho, there had undeniably been a need for urgent and bold action; the tiny nation had the world's fourth-highest HIV / AIDS prevalence rate at the time (estimated at 30 percent). After receiving his own test, the prime minister had said, "the more and more Basotho know their status, they will be more able to care for and support one another, as well as protect themselves and their partners, and thereby break down the walls of secrecy and denial, which feed the social stigma and discrimination." The WHO Representative to Lesotho had remarked that the prime minister's actions would go down in history as something unique: "This is not only a great day for Lesotho, but for the world. With universal voluntary testing we will be able to know how to better manage the pandemic and make best use of the medical and technical interventions now available to treat people with HIV / AIDS and to mobilize resources effectively."[10]

After the facilitators related this uplifting story to the group, the children used the example to develop a skit on universal voluntary counseling and testing. They hoped Lesotho's action could inspire other countries in the region, including Tanzania, to think of assessments and actions that they might adopt. A number of questions occurred to the young citizens: How would we assess community attitudes in Moshi about such an action? What kind of actions could young citizens take to encourage universal voluntary counseling and testing? How would we assess the impact of such an action?

The neighborhoods of Moshi already seemed primed for such a program as some residents liked what young citizens were doing with their surveys and at performances, but also asked: "Why do you come to the community with all this information about HIV transmission, testing, and treatment, and yet you don't bring any services to us?" These requests suggested that the young citizens might go beyond their initial and unanimously chosen goal of reducing the stigma of HIV / AIDS. While it was already possible for residents to receive free voluntary counseling and testing at local municipal health centers and other nongovernmental facilities, it seemed that people's desire to know their own health status was not the only problem. Some local people wanted to improve the health of the community. In response, the Young Citizens program began to provide sheets of paper listing the addresses of all the local voluntary counseling and testing services. This information still did not satisfy some of the more informed and determined community members, who continued to wish for universal voluntary counseling and testing. Finally, in February 2007, circumstances allowed for the young citizens to begin a major effort along the lines of the Lesotho prime minister's campaign of three years before.

So now we go back to the assessment issues which were the focus of at least half the Module Four sessions. The session scripts for Module Four contained activities incorporating the full range of survey research competencies the young citizens had acquired. They worked again with GPS equipment and GIS maps to determine a representative spatial sampling plan for households, and developed survey instruments for adult residents in the fifteen intervention neighborhoods. Their questions tested how much people knew about their mitaa and its leaders, whether people thought of children as capable of educating the community, what knowledge people had of HIV / AIDS, and what actions people thought should be taken in the community to increase its competence in tackling HIV / AIDS. Within each of these broad topic areas, they worked to choose two or three questions, with an eye to crafting a survey composed of no more than ten questions. The young citizens were given a few more sessions to practice interviewing techniques first introduced in Module Two. Survey teams were trained to mobilize each of the fifteen communities where the intervention had been done; they distributed fliers announcing when and where the survey team would be asking for input in conjunction with skit performances by other young citizens.

The fifth session of Module Four was devoted to "reflecting on the community survey" and that day's discussion came to a clear conclusion: everything else can be done well about a survey effort, but if your fliers don't work, you don't have a useful assessment. The top finding about the survey was captured in a comment in one group's session: "It turns out that the initial assessment results were disappointing, and the young citizens immediately identified the problem as too much dependence on fliers." Results for the survey were similar across all mitaa. "The fliers did not always create the effect we anticipated and did not make people come to the survey site," another young citizen noted. "Many people surveyed simply walked by the survey site." Still, despite low participation, some patterns could be detected. For example, groups also noted:

> In some neighborhoods most people thought that the young citizens could educate the community about issues like malaria and HIV / AIDS.

The majority of people surveyed think that HIV infection and stigma will decrease if people know more about the way in which HIV infects the body's immune system.

Most people surveyed think that only a moderate number of people will get tested for HIV over the next six months.

Many also think that this number will not change much over the next six months.

People are also not convinced that many more HIV+ people will seek HIV treatment over the next six months.

"Time will tell," one group simply concluded. They would make no more use of fliers but wait for universal voluntary counseling and testing statistics to be reported in 2007 and 2008.

Inter-Acting

In this final module, the children make a habit of chanting and drumming as they walk through the community in advance of the weekly sessions, to encourage community members of all ages to come. Although there are tasks to complete at each session, there is also a community component with the young citizens doing their standard skits about the HIV virus and soldiers of the immune system, and other dramatic improvisations.

Their presentations encouraged vigorous debate among community members, who wanted to work with the young citizens in confronting the issues that this complex disease had brought to communities. The young citizens devised intricate and provocative dramas on themes such as the seduction of girls by older men, the abandonment of orphaned children, and the potential to develop drug resistance to antiretroviral medications. As the community's interest in universal testing grew, the children added a drama about that to their repertoire, depicting how it reduced stigma.

One of the more popular dramas produced by the young citizens centered on two characters: Kidogo (Swahili for *female little one*) and Bwana Mapesa (*Mister Money*). This drama had meaning for them as children, and it raised a serious issue for their communities. In the story, a young girl who has lost both parents to AIDS is living in desperation, with nowhere to turn for food and shelter. Sitting alone outside the schoolyard, she is approached by an older man. His fine shirt covers his large *tumbo*, or potbelly, a symbol of wealth. Holding a cell phone in his hand, he gestures to Kidogo as if to say, "everything is alright." As he briskly walks toward her, he pats his pocket, where his money must be. After a brief exchange they walk off together, out of sight. Fast forward. Kidogo appears, looking older and unwell. She finds Bwana Mapesa to ask for money for medicine. He first ignores her and then tells her to leave. As she drops to the ground to plead with him, he walks away and out of sight, leaving the now-infected girl once again without food and shelter.

While watching a performance of this drama near Soweto Primary School in Korongoni Ward one weekend day, Tony's clinical alarm went off. The child playing Kidogo was utterly convincing, slumped on the ground in grief and despair, but Tony perceived more than playacting in the sobbing. He turned to the facilitator to say that the show had to stop; "This might be a genuine post-traumatic reaction." Tony bent down to calm the girl. But when she looked up, he could see that the seemingly distressed child was really a boy. Instantly, the boy abandoned his role as a suffering girl and returned to himself. Noticing Tony's astonished gaze, he beamed with self-confidence.

Genuine perspective-taking had been a major achievement beginning in Module One and continued to be crucial throughout the months of deliberation in which the young citizens engaged. This was understandable given the content of what they learned, taught, and witnessed, not to mention what many had experienced within their own families.

The performance that fooled Tony was not a disrespectful melodrama, but rather a genuine outpouring of the children's deep and broad commitment to making their neighborhoods more knowledgeable and conversant on HIV. In this same community, some weeks earlier, a young citizen had lost his mother to AIDS. To everyone's surprise, he returned to his group and participated in a session within days of her burial. He had begged his father to let him come. It would seem there was some kind of comfort in knowing, acting, and sharing in this quest for HIV / AIDS awareness.

During the eight early weeks and seven later weeks of Module Four, the fifteen intervention groups performed once or twice a week in different locations throughout their neighborhoods, before an average audience size of sixty-four people. In total, 8,500 residents of all ages joined the young citizens' audiences from August to mid-November.[11] The children's actions had had real impact.

Know Your Status

In 2007, after the intervention had been extended to the former "control" neighborhoods in this randomized study (allowing the "YC2" group of children to participate in the same capacity-building activities), a challenge arose. Both the YC1 and YC2 groups wanted to continue holding their community sessions, but the funding had been for a research project of finite duration. To allow them to continue, we stretched the remaining funds in our Harvard budget, making cuts in administrative costs, including salaries, sufficient to cover another twenty-four months (until February 2009). And so, the young citizens continued their efforts to increase the rate of HIV testing in their neighborhoods. They had decided that universal testing was the key to decreasing stigma and building HIV / AIDS-competent communities. They decided to organize voluntary counseling and testing fairs, in collaboration with local health personnel, which they would promote and organize using their skills in teaching microbiology and in addressing the social realities of HIV infection.

Four young citizens groups composed of children from adjacent neighborhoods (now that the distinction between intervention and control groups was no longer relevant) started to make plans for health fairs to encourage and offer universal HIV testing at convenient locations in their communities. With facilitation from the project research team, the groups planned and executed all stages of these events. They began by meeting with their neighborhood leaders. Then they asked local health officers and voluntary counseling and testing counselors to administer those services in their neighborhoods. There was considerable skepticism among the counselors that testing in public places would work, but the young citizens' enthusiasm, matched with their knowledge and experience as public health agents, proved too full of promise to deny. To document their effort, they planned to conduct their own survey prior to each fair to assess community attitudes about testing in public, and then a repeat survey afterward to determine how attitudes may have changed. The place, time, invited guests, and sequence of mobilization strategies were all decided by young citizens themselves.

A few days before each voluntary counseling and testing fair, young citizens made announcements from project-owned vehicles using public broadcasting (known as "hello-hello") speakers. On the day of each fair, the young citizens marched through their neighborhoods, performing skits, drumming, and chanting to engage their adult and child neighbors in public discourse about HIV / AIDS while inviting them to join in the testing.

The first fair was held in two adjacent neighborhoods. Its success went well beyond expectations. Over the course of a day and a half, 114 residents were tested. Dozens were left waiting in line at the end of the day. Given the unexpected size of the crowd and the waiting times experienced, participants asked that the pre-test counseling be done in groups.

A particularly surprising result was that equal numbers of males and females were tested at the fair. In clinics, the usual experience was that females exceeded males by a ratio of three to one. Here, some men were even seen calling out to friends passing by to join them in line. Part of the counselors' routine questioning was to ask participants about their place of residence. The vast majority were from the same wards as the test sites they were visiting. The broad age range of those tested suggested that the campaign for universal testing was indeed casting a wide net. In the follow-up survey, many attributed their decision to be tested to the Young Citizens program and its public announcements.

Additional HIV testing fairs were planned in another three neighborhoods over the next four months. The second and third fairs attracted even greater numbers than the first fair, necessitating an even larger staff of voluntary counseling and testing counselors. Again, the majority of people being tested reported choosing to do so because of the young citizen's activities in their communities, providing further evidence that the campaign to achieve universal testing was working. The young citizens had learned what their neighbors most needed and wanted, and then they had delivered.

The fourth fair coincided with the International Day of the African Child, celebrated every June 16 since it was established in 1991 in remembrance of the hundreds of children killed in South Africa's Soweto uprising in 1976. Despite many other concurrent events on that day, the young citizens attracted large crowds with their skits. The 190 residents tested represented the maximum number the voluntary counseling and testing counselors could serve in a day. Altogether, 653 people had been tested at the four fairs. The municipal health officers and voluntary counseling and testing counselors were amazed at these numbers. They said that the volume of testing handled in a single day at a young citizens voluntary counseling and testing fair exceeded what was usually completed by their own clinics over a period of several months.

This practical, public display of the children's effectiveness showed that they were an important asset to their communities' pursuit of collective HIV competence. It further validated the results of the randomized trial, which had shown that children could effectively teach the scientific facts about HIV infection and reduce the stigma and discrimination associated with AIDS. In epidemiology, the kind of proof produced by a controlled experiment is referred to as *internal validity*. When the outcomes achieved within the experiment continue to operate outside the scope of the intervention, this is referred to as *external validity*. The latter is what we were observing in the young citizens' planning and orchestration of the health fairs.

The children planned a second series of voluntary counseling and testing fairs that would be organized in five adjacent neighborhoods, all within the same ward. This was one of the largest wards in Moshi. The principal reason for this decision was that health centers were available at the level of wards. They offered a broader range of services than the smaller and less well-equipped dispensaries, which provided services to neighborhoods. The centers had a wider base of voluntary counseling and testing and treatment services for AIDS.

In preparation for this second series of testing fairs, the young citizens and the project staff made several visits to a health center with the aim of meeting its medical staff and discussing the services they delivered. They learned that child immunization and voluntary counseling and testing services were available every weekday but not on Saturdays or Sundays. This meant that the young citizens' plan to hold voluntary counseling and testing fairs on weekends would not create any conflicts with staff responsibilities. This second round of fairs was planned in collaboration with the Elizabeth Glaser Pediatric AIDS Foundation. That organization's involvement brought a new level of experience to the project, especially in the realm of testing and treatment for maternal and infant AIDS. Its experts introduced provider-initiated testing and counseling, prevention of mother-to-child transmission, and delivery of antiretroviral therapy.

The young citizens visited a health center again to interview not only more health workers but also some of its clients. They prepared questionnaires to gain more understanding of mother-to-child transmission, seeking the perspectives of patients and providers on the availability of services and their prevention effects. The children interviewed more than two hundred residents in their homes in the five neighborhoods served by the health center.

They learned that roughly half the residents of the adjacent neighborhoods used the ward's health center. Approximately forty percent of these users indicated that they had been offered voluntary counseling and testing by their providers, and nearly ninety percent believed it to be a good idea. Half of all those interviewed reported having been tested in the past for HIV, many at a fair organized by the young citizens and others at local clinics or at an event by the national Presidential Campaign for testing and treatment. It was noted that those tested at the young citizens' fairs outnumbered those locally tested as part of that national campaign. Slightly less than fifty percent of respondents knew that the virus could be transmitted from mother to child. The main takeaway from this survey was a resolve on the young citizens' part to intensify their education on that form of disease spread—and on the integrated set of practices known as prevention of mother-to-child transmission. Making an effort to come to fairs more informed on this topic would help them mobilize the community more effectively.

The young citizens began their preparations for the voluntary counseling and testing fairs by meeting with leaders at the level of urban wards and street clusters and requesting approval to conduct HIV health fairs in their mitaa. They knew that in the first series of fairs, the presence of local leaders had strengthened the mobilization effort. Once again, the leaders all agreed to lend support and attend the fairs as honorary guests.

In the two weeks prior to the second set of fairs, young citizens and facilitators started a recruitment campaign featuring street theater performances. They distributed fliers house-to-house, made public and school announcements, mounted posters around communities, and contacted churches and mosques. As well as performing skits on prevention of mother-to-child transmission and on testing, they recited poems and sang songs they had composed, and went drumming throughout the neighborhoods. Their awareness-raising tactics were designed to encourage neighbors, friends, and family members to be tested, but also to disseminate information.

The fairs attracted large numbers of residents, and as the young citizens launched into their dramatic performances, the crowds became highly involved. Especially gratifying was the dialogue that developed around each performance and continued afterward. As in the first series of testing fairs, however, the young citizens knew they must be rigorous in their impact assessment. They formally interviewed individuals who came to be tested to determine which mobilization approaches had been most effective. Thirty percent of respondents said they were influenced by the young citizens' home visits—having a child tell them about the program and hand them a flier announcing the locations and timing of weekend testing fairs. Forty percent had been influenced by the public announcements from vehicles. Nearly seventy percent of those interviewed had witnessed the young citizens' presentations in the community and named those as a driver of their getting tested. Community posters were effective for only twenty percent, nine percent said that they were encouraged by religious leaders, and only a few said schools or mtaa leaders had influenced them.

Their data show that fairs in public spaces yielded many more persons agreeing to be tested than did health centers. It also seemed as if spillover into health centers of those not tested at fairs was occurring. Anonymous data collection indicated the number of people testing positive and whether they were referred for CD4 counts. A decline in these white blood cells, also called $CD4^+$ T cells, is an indication of the seriousness of HIV infection and need for drug therapy.

Among those requesting to be tested were many children under consenting age (eighteen years), who often arrived in groups, unaccompanied by their parents. These had to be told to come back with their parents—and some did manage to do so, with their parents consenting to the testing. Many children complained, however, that their parents or caregivers did not have time to accompany them to the testing site. Indicating their strong intent to be tested, they left their names and contact information so that they could be visited at home—or at school, provided their parents agreed to sign permission forms. Children were observed encouraging their peers to return home to bring their parents with them to test. Those who received parental permission appeared very excited about getting their results, showing no infection, and made promises to one another to avoid behaviors that put them at risk of contracting HIV.

Across the two series of fairs, gender parity did not change much; plenty of males continued to show up. Relative to the first series, many more children were tested in the second one, no doubt due to the mobilization effort's emphasis on children and the prevention of mother-to-child transmission. Out of 976 individuals tested, 187 (19 percent) were under the age of fifteen. Only one child in this age range had been tested in the first group.

Through our close collaboration with the health center, we were able to obtain anonymized data it had collected on seropositivity by age, which made it possible to compare patterns in the clinic's testing to patterns in our project's community testing. We were particularly interested in varying prevalence across different age groups. We divided the populations into three age groups for this purpose: those tested prior to expected sexual debut, those tested in the early range of risk for sexually transmitted infection (at fifteen to twenty years old), and those past their twentieth birthday, the group most likely to be sexually active. Awareness of seropositivity among the youngest group was especially important to us, as maternal transmission of HIV can happen *in utero*, during childbirth, or through breastfeeding and can remain undetected for years. It is important to detect seropositivity as soon as possible, for the health of the child, but also with regard to being unknowingly infectious to others. If a child is infected at birth, that is a child who could have benefited from a program focused on prevention of mother-to-child transmission, which could have been offered before conception, and throughout pregnancy, labor, and breastfeeding. It was heartbreaking to see that the youngest seropositive child in the data set was an infant.

The actions taken by the young citizens of Moshi made a difference to their community. Even beyond that, the success of their intervention has implications for other areas of Tanzania and sub-Saharan Africa. In many locales, a major transition from centralized administrations to local governance has placed enormous demands on local leaders and citizens to acquire knowledge, to develop deliberative skills, and to solve problems though assuming collective responsibility for action. The HIV / AIDS pandemic represents a daunting challenge to these communities and their local health administrations, as does the older, endemic problem of malaria. Overcoming such challenges will demand effective public health interventions as well as new biomedical technologies. Success will ultimately depend upon multidisciplinary strategies that integrate the social sciences with epidemiology and research into infectious diseases.

To design prevention and treatment services, a well-integrated approach must combine knowledge of the structural determinants of health (such as gender, age, education, and income) and understanding of how to manage behavioral risk factors (such as sharing syringes, having unprotected sex). Informed, locally based deliberation must be used to engage experts and lay citizens in collaborative appraisals of science, technology, and public health issues. This is precisely what happened in the deliberative groups we established in Chicago with the El Valor and the Mothers Struggling to Make a Difference groups (as described in Chapter 6). It was the key to the success of Brazil's Guardianship Councils, which combined elected local officials and health personnel (as seen in Chapter 3). Providing a venue for knowledge acquisition, deliberative skill development, and informed shared decision-making could allow the young citizens' successful mobilization in Tanzania to be extended to all citizens.

Our observation in Moshi was that the scene and spirit at the voluntary testing fairs were the antithesis of the solemn and distraught displays of shame and loss that HIV / AIDS had brought to so many areas of Eastern and Southern Africa. In a land where premature death had become a daily, wrenching phenomenon, the health fairs were, incredibly, festive and full of spontaneous camaraderie. In the long lines, which began to form in the early hours, a woman might ask someone near her in line to hold her spot—then merrily run off to drag her husband from his shop to be tested before noon, when the lines would get even longer.

A major celebrant in one crowded scene outside a fair site was the owner of the most popular local brew bar, located in the shed attached to the side of her small shack across the road. This hefty, jovial woman was decked out in a bright *kanga*—one of the traditional cotton fabrics, roughly three-foot wide by five-foot long, produced locally in Tanzania. Kangas typically have colored borders and center designs, often featuring proverbs or even political slogans. They take their name from the common guinea hen with its colorful, dotted feathers. Traditional uses include as shawls, skirts, head wraps, and most interesting of all, slings for carrying infants and toddlers. Many young citizens spent their first years in kangas, going along on the activities of their mothers, grandmothers, and sisters.

With kanga tied around her head and at her waist, Mama Pombe (KiSwahili for *brew*) was on a mission to find her male customers in the vicinity: "Godfrey, Rashidi, Goodluck, get over here and in this line right now. You want me to serve you this month, then let me see you in line to be tested, with these *ndugu* (brothers)." In the context of promoting "voluntary" HIV testing, we weren't sure what to make of her recruitment style, but at least it showed the young citizens that their efforts to inspire their neighbors were working.

Inspiring Bibi

As the sun sank lower across a dusty field at the end of one fair day, Maya was sitting on the school steps with Naomi, a facilitator, sharing the thrill of witnessing such a successful day for the young citizens, their families, and their community. They watched an elderly, stooped *bibi* (grandmother) with a subdued and dusty kanga tied over her shoulder coming in their direction to rest on the school steps where they sat. As she approached, she looked directly at Maya and smiled. Maya assumed she had been recognized as part of the project, since she was often the only *mzungu* (foreigner, or white person) in these neighborhoods, coming and going in the Land Cruiser Hardtop with the project's logo. Through Naomi, Maya asked the older woman if she had been watching the young citizens doing their skits today, and she nodded. Then she pulled her kanga back from her left arm and shoulder, extending her arm with her palm open. She displayed the crook of her elbow and the venipuncture from just having had her blood drawn.

Yikes, Maya thought. *Did she just stand in line with all the others throughout this hot, windy day to get tested for HIV?* The woman looked back and forth from Naomi to Maya, then spoke, prompting Naomi to translate her comments: "My husband has been dead many years and I live alone. I have no men friends," she said, looking away briefly as if embarrassed about sharing that private matter with strangers. She talked about having seen the young citizens doing their educational skits and parades for several months and said she had been wanting to join one of their community events.

"I was sure I wasn't infected," she said, again turning away sheepishly, "but I gave them my blood to show *mshikamano* (solidarity) with the children and my community." She was beaming as she wrapped her kanga loosely over her arm and shoulder again. We both smiled and nodded to show we understood, knowing that our just saying "thank you" would not be an appropriate response to such a profound expression of support. Her statement, coupled with the image of the venipuncture and her outstretched arm, struck us as incredibly poignant. In moments like this, we recognized Tanzanians as among the most generous and genuinely social people we could ever hope to meet.

Naomi and Maya sat there a few minutes longer, silently, waiting for their vehicle to return.

"Thank you for helping us . . . to be like we used to be," an older man had said at that early stakeholder meeting. And now, at the project's conclusion, an older woman had said, "I gave them my blood to show solidarity with the children and my community." These endorsements from elders represented the strongest kind of acceptance we could hope for from a community.

The degree to which the Young Citizens program was recognized and respected by parents, local government officials, and ordinary citizens suggested it would have a bright future. As the project research and HIV testing fair activities ended, we worked with the young citizens, former program facilitators and staff, and local leaders to help the project reinvent itself as a registered community-based organization in the municipality. We also organized an immediate plan with the remaining small staff to go about recruiting new community groups with a focus on malaria control. There were many challenges, of course, to think about: creating a new sample of young citizens; expanding the curriculum to focusing on the complicated microbiology of malaria transmission; showing that such program could be successful in the rural areas near Moshi; training some of the eldest among the young citizens to assume the role of facilitators and quality monitors. It remained a lofty goal to prepare children to effectively address community problems—perhaps any community problem in any region of Tanzania—but, we thought, an achievable one. It made writing this book all the more important.

10

Moving Forward

C an an intervention demonstrated to be beneficial in a small city like Moshi be just as vital in a rural community, or in the metropolis of Dar es Salaam? Might an approach originally designed to diagnose and prevent HIV infection also stem the spread of malaria or curb community violence? What about the coronavirus pandemic of 2020? Do young citizens who have demonstrated their capability to mobilize their communities to confront health challenges also have the potential to enhance the practice of everyday democracy? In this chapter we explore the relevance of the Young Citizens program across place and theme.

The Safety Audit

Usually, it was one of us making an appointment to secure some form of authorization for our project, but on this day it was the Moshi municipal director, an engaging woman with a genuine concern for children, who called us to her office. The waiting area was crowded with people looking nervously at one another, wondering who would be called next. Soon she emerged to free us from the queue and escort us back into her handsome, air-conditioned chamber. Over cups of famous

Kilimanjaro coffee she made a surprising request, inviting us to attend the Municipal Council's upcoming meeting with representatives of the UN-Habitat Safer Cities program. This group, due to arrive in a couple of days, was considering a partnership with the municipality to design and implement a safety audit based on the perspectives of children. She was clearly excited by the prospect. Her invitation signaled to us that she understood what the Young Citizens project was fundamentally about and could imagine its potential to address a problem other than HIV. We took it as a tremendous vote of confidence.

The Safer Cities program was launched in 1996 to address urban violence, as part of implementing the Habitat Agenda— the output of the Second United Nations Conference on Human Settlements, held that year in Istanbul. The main objectives of the program were to build capacities at the city level to adequately address insecurity, and to help establish cultures of prevention. Already, the program had successfully created a Women's Safety Audit in Tanzania's capital city, Dar es Salaam.[1] The director hoped that Moshi Municipality could partner in developing a Child Safety Audit.

In at least one respect, the timing of her invitation could not have been better for us. Mika Morse, a recent college graduate who had worked closely with our project team from 2005 to 2006, was interested in returning for the summer after her first year of law school. She had become proficient in Swahili during that year and was already well known to the rest of the staff, the community, and, most importantly, the young citizens.

In collaboration with a human rights program and with our guidance, Mika developed an eight-week project that engaged members of both our intervention groups (the control group having completed its first three modules).[2] The plan was to build on the deliberative capacities they had acquired in previous months and to involve their local mtaa leaders in brainstorming new approaches to improve community safety. From the thirty established young citizen groups combined, the new groups of around twenty young citizens each would meet for sessions lasting two to three hours once a week (after school or on Saturdays) with one adult facilitator and a recorder. The sessions were structured around child-friendly activities.

Using an approach Mika called "collective citizenship capability," the project was designed to develop five key skills; the children would learn to identify problems, prioritize issues, communicate ideas to other children and to adults, plan for future action, and collaborate with other community members. The idea was to show local leaders that the same principles that had been applied in a program to tackle an infectious disease could also help their communities confront public safety problems. Especially noteworthy in this program's action plan was this: it explicitly recognized the importance of training community leaders to integrate children into their local committee structures.

In the final section of a detailed report, Mika addressed the issues of generalizability and sustainability. "As of now, the Young Citizens program has the right elements to become a durable institution," she wrote. She noted that program leaders were working to strengthen a partnership with a legal aid program (the Kilimanjaro Women's Exchange and Community Organization) in hopes that this organization might take on the governance role of monitoring, evaluating, and sustaining their initiative. They had also begun training mitaa executive officers to become "guardians" of the Young Citizens program— although, Mika noted, "they are not trained to be competent in child facilitation skills." She concluded with a bottom-line concern: "Finding a sustainable way to recruit and train facilitators will continue to be a challenge, unless new sources of funding can be found to support this aspect of the project. The municipal and mitaa governments are very cooperative, but there are no special funds that can be earmarked for the project at this time."

Here was the sting of reality, the issue that has loomed over legions of students, professors, and veteran practitioners trying to secure and scale up successful interventions.

Control of Malaria

From the beginning of the program, we knew that expanding to rural communities would require developing a focus on malaria. Although Tanzania's demographics are trending heavily toward urbanization (in fact, the forecasted growth of Dar es Salaam over the next three decades is alarming), the country is still predominantly rural. Fortunately, our research assistants were prepared to make this adjustment because the Young Citizens original curriculum had made them familiar with the micro and macro worlds of malaria as well as HIV / AIDS. Confident that the group, having addressed HIV, could now succeed with malaria, one of our young citizens quoted a traditional saying: "If we have crossed the river, we cannot fail to cross the stream."

After the Young Citizens groups—the treatment group (YC1) and the control group (YC2)—had completed their intervention modules and participated in HIV testing fairs, some members had the time and interest to become facilitators themselves. They began helping to recruit and train the next generation of young citizens from the same communities—

YC3, YC4, and so forth. In this new role, they began by conducting surveys and were able to show that their urban communities lacked sufficient knowledge about the transmission and environmental management of malaria. Among the findings: only 20 percent of those surveyed knew that if a mosquito bit an infected person it could transmit malaria to another person; only 27 percent knew that malaria was caused by the *plasmodium* parasite; and only 23 percent had heard of biocontrol or environmental control of malaria.

Hoping to raise these percentages, they began by using a microworld skit to introduce the *plasmodium* life cycle. It portrayed the four stages of infectivity by which, first, an infected female *Anopheles* mosquito bites through skin and transmits the parasite to the bloodstream—which, second, infects the liver. Third, the *plasmodium* returns to the bloodstream and infects red blood cells. Fourth, a new mosquito is infected when she bites this infected person. And the cycle continues.

In the initial HIV program, young citizens had approached and engaged local community members through public performances, in part to avoid targeting families affected by a stigmatized disease. As the focus shifted to malaria transmission and environmental management, the best strategy for engaging fellow citizens also shifted. When making household visits for education, the young citizens could do important work with neighbors around their homes, demonstrating environmental approaches to disease control through mosquito monitoring and elimination. Confidentiality was not the issue it had been for HIV / AIDS. The young citizens' ability to collect GPS data, and access to the GIS maps from the project's previous work, enabled them to map the location of the households where mosquito populations were highest and to help residents identify the sources of standing water where breeding was occurring. They also provided scientific explanations and demonstrated environmental management practices, such as biocontrol with larvivorous (larva-eating) fish.

The Tanzanian fish species *Nothobranchius guentheri* is an annual species of the type known as killifish, which are native to several regions of Tanzania. Adults die off yearly, leaving their embryos in a state of suspended animation in dry dirt when the water recedes. When the rainy season begins, the embryos hatch and feed on the *Anopheles* mosquito larvae, which hatch around the same time. The young citizens worked with project staff to dig experimental ponds in a restricted region of the community, to create maps of existing ponds, and to take weekly larval counts before and after introducing larva-eating fish to their experimental ponds. This project was initiated on a large scale and also replicated in a rural area near urban Moshi.

When the project's supplier of killifish eggs went out of business, we searched scientific articles to learn where killifish had been studied nearby in the past. This led us, together with our wonderful driver, Mwakatobe, two facilitators, some local officials, and an experienced guide, to venture across dry plains in search of killifish dormant eggs in a dry riverbed. When we arrived at the banks of the Kifara River, we paused to enjoy the scenery while our local hosts walked our team up a ways, scouting beyond a bend. Eventually, Tony decided to follow and set out toward the point we had last seen them. But his steps across the "dry riverbed" became slower and slower until he realized he was sinking. A panicky look was exchanged as we realized Maya could hardly come to pull Tony out—we would only sink together. We shouted for the others as we knew he should remain motionless.

Tony was already knee-deep when they got to him, picking their way across fallen tree trunks to perform the rescue. When we returned to Moshi, we had our sample of dry river mud but also a new recognition that our glory days of fieldwork were in the past. We pondered what the traditional saying might be for those who had *failed* to cross the river. We hoped it was better than for straying cattle, who could only provide a long, slow feast for the local crocodiles, the mamba!

Becoming a Community Organization

Community members began to ask: What is happening with your project? For a while there were several promising events to savor. Recall that the Young Citizens program intervention began with its YC1 treatment group and YC2 control group, and that the latter set of fifteen neighborhoods also went through the treatment process after it had proven beneficial. As YC2 approached completion of the final modules, a committee was convened of parents, neighborhood ward counselors, all department heads of the municipality, and the mayor and municipal director. At its first meeting, the research team presented an overview of the progress made over the past year, and the young citizens performed their popular macroworld and microworld dramas. Then there was an open discussion. After this meeting, the municipal council endorsed the program and strongly supported the idea that Moshi should become a demonstration site for other localities in Tanzania and the region.

The project and the entire staff entered a transitional period in which the objective was to go beyond carrying out the Young Citizens program in the intervention and control communities (representing half the municipal population). They began actively considering how all children could by age ten, if not sooner, be drawn permanently into participation in Tanzania's decentralized and democratically elected neighborhood governing structure. To be sure, this idealized intention was challenged by political reality: making such a change would require authorization from the national government. No matter that young citizens had demonstrated their competence and confidence in hugely successful HIV-testing fairs, easily taking on major responsibilities for most aspects of planning, execution, and evaluation. Local authorities still anticipated that the process of getting such a proposal endorsed by the central government would be prolonged and burdensome.

In 2009, as the program prepared to transfer stewardship to the municipality, its research assistants conducted an exit survey in which community leaders and parents in all thirty neighborhoods involved in the trial participated. The survey questions probed the community's level of interest in the program and their willingness to support its continuation. It was during this same period that the program began working in collaboration with the Elizabeth Glaser Pediatric AIDS Foundation, the organization which supported the second round of HIV health fairs described in Chapter 9.

The young citizens, their parents, and their community leaders reached a consensus: the project should become an official community-based organization. This would give it a degree of independence and allow it to receive funding as a member of civil society. And it would preserve the project in Moshi to serve as a demonstration site for other areas of the country and region.

The fact that this program has always been designed as a structural intervention, with methods and goals aligned with the local government's way of working, would establish a basis for its ongoing security and maintenance. An expansion of the Young Citizens curriculum to establish deliberative councils with elected local officials and health personnel would provide venues for knowledge acquisition and the continuing practice of deliberative citizenship for all children in the municipality.

While the prospects for replicating and expanding the reach of the program in Tanzania were encouraging, there were also challenges to acknowledge. Mounting this first large-scale rendition of the Young Citizens curriculum and realizing its results had involved a commitment of resources and attention that would be difficult to replicate outside the context of a rigorously conducted and well-funded research study. Several aspects of its design would be difficult to scale to even a modest community program—including its supervision of facilitators by a college-educated research staff, provision of transportation to and from sessions for children who attended schools outside their communities, and vigilant follow-up with participants who were persistently late or frequently absent from sessions. One exciting idea afloat was that new waves or cohorts of new young citizens could take the role of assistant facilitators and supervised and guided by seasoned lead facilitators. They would sustain a continuous process, guided by a shared mantra: Once a citizen, always a citizen. By definition, a community-based organization would operate close to home and work in coordination with the public.

A big part of the project's success had been its collaborative planning and managing with the local health department and the Elizabeth Glaser Pediatric AIDS Foundation. As it transitioned to a community-based organization, a primary objective would be to identify municipal departments and appropriate agencies to become partners in community projects. There was another proposal envisioned, expanding the Young Citizens program into the extensive network of villages and rural areas surrounding Moshi's urban district. One challenge would be maintaining standards in the recruitment of new waves of young citizens. Another would be ensuring that the curriculum could be appropriately implemented by facilitators with less than a college education. Support would be crucial.

News of the project's success was spreading. The Bill and Melinda Gates Foundation's Grand Challenges for Global Health Program paid a two-day visit in October 2009. The young citizens themselves organized and executed activities to actively engage dozens of Gates Fellows—a select group of around fifty graduate students and established infectious disease scientists—in discussions and dramatizations about HIV and malaria. The young citizens and Gates groups exchanged ideas about each other's activities. The young citizens also engaged them in a few of the routine community dramas they had used to educate and mobilize their communities. The most lively drama proved to be the story of Kidogo and Bwana Mapesa; the visitors' efforts to entice Bwana (the antagonist) away from the protagonist (Kidogo) included such amusingly weak ploys as "Hey, Bwana, come with me and share a couple of beers!" Another special moment occurred when one of the young citizens asked a researcher who studied the early stage of the malaria infection in the liver a question: Why does the parasite choose the liver as a place to hide? The researcher, unprepared for the moment, had to admit that it was a tough question. Three months later, the US Ambassador to Tanzania visited the project. Moved to reflect on his own childhood, he described how, as a child, he had sought to join this kind of enrichment program in his neighborhood. Comfortably, he engaged the staff and children in a lively exchange on the meaning of child citizenship. This was a hopeful moment for the program.

At an earlier time, we would certainly have arranged our back-and-forth travel schedules to be present and preside over such events. Now, we believed the time had come that the young citizens themselves, with the presence of their facilitators, could organize their events. They had always done a splendid job performing skits, trading stories, and posing and answering questions about HIV and malaria. Later, watching recorded videos of subsequent events, we found it thrilling to see the knowledge they displayed and the maturity of their interactions with guests. They made it clear that they did not need our hand-holding; the transfer of this research-based endeavor to the community had begun.

Despite community-wide support and demonstrated applicability to HIV, malaria, and public safety, intensive efforts to establish a new entity were not realized. Once the funding from our research grant was exhausted, the community-based organization faltered. After twelve years on the ground in Moshi, we knew at least part of the reason. Chronic poverty produces a sense of dependency on external beneficence, which over time can weaken the confidence needed to take risks. This state of mind is exactly what President Nyerere was driving at in his speeches on self-reliance. And it is reflected in what our research project was attempting to accomplish in its experiment to enhance self- and collective efficacy.

Yet, Tanzania represented an important context to test the merits of this intervention. As a nation, it is democratic, culturally unified, and politically stable. A high degree of religious and ethnic tolerance exists. The local government reform conducted in the 1990s has encouraged a participatory, democratic ethos among its people. This nation has also been a vigorous supporter of implementing child rights as enshrined in the UN Convention on the Rights of the Child and the African Charter on the Rights and Welfare of the Child. Although a highly conservative posture towards child-rearing continues in families and schools, the concept of child rights is not viewed as contradictory to that. It is widely acknowledged that the profound level of poverty characterizing this society, rather than political will, acts more than any other factor as a constraint on implementing the principles of provision, protection, and participation that are enshrined in these declarations.

While our near vision was focused on the experiment in Moshi, our far vision was trained on other issues, from local to global ones, including chronic diseases and violence. How could the principles and methods of the Young Citizens program address these other public health and social problems? Could the ideas, curriculum, and training manuals inform and guide social policy and evidence-based practice for children addressing other challenges? A particularly tough and persistent question presented itself: Would we be able to identify circumstances that would bode well for the durability of a new Young Citizens entity?

We encountered an inspiring answer to this question in Costa Rica as collaborators with the Deliberative Capabilities in School-Age Children project (abbreviated to CADE, from the Spanish *capacidades deliberativas*). CADE is one of several educational programs organized and guided by the Omar Dengo Foundation through a public-private collaboration with the Costa Rica Ministry of Public Education.[3] This nation has strong democratic traditions, one of which is to encourage children as young as ages three and four to vote in mock presidential elections. We discovered it to be an ideal setting in which to engage children in the practice of deliberative citizenship. CADE adopted our synthesis of collective efficacy, capability, and deliberation as a framework for a school-based curriculum that became a national program founded on two premises. The first recognized that the legal changes brought about by the Convention on the Rights of the Child had caused Costa Ricans to rethink the basis of education for citizenship. This could no longer be conceived as preparation for future political and civic responsibilities. Rather, it would be understood as a process of respecting the participation rights that children already have and guiding their participation in public issues as students. The second premise behind CADE has to do with the value of applying a digital dimension in citizenship. Digital technologies include powerful educational tools that can enrich the ways in which students understand the views and positions of others, spread their own ideas and proposals, and join different networks and spaces for communication and dialogue. CADE developed its own "preferendum online," a powerful web-based tool for discussing topics, voting, and reaching agreements among children from schools across the country.[4]

Summing up, we initiated a large and complex experimental project with the enthusiastic participation of local democratic government, residents, parents, and children themselves. As well as having a positive impact locally, that project made progress on some of democracy's unfinished business: How should children be included as participants in government and civil society? Citizenship is variously defined, we know;

our definition centers on active, competent participation in multigenerational, local contexts. To regard the child as a citizen is to accept a new dimension of childhood. The Young Citizens program provided the space and established a procedure to bring the idea of the citizen child into higher resolution. The young citizens accomplished two things. Through their actions they helped to *heal* their communities from the attack of a deadly virus that had the potential to destroy their society. Their informed participation also strengthened the foundation of their everyday democracy.

Epilogue

This book has been our effort to help the world turn to a new and compelling chapter in the history of childhood— one that has the child embedded not just in the family and school but in the community, as well. We have tried in our account of the Young Citizens program to tell a story of moving beyond the child as *rightsholder* to a vision of the child as *citizen.*

We began, in our Prologue, by posing two challenging questions to our adult readers: How can we claim to see our world clearly and completely without incorporating the perspectives of its youngest inhabitants, its children? And what will we adults—parents, neighbors, educators, scholars, and leaders—do to engage them? We hope you are now better prepared to answer. Our text has explored the issues these questions raise by drawing on the science and philosophy of human development, but also on the personal vignettes and profiles of children we have encountered. These have equally fueled our enthusiasm for a movement we now believe is well underway—the movement we invite you to join.

Our ethical approach was guided by Habermas's communicative action theory, by which a group's members first build trust by sharing perspectives and then use critical thinking to reach mutual understanding in preparation for action. If the ultimate objective is to take collective action, these are the necessary steps. In our own three-pronged process of voice, choice, and action, this is the essence we have tried to capture, finding a way for voices to become rational and consensual, choices to become informed and critical, and joint actions to become achievable. This is the durable model represented in the Young Citizens program to engage the community in participatory exchanges about health and science-based scenarios. It brings a new, ethical dimension to public deliberation.

The capability approach developed by Sen grew out of his work to find a better way to define and measure human inequality. His new approach began with a question: Freedom of *what*? His answer is a new focus on people's freedom to choose among the opportunities they have to live a life they value. The most important choices in life opportunities, he believes, have to do with the roles one can play (What can I be?) and the activities in which one can engage (What can I do?). From this perspective, the participants in the Young Citizens program experienced high levels of well-being: they freely chose to become deliberative citizens and health agents in their communities. Having the opportunity to choose these roles in their communities enabled them in turn to choose the actions they would take to improve their communities' health. When we subtitled this book "the potential of young citizens to heal democracy," this is the kind of choice-making we had in mind.

For us, the question has never been whether children have something to say. It is whether they will be expected and how they can be encouraged to voice their opinions, make informed decisions, and coordinate their chosen actions. The design and execution of the Young Citizens program offers a promising approach. It has been demonstrated to be a durable yet flexible model for guiding the development of deliberative citizenship in children.

We have both short-term and long-term expectations for what may happen next. Looking out just five years, the idea of the child as a citizen will gain more traction, not only as adult "authority figures" grapple with the concepts and principles involved but more importantly as positive change is increasingly and visibly driven by societies' youngest members. Looking out much further, to the future generations of a demographically altered world, we expect the time will come when no successful social action will fail to engage the capabilities of children.

Most of all, we expect that adults will not do this alone. This book has been written to audiences whose conceptual proficiencies and reading levels are mature. But its ideas and stories are accessible to children and can be expressed in many ways—just as the science of HIV / AIDS and malaria can be. As ideas about child citizenship make their way into child-engaging formats, children will contribute more to realizing this vision of the future.

The decision to portray health and disease through the representation in the microworld of human biology simultaneously with the macroworld of society became a pivotal device in capturing the ingenuity and unadulterated perspectives of children. We rest our case with a vignette that reveals a spontaneous display of critical thinking and decision-making. The following exchange was observed in a deliberative session toward the beginning of Module Four.

Two facilitators open the classroom scene: Clara takes on the animated role of a traditional healer, displaying her charms and tree leaves and chanting away. John plays the

more understated part of the "western" doctor, equipped
with notepad and stethoscope. He appeals to the roughly
twenty young citizens looking on: Whose remedy would they
trust more? The group, clearly dazzled by Clara's performance, seems ready to rush to judgment. But one member, a
normally reserved boy, jumps up from his desk. Running to
the window, he points to a nearby Mwarobaini tree. Its name
means "forty" and refers to the number of maladies said to be
cured by its bark, seeds, and leaves. He begs his friends to
recall what they learned about HIV and the "soldiers" of the
human immune system. "This tree has never heard of T4, the
Commander cell," he declares, "so how could its leaves protect anyone's T4 cells from infection?"

Somewhat stunned by this outburst, the others begin
speaking among themselves, and remembering those lessons. For several minutes they trade scientific facts from their
dramatization of the struggles between the virus, the B cell,
and the antibodies. They talk about the near demise of the T4
Commander, and how rescue arrived at the last moment in
the form of a proven treatment.

Clara and John gently intrude: "Are you ready to share
your understanding of science with your parents and the
community?" United in their resolve to take action they listen
again to the quiet boy. "Science is real," he says. "The medicine stops the virus from multiplying, but does not kill the
virus—but it allows people to live." The group has reached a
new level of knowledge and comprehension. This is about life
and death. Their efforts have been about communities caring
for one another, and about children being seen as informed
and responsible by other members of the community. This is
not simply entertainment, and there is no going back.

NOTES

ACKNOWLEDGMENTS

INDEX

Notes

Introduction

1. Amy Gutmann and Dennis Thompson, *Why Deliberative Democracy?* (Princeton, NJ: Princeton University Press, 2009).

2. United Nations Population Fund, "Total Population in Millions, 2019," World Population Dashboard, https://www.unfpa.org/data/world-population-dashboard.

3. Jürgen Habermas, *Moral Consciousness and Communicative Action*, trans. Christian Lenhardt and Shierry W. Nicholson (Cambridge, MA: MIT Press, 1990).

4. Amartya K. Sen, *The Idea of Justice* (Cambridge, MA: Belknap Press of Harvard University Press, 2009).

5. It was the 1805 vision of an early University of Wisconsin president that education should influence people's lives far beyond the scholarly pursuits of the classroom. What became known as the "Wisconsin Idea" signifies a guiding philosophy that the university should be committed to public service: As President Theodore Roosevelt wrote in 1912, the state became "literally a laboratory for wise experimental legislation aiming to secure the social and political betterment of the people as a whole." Charles McCarthy, *The Wisconsin Idea* (New York: Macmillan, 1912), xvi.

6. Felton Earls, "Prevalence of Behavior Problems in 3-Year-Old Children: A Cross-National Replication," *Archives of General Psychiatry* 37, no 10 (1980): 1153–1157.

7. Robert J. Sampson, Stephen W. Raudenbush, and Felton Earls, "Neighborhoods and Violent Crime: A Multilevel Study of Collective Efficacy," *Science* 277, no. 5328 (1997): 918–924.

8. United States Senate, "Have You No Sense of Decency?: Account of Proceedings on June 9, 1954," Historical Highlights, US Senate website, https://www.senate.gov/artandhistory/history/minute/Have_you_no_sense_of_decency.htm.

9. E. Mavis Hetherington and Mary Carlson. "Effects of Candidate Support and Election Results upon Attitudes to the Presidency." *Journal of Social Psychology* 64, no. 2 (1964): 333–338.

10. J. Anthony Lukas, *Common Ground: A Turbulent Decade in the Lives of Three American Families* (New York: Vintage, 1986).

11. Matthew Delmont, "The Lasting Legacy of the Busing Crisis," *Atlantic*, March 29, 2016.

12. Brown Bavusile Maaba, "Alternative Schooling for South Africans: Notes on the Solomon Mahlangu Freedom College in Tanzania, 1978–1992," *International Journal of African Historical Studies* 37, no. 2 (2004): 289–308.

13. This meeting was arranged by Dumisani Kumalo, trained as journalist and forced into exile in the United States where he became the national organizer of the divestment campaigns (including the St. Louis Coalition Against Apartheid, which we helped to organize with wise counsel) while project director from 1979 to 1997 at the American Committee on Africa. As the apartheid regime ended, Kumalo returned home to an appointment as director of the United States desk of the Department of Foreign Affairs. He later returned to the United States, in 1999, and served as South Africa's permanent representative to the United Nations until 2009.

14. Cristina Szanton Blanc, ed., *Urban Children in Distress: Global Predicaments and Innovative Strategies* (Luxembourg: Gordon and Breach for UNICEF, 1994). Also see Felton Earls, "Review: *Urban Children in Distress: Global Predicaments and Innovative Strategies*," *Childhood: A Global Journal of Child Research* 3, no. 1 (1996): 121–125.

15. Margaret Burchinal, Lauren Nelson, Mary Carlson, and Jeanne Brooks-Gunn, "Neighborhood Characteristics and Child Care Type and Quality," *Early Education and Development* 19, no. 5 (2008): 702–725.

16. Unnamed child delegate, *Raised Voices*, Caroline Webb, director and producer (London: Moving Times, 1993), quote at 3:55, https://www.youtube.com/watch?v=vHs99jD95MY.

17. Caroline Webb, *Raised Voices*, quote at 28:36.

1. Known City

1. William Lee and Madeline Buckley, "11-Year-Old 'Yummy' Sandifer Was on the Run for Killing a Teenage Girl. Then He Was Killed By His Own Gang in

a Chicago Story that Shocked the Nation 25 Years Ago," *Chicago Tribune*, August 30, 2019; Nancy Gibbs, "Murder in Miniature," *Time*, September 19, 1994. The *Time* cover, which reads "So Young to Kill, So Young to Die: The Short Violent Life of Robert "Yummy Sandifer," can be viewed at http://content.time.com/time/magazine/0,9263,7601940919,00.html.

2. United States Government, "Report of the National Advisory Commission on Civil Disorders," Otto Kerner, Chairman (Washington, DC: Government Printing Office, 1968).

3. Robert J. Sampson, Stephen W. Raudenbush, and Felton Earls, "Neighborhoods and Violent Crime: A Multilevel Study of Collective Efficacy," *Science* 277, no. 5328 (1997): 918–924.

4. Albert Bandura, "Exercise of Human Agency through Collective Efficacy," *Current Directions in Psychological Science* 9, no. 3 (2000): 75–78, quote on 76.

5. Gerald D. Suttles, *The Social Construction of Communities* (Chicago: University of Chicago Press, 1972).

6. One of the most influential theories on the causes of crime is *social disorganization theory*, developed by the Chicago School of Sociology in the first two decades of the twentieth century. The basic idea is that an *organized* neighborhood puts constraints on delinquent and criminal behavior, and *disorganized* neighborhoods are characterized by a breakdown in these social controls. A criticism of the theory, however, is that different controls from those identified by the theory may be present. Considering the effects of trust and cohesion among neighbors, and whether there is an expectation that neighbors will exert control over antisocial behavior, led to the more comprehensive concept of *collective efficacy*.

7. Robert J. Sampson, *Great American City: Chicago and the Enduring Neighborhood Effect* (Chicago: University of Chicago Press, 2012).

8. The Project on Human Development in Chicago Neighborhoods was supported by a public-private partnership of the National Institute of Justice and the John D. and Catherine T. MacArthur Foundation from 1990 to 2005. Felton Earls was the Principal Investigator. Scientific Directors were Robert Sampson, Stephen Raudenbusch, and Jeanne Brooks-Gunn.

9. Longitudinal studies provide opportunities to observe the changes and consistencies that mark the personal ways in which children grow up. The project separately interviewed parents and children about the children's health, education, and behavior. Seven age cohorts, each consisting of eight

hundred to a thousand children were followed over seven years. These included newborns and children at ages three, six, nine, twelve, fifteen, and eighteen; by the end of the study, the youngest participants were seven years old and the oldest participants were twenty-five. In this way, the study of twenty-five years of growth and development was compressed into seven years of data collection. If families moved from their initial addresses, research assistants remained in touch with them. The same children were contacted on three occasions (at intervals of roughly eighteen months). Forty to forty-five staff members handled data acquisition, processing, and storage. In the vanguard of this group were the twenty-eight to thirty well-trained research assistants (nearly all college graduates) who conducted interviews and collected data during home visits.

10. Felton Earls and Stephen L. Buka, "Project on Human Development in Chicago Neighborhoods," Technical Report 163495, National Institute of Justice, US Department of Justice, March 1997, https://www.ncjrs.gov /pdffiles1/Digitization/163495NCJRS.pdf.

11. Stephen W. Raudenbush and Robert J. Sampson, "Ecometrics: Toward a Science of Assessing Ecological Settings, with Application to the Systematic Social Observation of Neighborhoods," *Sociological Methodology* 29, no. 1 (1999): 1–41.

12. Jeffrey D. Morenoff, "Neighborhood Mechanisms and the Spatial Dynamics of Birth Weight," *American Journal of Sociology* 108, no. 5 (2003): 976–1017.

13. Christopher R. Browning, Tama Leventhal, and Jeanne Brooks-Gunn, "Sexual Initiation in Early Adolescence: The Nexus of Parental and Community Control," *American Sociological Review* 70, no. 5 (2005): 758–778.

14. Project on Human Development in Chicago Neighborhoods, "Neighborhoods Matter: Selected Findings from the Project on Human Development in Chicago Neighborhoods," paper prepared for New Directions in Housing Research: An Exploratory Discussion, sponsored by the John D. and Catherine T. MacArthur Foundation, Cambridge, MA, July 13–14, 2004.

15. Project on Human Development in Chicago Neighborhoods (PHDCN): Flagged Instrument List, Wave 3, 2000–2002 (ICPSR 13702), National Archive of Criminal Justice Data, Ann Arbor, MI. Version Date: Apr 27, 2007.

16. Robert J. Sampson, J. D. Morenoff, and Felton Earls, "Beyond Social Capital: Spatial Dynamics of Collective Efficacy for Children," *American Sociological Review* 64, no. 5 (1999): 633–660.

17. Douglas S. Massey and Nancy A. Denton, *American Apartheid: Segregation and the Making of the Underclass* (Cambridge, MA: Harvard University Press, 1993).

18. Tim Wadsworth and Charis E. Kubrin, "Hispanic Suicide in U.S. Metropolitan Areas: Examining the Effects of Immigration, Assimilation, Affluence, and Disadvantage," *American Journal of Sociology* 112, no. 6 (2007): 1848–1885.

19. This pattern of residential stratification by race and class was evident in the 1990 census data used as the template for drawing the samples for the community and longitudinal components of the project.

20. Sampson, *Great American City.*

21. Four teams, each composed of ten to twelve research assistants and two supervisors, were staffed by full-time, off-site employees of Harvard University who were carefully trained in conducting interviews and recording data accurately and respectfully. Amazingly, as they drove the streets and walked the neighborhoods for seven years, none fell victim to serious assault. By the conclusion of the project, they knew the exterior and interior lifeworlds of Chicago as well as anyone.

2. Lonely Cradles

1. William Moskoff, "Pronatalist Policies in Romania," *Economic Development and Cultural Change* 28, no. 3 (1980): 597–614.

2. "Romania's Orphans: A Legacy of Repression," *Human Rights Watch / Helsinki* 2, no. 15 (1990), https://www.hrw.org/sites/default/files /report_pdf/romania1290.pdf.

3. Dimitris Papadimitriou and David Phinnemore, *Romania and the European Union: From Marginalisation to Membership?* (New York: Routledge, 2008).

4. Spitz used film to document his research on orphans and abandoned infants in institutions in South America. See especially René A. Spitz and Katherine M. Wolf, *Grief, A Peril in Infancy* [film] (New York: Psychoanalytic Research Project on Problems of Infancy, 1947), https://collections .nlm.nih.gov/catalog/nlm:nlmuid-9505470-vid.

5. John Bowlby, *Maternal Care and Mental Health* (Geneva: World Health Organization, 1951).

6. Gerald C. Ruppenthal, Gary L. Arling, Harry F. Harlow, Gene P. Sackett, and Stephen J. Suomi, "A 10-Year Perspective of Motherless-Mother

Monkey Behavior," *Journal of Abnormal Psychology* 85, no. 4 (1976): 341–349.

7. Research conducted at Yerkes Laboratories of Primate Biology in Orange Park, Florida, and at the Max Planck Institute for Brain Research in Frankfurt am Main, Germany, respectively: Mary C. Randolph (Carlson) and Barbara A. Brooks, "Conditioning of a Vocal Response in a Chimpanzee through Social Reinforcement," *Folia Primatologica* 5, no. 1–2 (1967): 70–79; Mary C. Randolph (Carlson) and W. A. Mason, "Effects of Rearing Conditions on Distress Vocalizations in Chimpanzees," *Folia Primatologica* 10, no. 1–2 (1969): 103–112.

8. Mary Carlson, "Development of Tactile Discrimination Capacity in Macaca Mulatta. I. Normal Infants," *Developmental Brain Research* 16, no. 1 (1984): 69–82; Mary Carlson, M. F. Huerta, C. G. Cusick, and J. H. Kaas, "Studies on the Evolution of Multiple Somatosensory Representations in Primates: The Organization of Anterior Parietal Cortex in the New World Callitrichid, Saguinus," *Journal of Comparative Neurology* 246, no. 3 (1986): 409–426; Mary Carlson, "The Role of Somatic Sensory Cortex in Tactile Discrimination in Primates," in *Cerebral Cortex, Volume 8B: Comparative Structure and Evolution of Cerebral Cortex, Part II*, ed. Edward G. Jones and Alan Peters, 451–486 (Boston, MA: Springer, 1990); Mary Carlson, "Ontogenetic and Phylogenetic Perspectives on Somatic Sensory Cortex and Tactile Function," in *Information Processing in the Somatosensory System*, ed. Ove Franzén and Jan Westman, 177–192 (London: MacMillan, 1991); Mary Carlson and Pia Nystrom, "Tactile Discrimination Capacity in Relation to Size and Organization of Somatic Sensory Cortex in Primates: I. Old-World Prosimian, Galago; II. New-World Anthropoids, Saimiri and Cebus," *Journal of Neuroscience* 14, no. 3 (1994): 1516–1541.

9. Dong Liu, Josie Diorio, Beth Tannenbaum, Christian Caldji, Darlene Francis, Alison Freedman, Shakti Sharma, Deborah Pearson, Paul M. Plotsky, and Michael J. Meaney, "Maternal Care, Hippocampal Glucocorticoid Receptors, and Hypothalamic-Pituitary-Adrenal Responses to Stress," *Science* 277, no. 5332 (1997): 1659–1662; Tie-Yuan Zhang, Rose Bagot, Carine Parent, Cathy Nesbitt, Timothy W. Bredy, Christian Caldji, Eric Fish, Hymie Anisman, Moshe Szyf, and Michael J. Meaney, "Maternal Programming of Defensive Responses through Sustained Effects on Gene Expression," *Biological Psychology* 73, no. 1 (2006): 72–89.

10. Bruce S. McEwen, "Protective and Damaging Effects of Stress Mediators," *New England Journal of Medicine* 338, no. 3 (1998): 171–179; Bruce S.

McEwen, "Stress, Adaptation, and Disease: Allostasis and Allostatic Load," *Annals of the New York Academy of Sciences* 840, no. 1 (1998): 33–44.

11. Clemens Kirschbaum and Dirk H. Hellhammer, "Salivary Cortisol in Psychoneuroendocrine Research: Recent Developments and Applications," *Psychoneuroendocrinology* 19, no. 4 (1994): 313–333.

12. Katrin Ivars, Nina Nelson, Annette Theodorsson, Elvar Theodorsson, Jakob O. Ström, and Evalotte Mörelius, "Development of Salivary Cortisol Circadian Rhythm and Reference Intervals in Full-Term Infants," *PloS One* 10, no. 6 (2015): e0129502.

13. Joshua A. Rash, Jenna C. Thomas, Tavis S. Campbell, Nicole Letourneau, Douglas A. Granger, Gerald F. Giesbrecht, and APrON Study Team, "Developmental Origins of Infant Stress Reactivity Profiles: A Multi-System Approach," *Developmental Psychobiology* 58, no. 5 (2016): 578–599.

14. Laurie C. Miller, "Initial Assessment of Growth, Development, and the Effects of Institutionalization in Internationally Adopted Children," *Pediatric Annals* 29, no. 4 (2000): 224–232.

15. Joseph Sparling, Cristiana Dragomir, Sharon L. Ramey, and Laura Florescu, "An Educational Intervention Improves Developmental Progress of Young Children in a Romanian Orphanage," *Infant Mental Health Journal* 26, no. 2 (2005): 127–142.

16. Joseph Sparling and Kimberly Meunier, "Abecedarian: An Early Childhood Education Approach that Has a Rich History and a Vibrant Present," *International Journal of Early Childhood* 51, no. 2 (2019): 207–216.

17. Leah Nellis and Betty E. Gridley, "Review of the Bayley Scales of Infant Development—Second Edition," *Journal of School Psychology* 32, no. 2 (1994): 201–209.

18. William K. Frankenburg and Josiah B. Dodds, "The Denver Developmental Screening Test," *Journal of Pediatrics* 71, no. 2 (1967): 181–191.

19. Katrin Ivars, Nina Nelson, Annette Theodorsson, Elvar Theodorsson, Jakob O. Ström, and Evalotte Mörelius, "Development of Salivary Cortisol Circadian Rhythm and Reference Intervals in Full-Term Infants," *PloS One* 10, no. 6 (2015); Joshua A. Rash, Jenna C. Thomas, Tavis S. Campbell, Nicole Letourneau, Douglas A. Granger, Gerald F. Giesbrecht, and APrON Study Team, "Developmental Origins of Infant Stress Reactivity Profiles: A Multi-System Approach," *Developmental Psychobiology* 58, no. 5 (2016): 578–599.

20. Infants who were to participate in the study had been placed in the leagăn nursery when they were between two and three months old, most coming directly from the nurseries in nearby state-run maternity homes. At the age of six months, infants were selected from the current nursery population and randomly assigned to the intervention (enriched) group or to remain in the standard programs.

21. Regarding "age-appropriate percentiles," the score for an individual test-taker indicates the percentage of individuals in the comparison group scoring lower than the focal test-taker. Percentile scores range from first (meaning that 1 percent of test-takers scored below that score) to ninety-ninth (99 percent of test-takers scored below that score).

22. Mary Carlson, Cristiana Dragomir, Felton Earls, Marie Farrell, Olimpia Macovei, Pia Nystrom, and Joseph Sparling, "Effects of Social Deprivation on Cortisol Regulation in Institutionalized Romanian Infants," *Society of Neuroscience Abstracts* 218, no. 12 (1995), 524; Mary Carlson, Cristina Dragomir, Felton Earls, M. Farrell, Olimpia Macovei, Pia Nystrom, and Joseph Sparling, "Cortisol Regulation in Home-reared and Institutionalized Romanian Children," *Society of Neuroscience Abstracts* 218, no. 12 (1995); Mary Carlson and Felton Earls, "Psychological and Neuroendocrinological Sequelae of Early Social Deprivation in Institutionalized Children in Romania," *Annals of the New York Academy of Sciences* 807 (1997): 419–428.

23. Bruce S. McEwen, "What Is the Confusion with Cortisol?," *Chronic Stress* 3 (2019).

24. Michael Rutter, *Maternal Deprivation Reassessed* (London: Penguin Books, 1981).

25. Frank C. Van der Horst, Helen A. LeRoy, and René Van der Veer, "'When Strangers Meet': John Bowlby and Harry Harlow on Attachment Behavior," *Integrative Psychological and Behavioral Science* 42, no. 4 (2008): 370–388. The title of this excellent article on the lengthy correspondence between Bowlby and Harlow, and the day in 1958 that they finally met in person, is wordplay on the "strange situation" technique developed by Mary Ainsworth, Bowlby's research associate, to measure attachment behavior.

26. Michael Rutter, Celia Beckett, Jenny Castle, Emma Colvert, Jana Kreppner, Mitul Mehta, Suzanne Stevens, and Edmund Sonuga-Barke, "Effects of Profound Early Institutional Deprivation: An Overview of Findings from a UK Longitudinal Study of Romanian Adoptees," *European Journal of Developmental Psychology* 4, no. 3 (2007): 332–350.

27. Edmund J. S. Sonuga-Barke, Mark Kennedy, Robert Kumsta, Nicky Knights, Dennis Golm, Michael Rutter, Barbara Maughan, Wolff Schlotz, and Jana Kreppner, "Child-to-Adult Neurodevelopmental and Mental Health Trajectories after Early Life Deprivation: The Young Adult Follow-up of the Longitudinal English and Romanian Adoptees Study," *Lancet* 389, no. 10078 (2017): 1539–1548.

3. Mean Streets

1. Amnesty International, "Brazil: Torture and Extrajudicial Execution in Urban Brazil," Amnesty International, London, June 1990, https://www.amnesty.org/download/Documents/200000/amr190051990en.pdf. See also "Child Victims of Killing and Cruelty," *Amnesty International Newsletter* 10, no. 9 (September 1990), 3–6, https://www.amnesty.org/download/Documents/200000/nws210091990en.pdf.

2. William A. Lavelle, "State Terrorism and the Death Squad: A Study of Phenomenon," Master's thesis, California State University, Sacramento, January 1, 1992, 58, Archives of Defense Technical Information Center, https://archive.org/details/DTIC_ADA267650/page/n73/mode/2up/search/contempt.

3. Brazilian Institute of Social and Economic Analysis, "Children and Adolescents in Brazil: The Silenced Life," São Paulo, IBASE Press, 1989.

4. The report of the Comissão Parlamentar de Inquérito para Apuração de Responsabilidades Pelo Extermínio de Crianças e Adolescentes no Estado do Rio de Janeiro (Parliamentary Commission of Inquiry to Investigate the Extermination of Children and Adolescents in Rio de Janeiro State), set up in March 1991 by the State Assembly of Rio de Janeiro, was published in September 1991. For a summary of its findings, see Amnesty International, "Brazil: Impunity and the Law: The Killing of Street Children in Rio de Janeiro State," April 1992, https://www.amnesty.org/download/Documents/192000/amr190051992en.pdf.

5. Donna Bowater, "Brazil Marks 20 Years Since the Candelaria Child Massacre," BBC News, July 24, 2013, https://www.bbc.com/news/world-latin-america-23417669.

6. For data on how the economic downturn in 1980s Brazil affected children, see, for example, Suzanne Duryea, David Lam, and Deborah Levison, "Effects of Economic Shocks on Children's Employment and Schooling in Brazil," *Journal of Development Economics* 84, no. 1 (2007): 188–214.

7. Irene Rizzini, Irma Rizzini, Monica Munhoz, and Lidia Galeano, "Childhood and Urban Poverty in Brazil: Street and Working Children and Their Families," UNICEF Office of Research, Innocenti Occasional Paper, Urban Child Series, no. 3, August 1992, https://www.unicef-irc.org /publications/96-childhood-and-urban-poverty-in-brazil-street-and -working-children-and-their-families.html.

8. See, for example, Salah Abdelgalil, Ricardo G. Gurgel, Sally Theobald, Luis Eduardo Cuevas, "Household and Family Characteristics of Street Children in Aracaju, Brazil," *Archives of Disease in Childhood* 89, no. 9 (2004), 817–820, https://adc.bmj.com/content/89/9/817.

9. Jorge Amado, *Captains of the Sands,* trans. G. Rabassa (1988; New York: Penguin Classics, 2013).

10. National Movement of Street Boys and Girls, "Objectives, Actions and Achievements," Pangaea Street Children–Community Children Worldwide Resource Library, October 18, 1994, http://pangaea.org/street_children /latin/mnmmr.htm.

11. For a history of FUNABEM, see Aldaiza Sposati, "Displacement of Social Security and Social Disprotection in Brazil," *Ciência & Saúde Coletiva* [Science & Collective Health]. 23, no. 7 (2018), 2315–2325. Available in English online at http://www.scielo.br/scielo.php?script=sci_arttext&pid =S1413-81232018000702315&lng=en&nrm=iso&tlng=en.

12. *Raised Voices,* Caroline Webb, director and producer (London: Moving Times, 1993), segment beginning at 19.01, https://www.youtube.com /watch?v=vHs99jD95MY.

13. Child and Adolescent Statute (*Estatuto da Criança e do Adolescente*), Law No. 8,069, July 13, 1990, art. 1, website of the Brazilian Presidency, http://www.planalto.gov.br/ccivil_03/leis/l8069.htm. For discussion, see Eduardo Soares, "Children's Rights: Brazil," Legal Report, Law Library of Congress, January 2009, https://www.loc.gov/law/help/child-rights/brazil .php#f41.

14. Art. 227, Chapter VII (Family, Child, Adolescent, Youth and Elderly), Title VIII (Of the Social Order), Constitution of the Federative Republic of Brazil, 1988, website of the Brazilian Presidency, http://www.planalto.gov .br/ccivil_03/constituicao/constituicaocompilado.htm.

15. Benedito Rodrigues dos Santos, interview with Tony Earls and Maya Carlson, November 21, 1993. UNICEF had arranged our visit to the São Paulo office of the National Movement of Street Boys and Girls, where we were

fortunate to meet Benedito, one of the movement's adult supporters, who was eager to explain the remarkable accomplishments of this coalition.

16. For details on the circus program and its outcomes, see Mary Garcia Castro, *Cultivating Life, Disarming Violence: Experiences in Education, Culture, Leisure, Sports, and Citizenship with Youths in Poverty Situations* (Rio de Janeiro, Brazil: UNESCO Brazil Editions, 2002), Section 4.2.5 "Circo Picolino," 143–150, https://unesdoc.unesco.org/ark:/48223/pf0000127895.

17. In collaboration with Irene Rizzini and another Brazilian colleague, Cristina Duarte, we continue to track the development of the Brazilian Child Rights Councils and Guardianship Councils as legislated models of community-based, rights-informed care and protection for children. It is important to understand if these entities of local, decentralized government generate and maintain high levels of collective efficacy for children.

18. Cristiane S. Duarte, Irene Rizzini, Christina W. Hoven, Mary Carlson, and Felton J. Earls, "The Evolution of Child Rights Councils in Brazil," *International Journal of Children's Rights* 15, no. 2 (2007), p. 269–282; Anthony Dewees and Steven J. Klees, "Social Movements and the Transformation of National Policy: Street and Working Children in Brazil," *Comparative Education Review* 39, no. 1 (1995): 76–100.

4. Wishes of the Community

1. Felton Earls was a principal investigator on the five-year epidemiological study launched in 1995 to examine the causes and consequences of children's exposure to violence, funded by the National Institute for Mental Health and the John D. and Catherine T. MacArthur Foundation.

2. Jane Fonda, The Turner Foundation, and the Center for Child Well-Being supported the Chicago and Cambridge Young Citizen programs with seed grants.

3. Sharon Detrick, "Saint Xavier University Sesquicentennial Conference, 'Children in the World: Exploring the Rights of the Child,' 20–23 March 1997" [conference announcement], *International Journal of Children's Rights* 4, no. 4 (1996): 417–418.

4. Joel E. Oestreich, "UNICEF and the Implementation of the Convention on the Rights of the Child," *Global Governance* 4, no. 2 (1998): 183–198.

5. United Nations, Universal Declaration of Human Rights, proclaimed by the UN General Assembly in Paris December 10, 1948 (General Assembly resolution 217 A), https://www.un.org/en/universal-declaration-human

-rights/. For background, see Mary Ann Glendon, *A World Made New: Eleanor Roosevelt and the Universal Declaration of Human Rights* (New York: Random House, 2001).

6. Article 27 specifies that "States Parties recognize the right of every child to a standard of living adequate for the child's physical, mental, spiritual, moral and social development . . . to provide them with the conditions of living necessary for the child's development." Governments are expected to assist parents with material assistance and programs when needed. United Nations Convention on the Rights of the Child, November 20, 1989, https://www.ohchr.org/en/professionalinterest/pages/crc.aspx.

7. Jürgen Habermas, *A Theory of Communicative Action*, vol. 1: *Reason and the Rationalization of Society;* vol. 2: *Lifeworld and System,* trans. Thomas McCarthy (Boston: Beacon Press, 1984).

8. United Nations Convention on the Rights of the Child.

9. Roger A. Hart, Children's Participation: *The Theory and Practice of Involving Young Citizens in Community Development and Environmental Care* (New York: Earthscan, 1997).

10. The first publication of the Delphi method came some years after its initial, confidential use by RAND. Norman Dalkey and Olaf Helmer, "An Experimental Application of the DELPHI Method to the Use of Experts," *Management Science* 9, no. 3 (1963), 351–515.

11. Beverly D. Tatum, *"Why Are All the Black Kids Sitting Together in the Cafeteria? And Other Conversations about Race* (New York: Basic Books, 1997).

12. Mary Carlson and Felton Earls, "Adolescents as Deliberative Citizens: Building Health Competence in Local Communities," *Annals of the American Academy of Political and Social Science* 633, no. 1 (2011): 223–242.

13. Etienne van de Walle, "The Social Impact of AIDS in Sub-Saharan Africa," *Milbank Quarterly* 68 (1990): 10–32.

5. Big Ideas in Small Places

1. Etienne van de Walle, "The Social Impact of AIDS in Sub-Saharan Africa," *Milbank Quarterly* 68 (1990): 10–32.

2. For an overview of Child to Child and its mission, see the organization's website: http://www.childtochild.org.uk/about/.

3. Mary Carlson and Felton Earls, "Adolescents as Deliberative Citizens: Building Health Competence in Local Communities," *Annals of the*

American Academy of Political and Social Science 633, no. 1 (2011): 223–242.

4. Jürgen Habermas, *A Theory of Communicative Action*, vol. 1: *Reason and the Rationalization of Society;* vol. 2: *Lifeworld and System,* trans. Thomas McCarthy (Boston: Beacon Press, 1984).

5. Urie Bronfenbrenner, *The Ecology of Human Development* (Cambridge, MA: Harvard University Press, 1979).

6. Mary Carlson and Felton Earls, "A Health Promotion Curriculum for Adolescent Young Citizens: Deliberation and Public Action for HIV / AIDS–Competent Communities," *American Journal of Orthopsychiatry* 81, no. 4 (2011): 453.

7. Abraham Flexner, *Medical Education in the United States and Canada: A Report to the Carnegie Foundation for the Advancement of Teaching,* Bulletin No. 4, Carnegie Foundation for the Advancement of Teaching, New York, 1910, http://archive.carnegiefoundation.org/pdfs/elibrary/Carnegie _Flexner_Report.pdf.

8. For a complete account of the design of the cluster randomized controlled trial, including its theoretical framework, sampling, measures adopted, and data analysis employed, see Mary Carlson, Robert T. Brennan, and Felton Earls, "Enhancing Adolescent Self-Efficacy and Collective Efficacy through Public Engagement around HIV/AIDS Competence: A Multilevel, Cluster Randomized-Controlled Trial," Social Science and Medicine 75, no. 6 (2012): 1078–1087.

6. Reaching Mutual Understanding

1. Jürgen Habermas, *A Theory of Communicative Action,* vol. 1: *Reason and the Rationalization of Society;* vol. 2: *Lifeworld and System,* trans. Thomas McCarthy (Boston: Beacon Press, 1984), 1: 308.

2. Jürgen Habermas, *Moral Consciousness and Communicative Action,* trans. Christian Lenhardt and Shierry W. Nicholsen (Cambridge, MA: MIT Press, 1990), quote at 93, note 2; Jürgen Habermas, *Justification and Application,* trans. Ciaran P. Cronin (Cambridge, MA: MIT Press, 1993).

3. The Health and Human Services agency details additional protections required for children participating in human subject research in its regulation's manual. See "Subpart D—Additional Protections for Children Involved as Subjects in Research" of the HHS Code of Federal Regulations

(CFR) at 45 CFR part 46, https://www.govinfo.gov/content/pkg/CFR-2016
-title45-vol1/pdf/CFR-2016-title45-vol1-part46.pdf.

4. "The Temporary Assistance for Needy Families (TANF) Block Grant: A
Legislative History," CRS Report R44668, Congressional Research Service,
April 2, 2019, https://fas.org/sgp/crs/misc/R44668.pdf

5. National Campaign for Jobs and Income Support, "States Behaving
Badly: America's 10 Worst Welfare States," report issued by Make TANF
Work campaign, Washington, DC, February 2, 2002, http://lobby.la.psu
.edu/_107th/110_TANF_Work_Training/Organizational_Statements
/NCJIS/NCIJS_States_Behaving_Badly.pdf.

6. This work was supported by the Jules and Doris Stein Foundation.

7. For background on childcare quality rating systems, see Arthur C. Emlen
and Roberta B. Weber, "Parental Use of Child Care: A Guide for Constructing
Parent Surveys," Oregon Child Care Research Partnership Family Policy
Program, Oregon State University, January 2007, https://www.research
connections.org/childcare/resources/7992/pdf. On the Environment Ratings
Scales developed by Thelma Harms, Debby Cryer, and Richard M. Clifford,
see "A Brief History of the Environment Rating Scales," Environment Rating
Scales Institute (website), https://www.ersi.info/scales_history.html.

8. *Rage of Innocents: The Project on Human Development in Chicago
Neighborhoods,* Noah Erenberg, producer (Princeton, NJ: Films for the
Humanities & Sciences, c1999), Discovery Channel, March 2000. Viewable
at http://youtu.be/AtggL6aq30U.

9. Gerald H. Fairtlough, "Habermas' Concept of 'Lifeworld,'" *Systems
Practice* 4 no. 6 (1991): 547–563.

10. Habermas, *Theory of Communicative Action,* vol. 2: *Lifeworld and Systems.*

11. Christopher J. Howe and David J. Handelsman, "Use of Filter Paper for
Sample Collection and Transport in Steroid Pharmacology," *Clinical
Chemistry* 43, no. 8 (1997): 1408–1415.

12. Mary Carlson, "Vulnerable Children and Families: The Critical Role of
Touch in the Early Regulations of Stress Hormone," presented at the
Wisconsin Symposium on Emotion: Affect and Plasticity, HealthEmotions
Research Institute, Madison, April 23–24, 1999; Charles A. Morgan, Sheila
Wang, Steven M. Southwick, Ann Rasmusson, Gary Hazlett, Richard L.
Hauger, and Dennis S. Charney, "Plasma Neuropeptide-Y Concentrations in
Humans Exposed to Military Survival Training," *Biological Psychiatry* 47,
no. 10 (2000): 902–909.

7. Promoting Human Capability

1. Sidney Verba, Kay Lehman Schlozman, and Henry E. Brady, *Voice and Equality: Civic Voluntarism in American Politics* (Cambridge, MA: Harvard University Press, 1995).

2. "Amartya Sen, Biographical," NobelPrize.org, n.d., https://www.nobelprize.org/prizes/economic-sciences/1998/sen/biographical/.

3. In collaboration with Mahbub ul Haq, a special advisor to the United Nations Development Program, Sen helped design and construct the first Human Development Index, in which statistics on life expectancy, educational achievement, and per-capita income are combined to indicate "development" levels. The index allows for comparing UN member nations on their people's well-being, in contrast to gross national product figures and rankings which draw only on economic output data.

4. "Constitution of the World Health Organization," in Basic Documents, Forty-Ninth Edition, World Health Organization, 2020, 1, http://apps.who.int/gb/bd/pdf_files/BD_49th-en.pdf#page=7.

5. Albert Bandura, "Health Promotion by Social Cognitive Means. *Health Education and Behavior, 31*(2): 143–164; Kenneth R. McLeroy, Daniel Bibeau, Allan Steckler, and Karen Glanz, "An Ecological Perspective on Health Promotion Programs," *Health Education and Behavior* 15, no. 4 (1988): 351–377

6. Amartya Sen, *Inequality Reexamined* (Cambridge, MA: Harvard University Press, 1992); Amartya Sen, *Development as Freedom* (New York: Alfred A. Knopf, 1999).

7. Felton Earls and Mary Carlson, "Promoting Human Capability as an Alternative to Early Crime Prevention," in *Integrating Crime Prevention Strategies: Propensity and Opportunity,* ed. Per- Olof H. Wikström, Ronald V. G. Clarke, and Joan McCord, 141–168 (Stockholm: National Council for Crime Prevention, 1995).

8. Eloisa Valenza, Yumiko Otsuka, Hermann Bulf, Hiroko Ichikawa, So Kanazawa, and Masami K. Yamaguchi, "Face Orientation and Motion Differently Affect the Deployment of Visual Attention in Newborns and 4-Month-Old Infants," *PloS One* 10, no. 9 (2015): e0136965; Harriet L. Rheingold, Jacob L. Gewirtz, and Helen W. Ross, "Social Conditioning of Vocalizations in the Infant. *Journal of Comparative and Physiological Psychology* 52, no. 1 (1959): 68–73.

9. Ingrid Robeyns, "The Capability Approach," *Stanford Encyclopedia of Philosophy*, published April 14, 2011, revised October 3, 2016, https://plato .stanford.edu/entries/capability-approach/.

10. Benjamin S. Bloom, ed., *Taxonomy of Educational Objectives*, vol. 1: *Cognitive Domain* (New York, NY: McKay, 1956).

11. John Dewey and Evelyn Dewey, *Schools of To-Morrow* (New York: E. P. Dutton, 1915), 304.

12. Martha Nussbaum, "Tagore, Dewey, and the Imminent Demise of Liberal Education," in *The Oxford Handbook of Philosophy of Education*, ed. H. Siegel (Oxford: Oxford University Press, 2009); Francis A. Samuel, "Educational Visions from Two Continents: What Tagore Adds to the Deweyan Perspective," *Educational Philosophy and Theory* 43, no. 10 (2011): 1161–1174.

8. Educating Our Community

1. Julius K. Nyerere, "Education for Self-Reliance," *Ecumenical Review* 19, no. 4 (1967): 382–403; reprinted in Nyerere, *Man and Development* (Dar-es-Salaam: Oxford University Press, 1974).

2. A video was made of Moshi young citizens learning and performing HIV skits in their community. View it on YouTube: https://www.youtube.com /watch?v=ZxzdkuIgf2s&t=36s.

3. Norifumi Kamo, Mary Carlson, Robert T. Brennan, and Felton Earls, "Young Citizens as Health Agents: Use of Drama in Promoting Community Efficacy for HIV / AIDS," *American Journal of Public Health* 98, no. 2 (2008): 201–204.

4. Mary Carlson and Felton Earls, "Adolescents as Deliberative Citizens: Building Health Competence in Local Communities," *Annals of the American Academy of Political and Social Science* 633, no. 1 (2011): 223–242.

9. Inspiring Our Community

1. Doris Sommer, Director of the Cultural Agents Initiative at Harvard, had invited Boal for a visit to the campus. Betsy Bard, a drama instructor at Cambridge Rindge and Latin School who participated in planning Boal's visit, organized the forum theater event for the high school.

2. Augusto Boal, *The Rainbow of Desire: The Boal Method of Theatre and Therapy*, trans. Adrian Jackson (London: Routledge, 1995); Augusto Boal,

Theatre of the Oppressed, new ed., trans. Charles A. McBride and Maria-Odilia Leal-McBride (London: Pluto, 2008). Boal was influenced by the view of a fellow Brazilian: Paulo Freire, *Pedagogy of the Oppressed*, trans. Myra B. Ramos (New York: Seabury Press, 1970) is a combination of philosophical, political, and educational perspectives in a treatise of oppression. Boal's dramatic theory shared with Freire the belief that the key to liberation is in the awakening of critical awareness and thinking leading to collaborative effort to overcome existing exploitation.

3. A superb example of a Joker addressing a community session is captured on video by Norris Kamo, as professionally produced by an undergraduate, Lucy McKinnon, in 2005, https://youtu.be/8sAX3FyJ3Ko.

4. Robert C. Gallo and Luc Montagnier, "The Discovery of HIV as the Cause of AIDS," *New England Journal of Medicine* 349, no. 24 (2003): 2283–2285.

5. Thomas S. Alexander, "Human Immunodeficiency Virus Diagnostic Testing: 30 Years of Evolution," *Clinical and Vaccine Immunology* 23, no. 4 (2016): 249–253.

6. G. Somi, M. Matee, C. L. Makena, J. van den Hombergh, B. Kilama, K. I. Yahya-Malimu, et al., "Three Years of HIV / AIDS Care and Treatment Services in Tanzania: Achievements and Challenges," *Tanzania Journal of Health Research* 11, no. 3 (2009): 136–143.

7. "Evaluation of the UNAIDS / UNITAR AIDS Competence Programme," Joint United Nations Programme on HIV / AIDS (UNAIDS), June 2005, http://data.unaids.org/publications/irc-pub06/jc1144-acp.evaluation_en.pdf.

http://data.unaids.org/publications/irc-pub06/jc1144-acp.evaluation_en.pdf.

8. Albert Bandura, *Self-Efficacy: The Exercise of Control* (New York, NY: W. H. Freeman, 1997).

9. Jürgen Habermas, *The Structural Transformation of the Public Sphere: An Inquiry into a Category of Bourgeois Society*, trans. T. Burger (Cambridge, MA: MIT Press, 1989).

10. "WHO Applauds Lesotho Prime Minister for Leading Universal Voluntary HIV Testing Drive," Three by Five Initiative, n.d., https://www.who.int/3by5/newsitem6/en/.

11. Mary Carlson and Felton Earls, "A Health Promotion Curriculum for Adolescent Young Citizens: Deliberation and Public Action for HIV / AIDS–Competent Communities," *American Journal of Orthopsychiatry* 81, no. 4 (2011): 453–460.

10. Moving Forward

1. "Women Safety Audit," Safer Cities Program, UN-Habitat, n.d., http://mirror.unhabitat.org/content.asp?typeid=24&catid=375&id=1466.

2. Mika Cori Morse, "Young Citizens: A Case Study of Institutionalizing Children's Participation in Community Decision-Making," *Children's Legal Rights Journal* 28, no. 3 (2008): 23–55.

3. Clotilde Fonseca and Maria Eugenia Bujanda, "Promoting Children's Capacities for Active and Deliberative Citizenship with Digital Technologies: The CADE Project in Costa Rica," *Annals of the American Academy of Political and Social Science* 633, no. 1 (2011): 243–262.

4. A video about the program was produced by the Omar Dengo Foundation to share its work with the public: *Learning How to Deliberate* (Producciones SA, 2005), https://youtu.be/ZlTr0x15cNc.

Acknowledgments

As late bloomers, we required a lot of encouragement to put ourselves to the task of writing this book. At strategic moments, the reassurance we required amounted to a form of foster care. The person who stands out in this regard is Sara Lawrence Lightfoot, our confidante and colleague. We began to discuss the merits of the book idea over a decade ago at a Sunday brunch at Commander's Palace in New Orleans. Since then, Sister Sara has never doubted that the multiple drafts we sent were benchmarks of a slow but steady progress toward a book that would be readable and perhaps interesting. For her probing honesty and diligence throughout this protracted gestation, she gets the first autographed copy.

We also had a persistent cheerleader in Dumisani Kumalo. He respected us as activists and scientists and guided our political aspirations in support of the transformation of South Africa's democracy. Whenever he spotted an opportunity, he would apply gentle pressure to keep turning the pages of our young citizens' story. Dumisani's passionate advocacy for our work surfaces in several places in these pages. He died in the year before the book was published, but will always claim a special place in our quest.

There were others who played their supporting roles in our effort to write for the general reader. Kate Medina, Shannon Ravenel, and Maurya Kilroy read substantial drafts and encouraged us to keep going. Larry Aber helped us secure Jim

Levine as an agent. Tony and Jim instantly recognized each other when we met in 2016 to discuss this book. Before becoming a literary agent, Jim was a child psychologist with a special interest in the role of fathers. In the 1980s, this was also a focus of Tony's research. They recalled being at the same meetings and sharing similar points of view. Jim won our hearts and minds by labeling our work and text as "radical."

Thanks to facilitation by Hilary Pennington, we were fortunate to receive a grant from the Ford Foundation that funded editorial support to the development of a book proposal and editorial assistance in writing for a general readership. That investment paid off when we met George Andreou, recently appointed director of Harvard University Press. He saw our unconventional text as a "biography of ideas" and his editorial vision for it remained a touchstone throughout the process.

Once the proposal was accepted, we opened our minds to receive guidance from other fine editors. Initial assistance was provided by a long-time friend, the South African journalist Joe Thloloe, who shared our wish to bring themes of childhood, community, and liberation to the forefront. Monica Jainschigg and Jim guided our ideas and words toward a successful proposal. We are especially indebted to Amanda Moon and Ben Platt, who helped us see how the book structure could highlight the themes of voice, choice, and action— and encouraged us to engage the reader by articulating the important questions we were addressing.

The final phase of editing was done at Harvard University Press. When we asked George Andreou what writers he most often refers his students to, he replied in one word: Aristotle. After duly consulting that philosopher's rhetorical advice, we took to heart this simple principle: A story that is whole has a beginning, a middle, and an end. We hope we have not disappointed George, as his unwavering encouragement has been key to our perseverance.

Robin Bellinger had the editorial role of critically reading our text with the perspective of the general reader, and her edits and recommendations were extraordinarily valuable. We were charmed when she confessed that her Habermas was a bit rusty. It was with the supportive and experienced guidance of Julia Kirby that we made it through the daunting steps that come between handing over a manuscript and having ink meet paper. She enhanced the energy of the text, and went back to catch errant commas in proof revisions when our own energy had faded.

We are fortunate to have had many colleagues providing invaluable scientific and scholarly advice over many years. Especially important were those whose critical reading of parts of the manuscript gave us greater confidence in it. Our gratitude goes to Robert Brennan, Lincoln Chen, Philip Graham, Steve Hyman, Bruce Jennings, Peter Levine, Micheal Meaney, Bruce MacEwen, Esther Mwaikambo, Martin Ruck, Robert Sampson, Amartya Sen, William Slayne, and Richard Weissbourg.

In Chicago, Deandre Minniefield, Jose (Paco) Lomeli, Percy Austin, Jeanette Rusiecki, and Lamar "Billy" Brooks confirmed the accuracy of our descriptions of the Young Citizens program. The Cambridge young citizens—Jessica Crews, Janelle Gibbs, Rachael Halton-Irwin, Lamar LaForce, Pedro Pedroza, and Sam Ryerson—showed us how deeply teenagers can probe a complex social issue. Brian Chan and Barbara Trickett were their facilitators. In Romania, Olimpia Macovei and Joseph Sparling made our observations and research possible. They read and gave sound advice on our study of the stress hormone cortisol in deprived infants and toddlers.

John Donohue, Dita Riefenberg, Irene Rizzini, and Benedito Rodrigues dos Santos provided seasoned advice and support on our visits to Brazil. Esther Mwaikambo, Alice Monyo, Abdullah Mufuriki, and Cliff Juma Tety also thoroughly reviewed those chapters describing the challenges and successes of the young citizens in Tanzania.

Our former students Mika Morse, Norris Kamo, and Brian Chan, who taught us so much throughout this journey, gained scientific and ethical command of the ideas and methods that propel us. This is evidenced by their independent contributions to the project, their own publications, and the extraordinary professional careers they have built over the last two decades.

Our two daughters, Leigh and Tanya, their spouses, Kevin and Khari, and our six grandchildren, Will, Julia, Zinzi, Elliot, Kossi, and Safina, more than anyone else, have witnessed the concentration and rugged persistence it has taken to bring our thirty-year quest to fruition. If the grandchildren were asked about our frequent absences for work in Tanzania, we think they might say they were compensated by their vast collections of Tinga Tinga paintings—the gifts they acquired from our constant travels between Boston and Kilimanjaro.

Index

Page numbers followed by *t* indicate tables.